BODY OF VISION

MICHAEL SINDING

Body of Vision

Northrop Frye and the Poetics of Mind

UNIVERSITY OF TORONTO PRESS
Toronto Buffalo London

Toronto Buffalo London
www.utppublishing.com

ISBN 978-1-4426-4391-8

Frye Studies

Library and Archives Canada Cataloguing in Publication

Sinding, Michael, 1970–
Body of vision : Northrop Frye and the poetics of mind / Michael Sinding.

(Frye studies)
Includes bibliographical references and index.
ISBN 978-1-4426-4391-8

1. Frye, Northrop, 1912–1991 – Criticism and interpretation. I. Title.
II. Series: Frye studies

PN75.F7S55 2014 801'.95092 C2013-901851-4

This book has been published with the help of a grant from the Michael G. De Groote family.

University of Toronto Press acknowledges the financial assistance to its publishing program of the Canada Council for the Arts and the Ontario Arts Council.

University of Toronto Press acknowledges the financial support for its publishing activities of the Government of Canada through the Canada Book Fund.

For Melissa

Contents

Preface and Acknowledgments

The interests that have finally resulted in this book came into alignment over the course of many years. It may help to orient the reader if I describe that process briefly. My first encounter with Frye was reading *The Educated Imagination* around 1989, as I was beginning a BA program at McGill University. For the next few years, Frye had priority in my reading, and I peppered my undergraduate essays with his ideas and words – not always inaptly, I hope. A copy of *The Great Code* loaned from my sister arrived at my door in 1991 on the day Frye died. As I remember it, my landlord handed me the package minutes before Frye's death was announced on CBC radio, so it seemed like a message from beyond the grave. About a year later, I found Frye's *Anatomy of Criticism* and Thomas Pynchon's novel *Gravity's Rainbow* at bookstores in different parts of Montréal. Both books were experiences of far-reaching mental disruption and reorganization. Reading the two more or less together inspired me to study the genre Frye called "anatomy" or Menippean satire, because of how well Pynchon's astonishing book matched Frye's exuberant account of the genre. This helped me make sense of Pynchon, as it put him in a tradition that included Lucian, Petronius, Erasmus, Rabelais, Cervantes, Burton, Swift, Sterne, Melville, Carlyle, Proust, and Joyce. Professor Kerry McSweeney at McGill supervised an independent study course that allowed me to read and write about many of those superb anatomy-novel hybrids. That project eventually grew into my master's and doctoral theses at McMaster University, where I luckily came across an engaged and welcoming group of Frye scholars. Frye is no longer a major part of most graduate school training, so it is important that there are places where his work is still studied seriously.

I had tried in various ways to bring together criticism, philosophy, and language theory – one would have thought it a natural connection – but with little success, until graduate school. The final piece of the puzzle came when I discovered cognitive linguistics and poetics. I was half way through my PhD program when I discovered Mark Turner's website on "Conceptual Blending and Integration" more or less by accident while searching for information on literary theory. The work presented there by Turner and his colleagues on imaginative thought in language and literature, and on metaphor in language and thought, was highly sophisticated and rigorous by the standards of linguistics and philosophy, as well as by those of literary criticism. Unlike most literary theory, it was not detached from linguistics and analytic philosophy. Unlike most linguistics and analytic philosophy, it was very illuminating about literary matters. Crucially, the cognitive scientific ideas about structure in language, metaphor, and literature powerfully echoed some of Frye's main insights. So Turner's and George Lakoff's books were another watershed for me. They presented the opportunity I had been looking for to begin to connect the study of literature, language, and thought, and to link analyses of the imagination at all its levels, from the smallest bits of text to the largest expanses of cultural history. My doctoral thesis metamorphosed into a cognitive approach to the anatomy and the concept of genre.

In all of this work, I found that the set of concepts and analyses Frye supplies, and the multidimensional structures and patterns he maps out, are highly revealing about literary texts and how literature, culture, and the imagination work. They are beautifully integrated into a vision that touches on almost everything a critic can touch on. Taken as a whole, they are much richer, more penetrating, and more plausible than those of any other theory I know of. Other forms of criticism can seem crude or narrow or one-sided by comparison. At the very least, Frye's studies constitute an indispensable perspective in the understanding of literature and culture. Yet in the marketplace of literary theory today, they are strangely under-valued. Thus, alongside the specific topic of my doctoral work, I began to work out ways to develop Frye's approach by linking key parts of his general framework with key parts of cognitive linguistics and poetics. I later realized that the dominance of other approaches to literature and culture meant that any such theoretical integration would probably not communicate very well with its main audience. The influence of Frye's analyses of literary form have given him a reputation for being a "formalist," and formal approaches to literature have been displaced over the past few decades by cultural and historical approaches. During my postdoctoral work I expanded my effort and began to link Frye's ideas with key elements of cultural studies and new historicism as well. The present book is the result of that long-term effort to weave these various strands of research into something that would cover the relevant bases and hold together as a unity.

This book would not have been possible without intellectual and financial support emanating from various sources. Those years of reading, writing, and trying out ideas with new colleagues have been immeasurably valuable. I thank Joseph Adamson, Alvin Lee, and Robert Denham for ongoing encouragement, discussion, and advice in all things Frye. Alvin's courteous but persistent inquiries about how the project was going were particularly helpful. A number of colleagues have assisted me in developing my interest in cognitive approaches to literature through their encouragement, writing, discussion and advice, hospitality, and collective reshaping of the institutions of literary study. I know many others have benefited from the enthusiasm and intelligence of Mark Turner, Margaret and Don Freeman, F. Elizabeth Hart, Isabel Jaén, Julien Simon, Michael Kimmel, Meir Sternberg, and Patrick Colm Hogan.

I am very grateful to the Social Sciences and Humanities Research Council of Canada, the Alexander von Humboldt Foundation, and the European Research Council for doctoral and postdoctoral fellowships supporting the development of this book. Profound thanks to Mark Turner, Ansgar Nünning, and Gerard Steen for supporting my fellowship applications, and supervising my work on Frye and other topics. The anonymous reviewers for University of Toronto Press provided very helpful advice. I thank the late Ron Schoeffel for supporting the project and helping me through the submission and publication process, Anne Laughlin and Carolyn Yates for copy-editing the manuscript, and Anthony Jenkins for kindly creating the drawing for the book's cover. Like so many other students of Frye, I am also very thankful to the de Groote Trust, of which Alvin is the manager, for a subvention in support of publication of this book. The fund has helped move many studies through various presses, and most importantly of all the Collected Works of Northrop Frye.

Parts of the book have appeared elsewhere. Chapter 1 adapts and revises about ten pages from chapter 4 of my doctoral dissertation. Chapter 3 is a revised and expanded version of a paper that was presented at the conference "Northrop Frye: New Directions from Old" held at the University of Ottawa in 2007, and later published as "Reframing Frye: Bridging Culture and Cognition," in *Northrop Frye: New Directions from Old*, edited by David Rampton (University of Ottawa Press, 2009). I thank Marie Clausén, Eric Nelson, and the University of Ottawa Press for permission to use that material. My introduction adapts parts of a review titled "The Turn to the Mind, Inside and Out," published in the *Journal of Literary Theory* (2010). I thank the editors for permission to use this material as well.

Finally, deepest thanks to my parents, family, and friends for the sort of ongoing personal support without which all other support would be meaningless. Most of all, thanks to my wife Melissa, for everything, and especially for gallivanting through Europe with me as the book slowly made its way to completion.

As usual, the remaining errors are my own.

Michael Sinding
Amsterdam

BODY OF VISION

Introduction
Landscapes and Prospects

Northrop Frye's ideas fundamentally changed the landscape of literary and cultural criticism and theory, and powerfully affected other disciplines. Today, however, Frye is somewhat marginal in literary and cultural studies, largely because much of the research in these fields over the past four decades has taken on theories, assumptions, and styles (broadly speaking, post-structuralist) that are incongruous with his in important ways. Yet there are good reasons to think that it is time to begin to reassess, recover, and develop what he has to offer. The topics in these fields are still Frye's main topics, and his compelling ideas about them have not been adequately digested and appreciated. At present, when many scholars are frustrated with the limitations of post-structuralist thinking and are searching for new ideas and approaches, a careful reconsideration of one of the great critical minds of the past century is timely indeed.

Post-Frye theories and assumptions differ from Frye most fundamentally in their ideas about meaning: what the structures of language and literature are, and how they work. But more recent research (broadly speaking, cognitive) on thought, meaning, language, narrative, and worldview is strikingly congruent with Frye's ideas. Thus, when considering the far-reaching implications of such work for the study of literature, culture, and ideology, Frye's work leaps into new prominence. I propose putting his core ideas into play with ongoing debates on some of the central questions and major approaches in literary studies and its adjacent fields. There are interesting parallels between Frye's views of the relation of literature to thought, language, and culture, and views developed in three lively intellectual undertakings: primarily cognitive poetics, but also two sociologically oriented schools of literary study, cultural studies and new historicism. I will show how these relationships of parallelism can develop into relationships of complementarity by conjoining various approaches into improved frameworks for analysing these topics and relations. Such a dialogue will clarify the implications and applications of theoretical concepts and offer some salutary correctives that may be invisible from within any one approach. To create this dialogue, I will relate cognitive poetics, cultural studies, and new historicism to Frye's ideas through three case studies. I will look at Dante's *Divine Comedy* in the light of cognitive poetics (the coherence of the metaphorical architecture of the storyworld), Hobbes and Rousseau in the light of cultural studies (how metaphors and story types create liberal and conservative worldviews), and Milton's pastoral elegy "Lycidas" in the light of new historicism (how cognitively universal and culturally particular aspects of metaphor and story interact in the poem and the genre). Through focused conversations and syntheses, I will develop all four approaches and illuminate their frameworks and subjects. While any one perspective may slight the forest or the trees, integrating perspectives on major aspects of literary production, transmission, and reception (small and large, in both structure and history) will create a sense of the whole system of interrelations connecting roots to branches, and trees to both seeds and forests.

Before delving into the details, in order to see what is at stake in this undertaking, one should appreciate the powerful effect Frye's ideas have had on their many audiences. Frye not only changed the scholarly landscape, but also spoke to generations of students and the public in ways that few critics have. He conveyed powerful ideas in clear, simple, highly readable language so his books could reach the widest possible audience, both academic and public (see WP xix–xx). He achieved his influence not through the usual route of extreme specialization, but through the synthesis of vast reading in which he discovered patterns that integrate his topics into encompassing, yet simpler, new wholes. These patterns often result from surprising shifts of perspective, which Frye creates by marshalling and knitting together disparate evidence and insights in unexpected ways. Often, he conveys these shifts and patterns through ingenious "verbal formulas," turns of phrase that impart turns of thought. Thus he developed a new schematology (he thought of his work as schematic rather than systematic, more diagrammatic than doctrinal) and new (or recreated) terminology that unified, rather than multiplied, specialist knowledge.

We can state in a few sentences what Frye's main topics and key ideas are, to suggest how and why they resonate with so many readers. Frye dealt mainly with literature and related it to its inner and outer workings: thought, meaning, and language on the one hand; and culture, society, and history on the other. In Frye's view, myth (or narrative) and metaphor are the basic structures of literature, and the imagination is the basic human capacity that creates them. The imagination is primarily constructive, not mimetic or referential. That is, it is geared toward (the writer) putting together ideas and (the reader) entertaining them. It engages a kind of attention that is centripetal more than centrifugal – writers use words hypothetically, and create stories and metaphors for their own sake, rather than for mapping the world beyond them. As a result, writing and reading individual stories builds up cosmologies, or mental worlds, which human desire founds and shapes. As another result, in a society, a certain group of stories tends to gain a canonical status and stick together to form a mythology. That mythology then builds up a cosmology for that society, rather than for an individual text. Social mythologies and cosmologies define the main concerns of their societies, and provide a larger sense of the human situation and destiny. There are recurring organizing principles and experiences in human life, and so there are recurring organizing principles and structures in human metaphors, myths, and mythologies. These are the conventions of literature, which include types of stories and genres, metaphors and imagery, characters, style, rhetoric, and more. Conventions are often extremely long-lived and widespread, and give literature both its coherence through history and its power to communicate across history. Both metaphor and myth are concerned with identity: the experience of unity between subject and object. Metaphor is concerned with establishing one thing's identity with another, typically an aspect of human personality with an aspect of nature. Myth is concerned with the story of the central experiential pattern of losing and re-establishing identity. Frye interweaves and elaborates on all of these ideas, each simple but powerful, on the basis of his remarkable knowledge of the cultural history of the West and beyond.

To contextualize this study, let us consider more closely the background of Frye's influence and legacy. His impact on literary criticism and theory is so deep and pervasive that it is difficult to gauge in any definite way.[1] However, Robert Denham has measured it as thoroughly as possible by examining and evaluating responses, applications, elaborations, and citations of Frye's work. Denham's "Auguries of Influence" cites Murray Krieger's 1966 remark that Frye "has had an influence – indeed an absolute hold – on a generation of developing literary critics greater and more exclusive than that of any one theorist in recent critical history" (78). Literary theorists who "have felt compelled to come to terms with Frye's work, even when they disagree with him ... include – to name only some of the most visible – Harold Bloom, Hayden White, Geoffrey Hartman, Murray Krieger, Jonathan Culler, Tzvetan Todorov, Paul Ricoeur, Terry Eagleton, Angus Fletcher, Paul Hernadi, Frank Kermode, Fredric Jameson, Robert Scholes, W.K. Wimsatt Jr., and René Wellek," and also Frank Lentricchia (81). There is also "the massive body of practical criticism Frye's theories have engendered." However, this kind of measurement does not always clearly show how Frye changed the way people think about literature. It is dizzying, inspiring, and a little unsettling to discover the extent and diversity of Frye's major and permanent contributions to the history of specific topics and questions in literary studies. Looking at topics I know reasonably well, genre and satire, recent studies and anthologies confirm this. In Ruben Quintero's *Companion to Satire* (2007), Frye's ideas are still prominent, if not quite as prominent as Mikhail Bakhtin's. Paul Simpson's *On the Discourse of Satire* (2003) says that Frye's *Anatomy* "shaped much criticism thereafter" and its "pithy definition" of satire is "more widely referenced perhaps than any other single formula" (52), though Simpson regrets that it has been little unpacked and probed (53). And Frye makes a respectable showing in John Frow's *Genre* (2006), along with Aristotle, Bakhtin, Derrida, and Todorov. These are rather different kinds of books, too. Quintero's *Companion* is fairly introductory but has many subtopics covered by many scholars, Simpson's is mainly a linguistic study, and Frow's is more post-structuralist, particularly Foucauldian (his book is in the New Critical Idiom series, which introduces key concepts in the light of recent theory). I expect this is true with many other topics, though no doubt some (e.g. genre, structure, and form) more than others. Scholarship on a number of individual authors – notably Blake, Milton, and Shakespeare – has not been the same since Frye. To return to the point: Frye changed the landscape – in fact, many landscapes – and although post-structuralism displaced him, it did not undo his influence. The landscape cannot be unchanged.

Today, critics no longer feel compelled to come to terms with Frye's work directly. Recent scholarship on Frye tends toward the contextual and comparative: it considers his intellectual influences and how his ideas compare with those influences (e.g., Denham's *Religious Visionary*; Gill, Cotrupi, Jonathan Hart, and Hamilton's *Anatomy*). (To some extent, this kind of focus may also be due to recent work that has prepared Frye's Collected Works and examined his unpublished writings.) Some of this scholarship situates Frye in relation to current debates in relevant fields, but opinion is divided about his relation to new historicism and cultural studies, the ruling schools of thought in literary and cultural scholarship. There does appear to be agreement that Frye's ideas are out of step with the politicization of literary studies in these schools (Denham, "Pity" 18–19). Yet some critical leading lights draw deeply on Frye's literary thought, though they do so with mixed feelings. Hayden White calls him the "greatest natural cultural historian of our time," ("Frye's" 28) and White's general theory of the literary structuring of history writing (*Metahistory*) is based in large part on Frye's scheme of mythic genres. Fredric Jameson's *Political Unconscious* similarly relies on Frye's analyses of genre and myth, even as it condemns a perceived anti-historical, formalist, and religious bias (see White, "Frye's" and "Ideology," for critics with similar attitudes, including Terry Eagleton and Frank Lentricchia). Other scholars give him respectful nods from time to time. In one of his early books, Stephen Greenblatt, the founder and main exponent of new historicism, mentions Frye as an "impeccable intelligence" on Shakespeare and alludes to him occasionally: Frye's concepts of "demonic parody," "fables of identity," and Shakespeare's "green world" appear in his other works (*Shakespearean* 23; *Learning* 120; Gallagher and Greenblatt, *Practicing* 38; "Theatrical Mobility" 85). Gallagher and Greenblatt's own introduction to their approach unconsciously echoes Frye's introductory dismissal of "all the literary chit-chat which makes the reputation of poets boom and crash in an imaginary stock exchange," such that "that wealthy investor Mr. Eliot, after dumping Milton on the market, is now buying him again; Donne has probably reached his peak and will begin to taper off; Tennyson may be in for a slight flutter but the Shelley stocks are still bearish" (*Anatomy* 18). In their version, the "literary stock market" is beneficial to the extent that it allows new investments: "Shares in Sir John Davies, say, decline, as capital shifts to Aemilia Lanyer and Lady Mary Wroth; John Denham gives way to Lucy Hutchinson and Gerard Winstanley," and so on (*Practicing* 10). Thus some Frye scholars have argued Frye's importance for these schools (see Hamilton, Salusinszky, Adamson, and Wang). But even favourable contextualizations tend to cast Frye as either an early contributor, in which case he is now superseded, or a late challenger, in which case he is now doomed. In either case, the shadow of the present obscures his work.

Sympathy for Frye's theories often seems to go along with the belief that cultures and cultural artefacts must be understood in terms of their similarities and general principles, whereas lack of interest or distrust seems to correlate with the belief that cultural study must focus on difference and particularity. However, considering the frequent exaggerations on both sides, it appears that a critic's general allegiance to similarity or difference is a matter of prejudice in the strict sense. That allegiance might begin as a matter of emphasis – what predominates, what comes first – and might remain so, if it were not that the need to dispute others' existing views tends to push a critic's own toward an opposite extreme and harden them into something more dogmatic than "focus" and "emphasis." For example, Jameson contrasts Frye's "positive hermeneutic" with his own "negative hermeneutic." That is, Frye illustrates a drive toward "historical *identity*" and "affinity between the cultural present of capitalism and the distant mythical past of tribal societies ... our psychic life and that of primitive peoples," which "tends to filter out historical difference and the radical discontinuity of modes of production and of their cultural expressions." Jameson, however, evinces a "sense of historical difference" that seeks to make vivid "what happens when plot falls into history ... and enters the force fields of the modern societies" (*Political* 130). Foucault's *Archaeology of Knowledge* places itself within a turn, in the disciplines of intellectual history, away from "vast unities like 'periods' or 'centuries' to the phenomena of rupture, of discontinuity" (4): one of his aims is precisely to avoid "the categories of cultural totalities ... to question teleologies and totalizations" (15–16). Greenblatt, a Foucault aficionado, insists the "disruptive forces" of "colonization, exile, emigration, wandering, contamination, and unintended consequences, along with the fierce compulsions of greed, longing, and restlessness" are what "principally shape the history and diffusion of identity and language, and not a rooted sense of cultural legitimacy" (*Cultural* 2).[2] Cognitive literary scholars, on the other hand, tend, like Frye, to emphasize commonalities and coherence. Turner urges the profession of English to pursue "a global continuity and a global unity" based on "a grounding, integrated approach to language and literature as acts of the human mind," which leads to a focus on the "vast space of systematic unconscious understanding" that is the context for nuance (*Reading* 6, 7, 18). Fauconnier and Turner say that disanalogy is "grounded on" and "coupled to" analogy: "We are not disposed to think of a brick and the Atlantic Ocean as disanalogous, but we are disposed to think of the Atlantic Ocean and the Pacific Ocean as disanalogous ... Psychological experiments show that people are stymied when asked to say what is different between two things that are extremely different, but answer immediately when the two things are already tightly analogous" (99). Citing Donald Davidson's remark that "even to understand and think about difference, we need to presuppose a vast range of similarities," Hogan points out that comparative literary study looks for distinctions and tends to exaggerate the specific differences it finds into group differences, which produces "a disproportionate sense of discrepancy and opposition" whereas "in fact there are far more numerous, deeper, more pervasive commonalities than differences" (*Mind* 3). Verbal art is produced not by nations and periods but by people, who are "incomparably more alike than not" (3). And critics interested in evolutionary theory emphasize the common nature of humans as a species. Put this way, these emphases seem to be products of temperaments, general assumptions and approaches, or worldviews, rather than of actual analysis or empirical investigation.

In fact, a number of figures of speech that have become part of folk wisdom express this contrast in strategies of understanding in less technical ways. To this end, Isaiah Berlin uses a fragment of the Greek poet Archilocus, which speaks of the hedgehog who knows one big thing as opposed to the fox who knows many small things. Several metaphors for the point are visual. If you are not a "big picture" person, you may be criticized for being "short-sighted." Frye, for his part, lamented the "academic tunnel vision" that sees his big pictures only as "sweeping generalizations" (WP 243). There is also the more recent contrast between people who are "lumpers" and those who are "splitters." Clancey has even suggested that there may be individual neural biases for processes of lumping and splitting, more elegantly termed *assimilation* and *distinction*, as learning strategies (4). However, this lumper versus splitter conflict should turn back into a matter of emphasis.

To attempt this, instead of contextualizing Frye in relation to past scholarship, I will try to look through the present to the future and continue the work of developing Frye's theories from the resulting vantage point. I find the most interesting responses to Frye to be just such developments of his ideas, in relation to either literary theory and criticism – e.g., on myth and genre, Fletcher's *Allegory* (1964), Todorov's *The Fantastic* (1973), Hernadi's *Beyond Genre* (1972) and "Entertaining

Commitments" (1981), and Jameson's *Political Unconscious* (1981) – or in other disciplines. As Denham notes, Frye's ideas,

> especially those that form his literary theory, continue to spill over into other disciplines, affecting them in substantive ways. His ideas have been applied by philosophers, historians, geographers, anthropologists, political scientists, and by writers in the fields of advertising, marketing, communication studies, nursing, political economy, legal theory, organization science, social psychology, and consumer research ... Interestingly, the debts to Frye come not from his writings about nonliterary topics: they derive, with a handful of exceptions, from the principles set down in *Anatomy of Criticism*. (*Handbook* 111)

The readiness of his concepts to "travel" is a highly valued quality of Frye's work, and is highly encouraging for the kind of interdisciplinary work I will attempt.[3]

Scholarship as Romance and as Comedy: From Quest and Battle to Dialogue and *Bricolage*

My study of figurative language and thought has made me quite conscious of the metaphors I use and how they guide my thinking, so it is worthwhile to reflect on those employed to characterize the nature of interdisciplinary study. There are interrelated metaphors for two aspects of this work – the general nature of the relation between fields, and the discourse that brings them together in various ways.

Frye warns of the dangers of vertical and horizontal metaphors for relations between literary study and other disciplines (SM 106–7). His concern is that such metaphors tend to deprive a field of its autonomy and coherence. Vertical metaphors of taking another field as a "base" or "foundation" for criticism (to which I add "grounding" and "hanging") are deterministic, and make literary study secondary to the foundation discipline (and perhaps defer the literary part indefinitely). Horizontal metaphors of "connecting, uniting, reconciling or bridge-building" between neighbouring intellectual edifices may be even worse, as they promote a way of bringing together ideas from different fields that tends to destroy the original contexts of each of those ideas. I have tried to avoid the liabilities of these metaphors, and instead let the ideas interpenetrate, as Frye advises – that is, to let cognitive ideas and thinkers "manifest themselves from within" literary criticism, like medieval angels (SM 107).

Recent cognitive criticism shows the imprint of some of these lessons. Increasingly, it emphasizes a balanced and reciprocal interchange between equal partners, and describes that interchange through metaphors of conversation, dialogue, debate, and other forms of fair meeting (e.g., Alan Richardson's introduction to his *Neural Sublime*; he later invites the cognitive side to reply, or at least overhear [78]). Cognitive literary critics have become wary of the way the "other" field can seem more authoritative, objective, and unquestionable, at the expense of the genuine progress and insights made within the home field. Several times, Richardson quotes Ellen Spolsky's salutary puncturing of "the common mistake of interdisciplinary studies," that is, "assuming that hypotheses presented from the area in which I am an amateur are (somehow) more reliable than the more familiar, but embattled assertions in my own field" (*Gaps* 41). Spolsky therefore recommends a "confrontation of the emergent theories of cognition with a suspicious reading of innovative texts," as literary scholars uniquely can "bring to the debate ... familiarity with complex texts and sophisticated interpretive practice" to rigorously challenge cognitive hypotheses (41, 2). Spolsky, Richardson says, calls for the "interpenetration" of cognitive and historicist literary studies – rather than the mere supplementation of one by the other, she argues that each must be "embedded" in the other (*Neural* 3). This is the voice of experience. Richardson and Spolsky have become close enough to the other field to have seen through the mirages of certainty and totality and gained a more realistic perception of the possibilities of exchange.

This sense of exchange has a further rhetorical outcome in the growth of metaphors of configuration, of putting together something new out of disparate parts (building, synthesis, integration, and blending). This, too, is as it should be, given the relative youth of both cognitive science and cognitive criticism. Richardson writes, apropos of the currently "sketchy" state of neuroscience, that "if our colleagues in the cognitive and neuroscientific fields are still (as V.S. Ramachandran puts it) 'tinkering' in productive and exciting ways in advance of a new scientific consensus, we can tinker with them, bringing additional objects of inquiry, different questions, and a certain healthy skepticism ... into the conversation ... we even have a fancy French name for it, *bricolage*" (*Neural* ix–x).

Conceptions of disciplines and their relations have implications, too, for the kinds of metaphors we write by – the metaphors by which we conceive and carry out scholarly discourse. George Lakoff describes three such metaphors: the guided tour, the heroic battle, and the heroic quest. In the guided tour, thought is motion, ideas are locations, reasoning moves step by step toward conclusions, and communication is a tour of an intellectual terrain given by a knowledgeable guide. In the heroic battle, the author's theory is a hero, an opposing theory is a villain, argument is war, and words are weapons. The argument-battle defends the hero's position and demolishes that of the villain. In the heroic quest, "knowledge is a valuable but elusive object that can be discovered if one perseveres," so the scholar is "the hero on a quest for knowledge, and the discourse form is an account of his difficult journey of discovery" ("Contemporary" 43–4). However, these are not the only metaphors that guide academic writing, and they may not be especially fitting for interdisciplinary research. Indeed, as the quest and battle are major events in the romance genre, the metaphors based on them seem to take a "romantic" view of scholarship: their attitude to learning and knowledge favours the individual, authoritative, and certain (the right trumping the wrong) over the cooperative, exploratory, and tentative.

Frye disliked the metaphor of intellectual "positions," for obvious enough reasons. It evokes the idea that opponents must fight things out until only one controls the whole territory. Any position affords only one perspective, and in battle positions get entrenched and movement gets difficult. Winning the battle becomes more important than the territory itself. Frye preferred metaphors of shared vision, and approvingly cited the etymological basis of "essay" as "trial or incomplete attempt" (AC 3) – an exploration, rather than a tour or quest. On the trials of interdisciplinarity, he turned a romantic metaphor in a comic direction: "A scholar in an area not his own feels like a knight errant who finds himself in the middle of a tournament and has unaccountably left his lance at home" (GC ix). Perhaps more typically, he also saw his own work in terms of construction, in which he as an "architect" built "palaces," "temples," or "museums" that readers could roam through or enter into more deeply (e.g., Salusinszky, "Art"; Denham, *Religious* 254–5). Evoking a more casual kind of building, he too used the term *bricolage*, to describe his book *The Great Code*, the Bible that is its topic, and the myth-making capacity in general: "Literature continues in society the tradition of myth-making, and myth-making has a quality that Lévi-Strauss calls *bricolage*, a putting together of bits and pieces out of whatever comes to hand" (GC xxi). I, too, prefer to follow metaphors like these, which have a bent toward the genre of comedy: as in the traditional turbulent wedding finale, they are more dialogic and social, more provisional and pragmatic, and more concerned with joining things together to create something new.

Thus, to round up these metaphors and apply them to *Body of Vision*, each of my chapters sets up a conversation between different forms of criticism, but each conversation takes place in Frye's house, so to speak, where he acts as presiding spirit, sets the topics and agenda, and guides the course of question, answer, and discussion. Across the table from one another are mainly cognitive and contextualist critics, but the conversation also devotes considerable energy to analysing texts. In time, each exchange becomes a configuration – each dialogue as it progresses goes some way toward building (or rebuilding) an approach that adapts and integrates selected elements from other approaches. As a result, each dialogue also points in new directions, raises new questions to explore, and locates new places for constructing, crafting, and embellishing.

To associate these metaphors of scholarly discourse with a congenial comic genre, observe that dialogue and debate are typical events in one of Frye's favourite genres, Menippean satire or anatomy. As the shorter "dialogue" or colloquy form of the genre, which has roots in Plato, develops into longer forms with more speakers joining the discussion, the setting is usually a *cena* or symposium in which the thinkers discourse around a table as they drink and dine late into the night (AC 310). Frye mentions Walter Savage Landor's book *Imaginary Conversations* as an example of the genre, and what I propose in the present book is in part a series of conversations that I have imagined within the theatre of my own mind. Gathering these thinkers around the same table can produce, I think, some valuable results that transcend the contribution of any single symposiast.[4]

This background should help clarify the organization of this book, and the time has come, as it usually does in an introduction, to sketch out that organization. The first part of my project develops an initial synthesis of Frye's theory of meaning with semantic theories in cognitive linguistics and poetics. The main topics of synthesis concern mental structures of metaphor, schematic imagery, and narrative. Once I establish certain basic lines of connection, I link that initial synthesis with major issues of cultural worldviews and literary history, as articulated in the critical schools known as cultural studies and new historicism.

The first chapter builds an agenda for comparing and integrating Frye's theory of literary imagination and structure with conceptual metaphor theory, especially its approach to literature, as represented mainly by the studies of George Lakoff, Mark Johnson, and Mark Turner, whom I will call the conceptual party. I introduce the two theories side by side; spell out their common principles, assumptions, and aims; and focus on their common concern with schematic structure in metaphor and myth. On the Frye side, I concentrate on the arguments in *Anatomy of Criticism*, and elsewhere, that myth and metaphor create schematic structure throughout human culture (in reason and philosophy as well as in art), as those arguments reveal Frye's affinities with the conceptual party better than do his explicit discussions of metaphor. I find that both parties view metaphor as conceptual, rather than as essentially linguistic. Hence metaphor is far from being merely ornamental; rather, it informs reasoning and knowledge by guiding inference. Moreover, both parties point to the existence of quasi-spatial conceptual models underlying thought and discourse as the basis of meaning and of certain effects. The conceptual party calls these structures image schemas and analyses them mainly in metaphors. However, where the conceptual party examines the relations among individual metaphors, poems, and cognitive models such as the Great Chain of Being, Frye considers the relation of metaphors and poems to what he calls a literary cosmology or cosmos – a kind of total world picture of a culture – and its continuing history. Hence Frye's theory of metaphor is intimately tied to his theory of myth and mythology or cosmology, and image schema research can inform the study of central elements of these structures. My preliminary analyses follow up this intuition, and consider how metaphoric image schemas correspond to Frye's structuring principles of literature, including, but not limited to, the *axis mundi*.

The second chapter applies the synthesis developed in chapter 1 to Dante's *Divine Comedy*. I show how large-scale metaphoric image-schematic structure is the basis of the coherence of Dante's storyworld, and hence of the text's meaning, values, and effect of aesthetic resonance. That storyworld structure is a particular version of medieval cosmology, which in turn builds on the broader tradition of literary cosmology mapped by Frye. It superimposes several major image schemas in a coherent picture, and this superimposition enables new inference and resonance with other images and concepts. For example, the cosmic VERTICAL SCALE of the *axis mundi* maps onto the cosmic structure of nested CONTAINERS, so that as Dante moves upward, he also moves outward.[5] Such coherence-based inferences have theoretical implications that deserve some airing out. This chapter demonstrates how the conceptual party's analysis of coherence across metaphors refines Frye's analysis of the literary cosmos as the main context for Western literature; yet it also shows how combining these analyses can spark original insights.

The next two chapters turn to another aspect of literary cosmology, and focus on narrative and metaphor in worldview, ideology, and history. Recent approaches to critical analysis have grown up alongside post-structuralism, and have incorporated its insights into the nature of textuality into their own focus on the relations of texts to the historical and cultural contexts of their producers and consumers. However, such approaches charge that post-structuralism tends to elide the world out there and its history, and thus they regard deconstruction as a too-hermetic practice that is just another technique for spinning out academic analyses. They want to consider the power of texts to operate in the actual struggles of human lives and societies. To do so, such approaches typically revise Marxist theories of the determination of mental life by material and social conditions to suit a richer understanding of the relations of mind, art, culture, and society. There are, of course, differences between cultural studies and new historicism, though they seem slight from a distance, as each school's assumptions overlap. One major difference is that new historicism sees society and history as more complex and less predictable – and specifically, less governed by material factors – so the school is less focused on the critique of capitalism. Both schools have palpable shortcomings, but they do make valuable contributions to central questions. What is really needed for continued progress is a synthesis of these approaches with Frygean and cognitive approaches.

Chapter 3 turns to social mythology. I present another perspective in which Frye's work creates important opportunities and means to connect cognitive linguistics with cultural studies, and cast some fresh light on their topics. Frye's approach to the relations among literature, society, and ideology in *The Critical Path* bears comparison with that of cultural studies, as represented mainly by Roland Barthes, one of the school's founders, and Stuart Hall, one of its most influential current voices. I consider some ways in which views of the effects of literature and culture, and of the relation of literature and culture to society and politics, follow from views of meaning. On that note, I introduce George Lakoff's account of the role of metaphor and conceptual framing in moral and political discourse. Lakoff claims that liberal and conservative worldviews are both based on the metaphor of the nation as a family, but use contrasting models of the family. These worldview frames guide our thinking about values and moral issues, as smaller-scale conceptual frames guide our grasp of expressions and words. By comparison, Frye's account bases conservative versus liberal psychology on stories of the social contract versus Utopia – which are in turn based on Biblical stories of the Fall and the Holy City. There are, however, important (though non-obvious) ways to link Lakoff's ideas about language and thought with those of Frye and cultural studies, to produce a richer account of how metaphor and story inform political thought in discourse. Lakoff offers a crucial supplementation and clarification of analyses of the construction of ideology in cultural media. Supplementation and clarification also goes the other way. Lakoff's analysis of the worldviews of liberalism and conservatism is incomplete. Those worldviews are not based solely on family metaphors, as he claims, but are also based on myths and on other metaphors. Two of the major myths are those of losing Paradise and regaining it (rooted in the literary cosmology, as Frye shows), and the major metaphors – insufficiently appreciated by Frye and Lakoff – are versions of the body politic. These additional factors are at work in the political discourse of Hobbes's *Leviathan* and Rousseau's *Social Contract*. Different metaphors and narratives have different degrees of importance and interact in various ways, and contrasting uses of these structures can account for the contrasting views of Hobbes and Rousseau. Both texts use all of the metaphors and stories described by Frye and Lakoff, but the body politic metaphor seems most important. In fact, this metaphor has a mythic aspect, as a decisive step in both texts is the story of the creation of the body politic.

Chapter 4 deals with literary history, particularly with how my cognitive version of Frye's theory views the relations between general principles of literary cognition and the cultural particulars of historical texts and contexts. Here, Frye's view of the topic once again confronts and converses with those of other approaches – in this case, the reigning historical school, the new historicism, and a narratological theory within cognitive poetics. Central among the basic differences of opinion between Frye and new historicism is that the latter downplays coherence, stability, and continuity in literary response and literary function, while Frye overplays these factors. In fact, new historicism's approach to genre was in part an explicit rejection of Frye's view of genres as long-standing structural conventions that tie literary texts more strongly to the context of literary tradition than to their local historical context. New historicism reverses this idea, and treats the context of local historical political struggles as more determining than tradition. Interestingly, some new historicists, such as Stephen Greenblatt, recognize the challenge for this view in the stability of valuation of certain texts and authors, and of some other features of literary structure and response. However, where they fail to explore this issue seriously, Frye addresses it directly and extensively in *Words with Power*. My aim is to develop an approach that can analyse the relative contributions of historical cultural factors and general cognitive factors in literary structure, response, and use, and how they interact. The history of the pastoral genre is apt for this purpose, as it appears decidedly dated in many ways, yet is still capable of powerful communication. Louis Adrian Montrose's essay on the "pastoral of power" can be connected with Frye's discussion of archetypal and anagogic perspectives on how Milton's "Lycidas" evokes the whole pastoral tradition and its role in Western culture, and with Patrick Colm Hogan's (Frye-influenced) theory of universal plots rooted in universal emotions. Here, too, Frye's approach can mediate between, and partly synthesize, cognitive and historicist approaches to literary history. Unlike either of them, it offers ideas of the general principles and shape of cultural history, and those general historical principles illuminate how general cognitive principles are specified and how they interact. "Lycidas" prompts reflection on how universals and particulars interplay in determining local thematic and ideological meanings, and longer-term literary value.

A brief conclusion looks back over the syntheses proposed and the arguments for them. I emphasize the potential for reviving and elaborating on Frye's core ideas and putting them to work again, and make some suggestions about important questions and directions for the future.

Turning from a fancy French word for what I will be doing to a fancy Latin word for what I will not be doing, I will now establish and review some caveats about the nature and scope of this project.

Books and Brains: Levels of Explanation in the Humanities and the Sciences

Any study of the relation of literature, and metaphor and narrative in particular, to cognition is liable to raise questions about the relation of those things to the brain. I will not try to answer such questions, nor will I go out of my way to raise them, and the reader may wonder why. To clarify the scope of the present study, I will talk briefly about the relation between the humanities and the sciences, and to talk about that I will need to talk about levels – of structure in the world, and of explanation in science. In short, while I am happy to see efforts to connect "hard" brain science (at the more solid lower levels of neurons and neural circuits and brain regions and processes) with humanistic matters (at the airier upper levels of what and how people think), I am not sanguine about most current attempts to do so. That is, what I understand of the state of knowledge in this endeavour seems patchy and tentative enough that further speculation or extrapolation on these topics is not useful for my project, however useful it may be in its own territory. It usually does not give literary studies enough to go on. Nor, in turn, does my project have much immediate bearing on such proposals. I expect these mind-matter connections will reveal themselves in time, but at present they remain well hidden. More looking is needed before such leaps can be made. Thus, I will leave aside speculation about how metaphor and story may connect to neuro-cognitive, neurobiological, neurochemical, and neuroscientific research generally. Instead, I will keep to the conceptual levels – that is, the levels at which Frye's analyses of myth and metaphor may connect to cognitive analyses of metaphor and narrative. There is even good reason to think that this conservative approach is a better way to make progress toward filling in the explanatory gaps than is impulsive level-collapsing. It is fair to ask that higher-level analyses be compatible with lower-level ones, but at present, the latter are often compatible with any number of the former, so it is more productive to specify the upper levels more fully.

Although most research in the humanities does not go deeply into neuroscientific waters, there are nonetheless many pages of speculation in these directions. Such speculation can be fascinating, but is sometimes extravagant and rarely convincing. A number of literary writers have found material in recent developments in the sciences of mind for their more hypothetical speculations (Tom Wolfe, David Lodge, Ian McEwan, Richard Powers, and others), but literary fiction at least eschews direct claims. Popularizations and extrapolations of science regularly offer simplifications, exaggerations, and hyperextensions, and some in popular media have started to deplore "neurobabble." This kind of commentary on what the mind sciences mean for humanistic matters, for the contemporary "world picture," tends to pump the most emotion possible into the farthest-reaching implications, swinging from the salvific to the cataclysmic. Several examples demonstrate the point. As exhibit A, I cite George Lakoff's claim in *The Political Mind* that the existence of mirror neurons proves humanity's inherently empathetic and therefore politically progressive nature (203–5, cf. 117–8). Neuroscientists at the University of Parma discovered mirror neurons in the 1990s. Specific actions, such as grasping an object, are correlated with the firing of specific groups of neurons. Vittorio Gallese and others discovered that when their macaque monkeys only *saw* other monkeys (or humans) performing that specific action, some of the *same* groups of neurons that fire in "monkey do" also fired in "monkey see." As Gallese puts it, "Action observation causes in the observer the automatic activation of the same neural mechanism triggered by action execution" (445). The same class of neurons exists in humans and possibly other species. When we see or imagine or read about a certain action, we run an unconscious "simulation" of that action on our own brains – at some level, we experience what we observe, which is one reason why pleasure and pain are "contagious." Ergo empathy is in the genome, and the future looks friendly. On the other side, a fitting exhibit B is Tom Wolfe's article on how neuroscience (brain imaging in particular) reveals that intelligence, thought, feeling, and behaviour are fully determined by the flickerings of genetically hardwired brain matter, and thus mind and self and soul, free will and discipline and accomplishment, are mirages emanating from a piece of machinery (Wolfe offers the telling title "Sorry, but Your Soul Just Died"). As neuroscience kills off these illusions, the human values bound up with them will also die, leading to worldwide catastrophe worse than that of the twentieth century following the death of God in the nineteenth. With evolutionary psychology, the tragic self-knowledge that there is no self will drag humanity back into chaos.

This variety of commentary, with these ambivalent qualities, is not confined to journalism and literature. Speculations are contested all the way up the ladder of expertise, even to the most knowledgeable specialists. In fact, the situation here suggests there is not always a clear line between popularizations and "real" science, particularly when it comes to open questions, and when experts venture beyond the bounds of their areas. Scientists themselves are also guilty, if that is the word, of following personal values and pet theories, looking for what they want to find, speculating energetically, and reflecting on and broadcasting the "implications" of what they take to be fact. Contrast, for example, the speculations in George Lakoff's political books with those of Steven Pinker in *The Blank Slate* (and see how science and values get entangled in their popular-press debate, noted in my citations for chapter 3).

On a more specific topic, metaphor is a major concern in both linguistics and literary studies. But linguistics, which is generally considered a major part of cognitive science, is closer to the sciences than literary studies is. There, too, there is a mixture of enthusiasm and scepticism on questions of how metaphor relates to the brain, and to "lower levels" of analysis generally. Consider some prominent and promising examples of speculation about metaphor and brain from linguists and cognitive scientists. V.S. Ramachandran and E.M. Hubbard link metaphor and even the origin of language with evidence for "natural constraints on the ways in which sounds are mapped onto objects" (e.g., people tend to associate nonsense names "kiki" and "bouba" with jagged and amoeboid shapes, respectively) plus a "sensory to motor synaesthesia" that would map sound contours to vocalizations ("Synaesthesia" 19). They further explain such synaesthesia in terms of connections that occur in the part of the brain known as the angular gyrus, which is concerned with cross-modal associations and is located at the "TPO junction," where the temporal, parietal, and occipital cortexes meet (18). Mark Turner suggests that conceptual blending (connecting disparate concepts in imaginative ways, including metaphor) is related to perceptual binding (perceiving objects as coherent entities, even though the brain processes their various properties, such as form, colour, and motion, in separate regions), though he is careful to draw the line between binding and blending (*Literary* 110–2). Rick Grush and Nili Mandelblit propose specific brain regions and processes as candidate mechanisms for conceptual blending. They also take their cue from studies of binding, and also focus on the "temporal-parietal-occipital association area" (233). In George Lakoff's recent accounts, the "neural theory of metaphor" (NTM) analyses concepts and mappings in terms of computations carried out by choreographed activations of various types of neural circuits ("Neural"). *The Cambridge Handbook of Metaphor and Thought* (ed. Gibbs, Jr., 2008) also contains chapters on computational theories, the brain, and artificial intelligence, and discusses evidence from psycholinguistics. These approaches are intriguing, and useful for work on the borders of linguistics and cognitive science, but what is the critic to do with them? One lesson here is that it is generally more worthwhile for critics to tinker about narrative and metaphor as mental structures than to tinker about brains. For one thing, linguistics-neurobiology links are controversial. Even in cognitive linguistics, for example, those who discuss the hard-scientific aspects of conceptual metaphor theory do not often take up Lakoff's NTM approach. In the *Cambridge Handbook*, only Lakoff discusses the NTM, and he himself recognizes the barriers raised by the difficulty of acquiring the needed expertise, though he then claims to have overcome them: "Metaphor analysts rarely know neural computation, and they shouldn't be expected to. The Neural Theory of Language Project has figured out a way to let linguists be linguists and not computer or brain scientists" ("Neural" 36). Yet Gerard Steen and others have somewhat soft-pedalled Lakoff's recent neuroscientific ambitions (Steen, "Contemporary"). Alan Richardson recognizes the value of neurobiological plausibility for such theories, and says the "postulates of the Lakoff-Johnson-Turner group have gained the serious attention of leading neuroscientists" ("Studies" 7). But he cautions that cognitive linguistics sometimes pretends to be more scientific than it is. It presents an accumulation of examples; but critics prefer the "controlled, randomized, and double-blind experiments that constitute the gold standard for empirical studies with human subjects" ("Studies" 7).

A broader lesson concerns the importance of careful philosophical thinking when it comes to tracing the webs of causality between books and brains and merging humanistic and scientific forms of explanation. Indeed, given that the nature of science and its role in humanistic scholarship is often misunderstood in literary studies, the philosophy of science could help to both introduce and contextualize cognitive and empirical approaches. This would help to clarify the issues without getting into the unnecessary technicalities of any specific science. Listening to philosophy of science means, among other things, respecting the fact/value dichotomy and the difficulty of reductive explanation. After all, even rigorous experiments do not guarantee permanent knowledge. Richardson observes "how often seemingly 'hard' empirical findings are overturned and how weakly supported some allegedly empirical work can turn out to be on a closer look" (*Neural* xi). Results may fail to be replicated, or may not be statistically significant, or may be marginalized by later results. A more general problem derives from the principle that theory and fact are inter-defined. That is, theories posit structures and processes that underlie what is observable, and observations are made in terms of such theories rather than being straightforwardly objective (see Kuhn, especially chapter 10). A simple example is the difference between how Ptolemy and Copernicus would see and describe what we still call "sunrise": the first would see the sun moving around the earth, while the second would see the earth moving around the sun. Both observations are tied into complex webs of categories, words, and conceptual models. These webs mean that scientific results do not necessarily have stable meanings or confirm or disconfirm theories in any unproblematic way. Even a wrongheaded approach may generate experimental results and create a veneer of success (e.g., behaviourism). Additionally, results are often pressed into the service of conflicting theoretical speculations. These may be just the risks of any scientific endeavour, but they show that empirical expertise does not confer an ability to generate satisfying explanations, or even to adjudicate the claims of competing frameworks, at least in the short term. This is not scepticism or relativism about science: in the long term, there is much that is not open to serious doubt.

The disputes between philosophers and scientists over how and why consciousness emerges from the brain quite clearly show the difficulties of connecting the mental and physical. This is where the mind-body problem now lives. Philosophers have long experience in grappling with this problem, and although scientists complain that long experience has not resulted in appreciable progress, philosophers rightly question over-hyped claims about science suddenly leaping over all imaginable obstacles with a few snazzy fMRI scans. David Lodge's *Consciousness and the Novel* contraposes two wildly differing views in its first few pages. The "Astonishing Hypothesis" of Nobel laureate Francis Crick (co-discoverer of the molecular structure of DNA) is that "'you,' your joys and your sorrows, your memories and your ambitions, your sense of personal identity and free will, are in fact no more than the behaviour of a vast assembly of nerve cells and their associated molecules. As Lewis Carroll's Alice might phrase it, 'You're nothing but a pack of neurons'" (qtd. in *Consciousness,* 2). Stuart Sutherland's *International Dictionary of Psychology,* on the other hand, blandly declares that "consciousness is a fascinating but elusive phenomenon; it is impossible to specify what it is, what it does, or why it evolved. Nothing worth reading has been written about it" (6). Some of the best philosophers of mind today would say that Sutherland gets closer than Crick does to the extreme intractability of even imagining how anything material can be conscious.[6]

Cognitive critics reflect, as part of their peculiar disciplinary position, on the comparably vexed relations between the humanities and the sciences: both how they can go wrong and how they ought to go right. David Bordwell proposes a mode of criticism that links interpretation with science without simply being either – that is, "not disguising culture as nature, but nibbling at the edges of philosophical doctrine with teeth sharpened by empirical inquiry" ("Case" 16). He addresses the concern that scientific approaches are irrelevant or worse because their reductive explanations ignore or eliminate all that is most important in culture. What Bordwell calls "good naturalization" implies a balanced relationship between philosophical and scientific fields. As philosophy of mind takes into account empirical scientific findings, science has a history of turning philosophy's traditional problems into "matters for empirical investigation" (e.g., "naturalizing epistemology") (14). Thus "an explanation of thought will be consistent with knowledge" from the rest of science, such as electrochemistry, evolution, and brain structure (15).[7] Coming from the other direction, Turner notes that literary scholars have the "crucial evidence" of "the imagination working at its highest pitch" (according to Richardson, "Studies" 2). Cognitive scientists need models of higher-order cognition and imagination in order to connect them with more basic cognitive structures and processes. In his review of and reflection on contrasting methodologies for literary study, Richardson concludes that empirical researchers should recognize that study constraints may screen out complexities and nuances, and should not minimize the value of trained introspection, informed intuition, and disciplinary expertise, while speculative critics should avoid making empirical claims or learn how to test them ("Field Map" 25). In addition, he concludes that literary scholars are poised to ask questions about "gender, culture, and history," which cognitive scientists are prone to neglect (2).

These opportunities and challenges have prompted calls for interdisciplinary cooperation and analyses for at least twenty-five years. In 1987, Turner argued that because metaphor is a principle of thought, critics should work with linguists, anthropologists, psychologists, neurobiologists, and philosophers of science (*Death* 13). Shortly after, Bordwell proposed that analyses of the arts should aim to "fit together physical, physiological, psychic, and social processes" ("Case" 21). Today, Ray Gibbs Jr. sees teasing apart the influences of brains, minds, language, and culture "in both enduring and novel patterns of metaphorical thought" as a major direction of future metaphor research ("Metaphor" 13). Interdisciplinary work is urgently needed, but if the "vertical" metaphor of "levels" is not used advisedly, the apparent virtues of such work could turn out to be, as early Christians liked to say about the virtues of the pagan gods, merely glittering vices.

Learn to Love Your Levels

Given what critics think about *what* we can and should do to work with our colleagues in the sciences, what can we discern about *how* to do these things? Science theorists often arrive at the idea that there are a number of "levels" of structure in the world and consequently that several levels of description and analysis are needed to explain that world. Depending on how the levels and their interrelations are understood, this view can allay concerns about "reducing" literature to some single narrow scientific explanatory scheme. Each discipline covers several levels, and the relations among levels are importantly reciprocal, and so no discipline need be seen as "based" or "founded" or "depending" on another.

What of specific hierarchies of levels? Few critics have suggested what exactly they should be, and none have agreed on them. Yet these hierarchies bear on how various apparently competing fields and frameworks might cooperate. One of the most pertinent, detailed, and balanced of these multi-levelled constructs is Hogan's in *Cognitive Science, Literature and the Arts* (202–10), which has definite implications for literary study. Hogan identifies what he calls the "standard levels of explanation" and the disciplines associated with them: society (political economics), mind (psychology), organic matter (biology), and inorganic matter (physics/chemistry) (202). Further, the hierarchy is a rough temporal sequence: each level both incorporates and is derived from the one that precedes it. He also makes a few crucial points about how these levels are related. First, the lower elements "provide necessary conditions" for the higher ones, and laws are conserved as we move up the explanatory ladder. For example, "laws of acoustics do not cease to operate in or bear on the psychological experience of music" (202). Next, "each level is defined by the emergence of some structure that is not accounted for by laws at the lower level" (203). The laws of inorganic matter do not capture the patterns of life, nor do the laws of biology capture the patterns of mind: organisms are much more than their molecules, and minds are much more than their neurons. Hogan says that this relationship is uncontroversial, but has potentially controversial implications; for example, while the mind is clearly contingent on brain function, this does not show that the mind is "really" just the brain, and does not mean that it is actually the "mind/brain." It is just that because lower-level laws continue to apply, any disruption of lower functions may also disrupt higher functions. Hogan quotes the Nobel laureate Robert Sperry: "The events of inner experience, as emergent properties of brain processes, become themselves explanatory causal constructs in their own right, interacting at their own level with their own laws and dynamics (qtd. in Holland *The Brain* 89)" (203).

In addition, Hogan argues that higher levels have profound consequences for lower levels. Specifically, "while laws are conserved upwards, *structures are projected downwards*" (207), and so an emergent structure organizes lower-level elements in its own terms. For example, "transportation systems," which are "integrated structures at the social level," project to the physical level and "tak[e] diverse bits of matter spread discontinuously across different regions and mak[e] them into a single structure" (207). This projection is a matter of organization, not causality. Treating lower levels in terms of higher ones is "interpretation," and treating higher levels in terms of lower ones is "explanation"; both of these "are important and neither is eliminable" (208). An implication of this downward projection that develops Sperry's point is fundamental for all sciences, for cognitive criticism generally, and for the focus and scope of the present book: "We should know as much as possible about the higher-level structure we are investigating before we go too far with the lower-level explanations ... Without a clear sense of higher-level structure, we cannot even know what there is to be explained ... cross-level explanation is inseparable from cross-level interpretation" (209).[8] Despite the metaphor in the word "fundamental," lower levels are not more real than higher ones, nor do we need to genuflect to the former to have a worthwhile conversation about the latter.

A cognitive approach to literary and other phenomena can accommodate elements at all levels. For the purposes of this book, the key point is that however the levels are carved up, my analysis will stay at the upper levels of the structures and processes of conceptualization, literature, and language, because that is where Frye's theories can connect with those of linguists, psychologists, and other critics. Yet my approach is also constrained by an awareness of the long-term goal of eventually connecting the various levels of explanation with one another. The minimal lesson is: do not allow the levels to conflict, given whatever you know about them.

Other metaphors that link body and mind lie behind my title. "Body of Vision" evokes, I hope, the sense of the relation of the body not just to sensory vision (the eyeballs, optic nerves, and other brain-related apparatus), but also to conceptual and imaginative vision. The "embodied" approach to cognition, which sees "the body in the mind" (as when metaphors map sensorimotor structures to "higher" conceptual structures, as per Lakoff and Johnson) has revolutionized the field, has been highly productive for literary studies, and matches some of Frye's early intuitions and later directions. The idea that such metaphor and kindred forms of imagination lie behind thought and meaning leads to postulations of a "poetics of mind" – a somewhat broader term than "cognitive poetics" (and also the title of a book by Gibbs Jr.). The other connotation of "body" draws on a different metaphor, that of a body as a coherent or organized (as in the bodily organs) assembly of things. It alludes to Frye's description of literature as a society's "body of vision" (e.g., CP 127), that is, an assembly of visions of human life in imaginative terms, parallel to but distinct from official ideologies and religions. These visions are coherent despite being unlimited in number and highly various in style, shape, feeling, and attitude, because they are intricately interwoven and work on the same principles. This view of literature is characteristic of what Frye calls the mythical or archetypal level of literary study, which is concerned with literature as communication and social fact. This level "attempts to fit poems into the body of poetry as a whole" by comparative study of conventions and genres (AC 99). This form of criticism also relates poems, conventions, and genres to the larger context of culture – as Frye provisionally defines it, "the total body of imaginative hypothesis in a society and its tradition" (AC 127). Seeing literature as a body of vision, then, is akin to seeing it as a "secular scripture" – an interconnected vision of the human situation, but with a special cognitive force that invites a hypothetical kind of response to possibility, rather than belief or disbelief in actuality. This is an essential perspective in the chapters that follow, which deal with recurring conventional metaphors and myths; their basis in bodily experience; their organization in texts, mythologies, and cosmologies; and their functions in culture and society. To investigate bodies of vision is to consider Frye's sense of the big picture: the whole panorama of mental models of literary imaginative worlds. As I will show, each approach to meaning in metaphor and narrative informs the other: embodied cognitive science's analyses of schematic conceptualization in language illuminate and are illuminated by the schematic imagination in literature and its embedding in culture and history. Let us open the symposium, then, and see where the talk takes us.

1 "Systems That Won't Quite Do": Schematic Structure in Literary Metaphor, Myth, and Models

I do not think of the *Anatomy* as primarily systematic: I think of it rather as schematic. The reason it is schematic is that poetic thinking is schematic. The structure of images that C.S. Lewis in *The Discarded Image* calls "the Model" was a projected schematic construct which provided the main organization for literature down to the Renaissance: it modulated into less projected forms after Newton's time, but it did not lose its central place in literature.

Northrop Frye, "Reflections in a Mirror," 1966

My first imaginary conversation will reveal important parallels between Frye's literary and cultural theory on the one hand, and cognitive literary studies on the other, which make it worthwhile to look at these theories in each others' lights.[1] The most important parallels concern the relation of metaphors to one another and to the larger mental models that structure culture, literature, philosophy, science, and moral and political worldviews and ideology. Determining their points of agreement and divergence will indicate how they may be developed in concert and supplement, extend, and correct one another's claims and arguments about common concerns. From this vantage, I see Frye as elaborating some of the broader cultural implications of the conceptual approach to meaning, and the conceptual party as able to support certain versions of Frye's theses about literature and culture by articulating the linguistic and conceptual details. (Putting them together, as I have suggested, reveals more of the forest and more of the trees than either one alone.) After a brief overview of some common aims, principles, and background, this chapter turns to detailed discussions of the former, then the latter. My ultimate aim is to describe the possible forms of coherence across metaphors and their imagistic structures. This will establish the groundwork for a study of metaphoric coherence in what Frye calls "literary cosmologies," which are metaphoric storyworlds. Storyworlds, as David Herman defines them, are "mental models of who did what to and with whom, when, where, why, and in what fashion in the world to which recipients relocate ... as they work to comprehend a narrative" (*Story Logic* 5). Literary cosmologies are metaphoric storyworlds, in that they are structured by compounds of metaphors (i.e., many aspects of the storyworld are metaphorical, and as they interact with one another, the metaphors combine). Chapter 2 will use this chapter's analysis to examine the metaphoric coherence of the cosmology of Dante's *Divine Comedy*. The chapters that follow connect the cosmology to social mythology and to literary history.

George Lakoff, Mark Johnson, and Mark Turner pioneered a revolutionary approach to figurative language and thought that captured imaginations across the world. At present, their approach constitutes a flourishing research program that invigorates many fields. It has roots in cognitive linguistics, which is also highly interdisciplinary and claims a very broad scope, examining metaphor, figures, and narrative in many areas, including literature, philosophy, religion, anthropology, politics, mathematics, and particularly worldview and common sense.[2] As with Frye, there is an impressive interdisciplinary range of sources and influences. Cognitive literary studies encompasses cognitive poetics, narratology, rhetoric, reader response, and more. Indeed, it may draw on any of the fields associated with cognitive science – not only linguistics, but also cognitive psychology, anthropology, and various divisions of neuroscience.

In fact, the theories of Frye and of Lakoff, Johnson, and Turner have had a comparable reception, which points to some of their common aims and assumptions. Early views of Frye tend toward hagiography or hatchet job, and the gamut remains narrow and polarized. While many critics find Frye's ingenious analyses, analogies, synopses, and pattern perception highly informative, others find them over-ingenious and over-idealized. Hamilton discounts genial praise, general abuse, and frequent misunderstanding, and sees serious critiques of Frye as containing chiefly a distrust of his systematicity, a concern that abstraction away from contextualized particulars can flatten textual complexity and literary experience, and a rejection of his totalizing ambitions (*Anatomy* 4–6). Dolzani notes the standard complaint of reductivism, and says that during the fifties and sixties Frye was attacked for being unscientific and not demonstrating his patterns empirically, and during the seventies and eighties for misinterpreting empirical findings. In the nineties, sociological critique questioned who decides on and interprets universals, and on what authority ("Wrestling" 98). Cognitive critics are also oriented toward form and structure, general principles, and universals, and Lakoff, Johnson, Turner, and others, have also been accused, in similar terms, of overstating their claims and simplifying their topics: reducing specifics to abstractions, flattening meaning and emotion, downplaying cultural and historical context, and insufficiently distinguishing literal from figurative.[3]

Without going into great detail, we may fashion one response for both: reductionism need not follow. Neither theory purports to explain everything about particular texts. Both address a clear need for larger perspectives by creating frameworks capable of bringing together arrays of related phenomena. Fine-grained facts may be the most immediately evident to the senses, especially with art, which trains and rewards heightened sensitivity to nuance. But they are not the only facts, and they do not vitiate the need to address those of coarser grain. Indeed, if Frye and the conceptual party are right about the importance of conceptual systematicity (or schematicity) in the creation of resonance for myth and metaphor, then their theories offer an explanation for some of the most powerful, and most specifically artistic effects of literature – an explanation of a kind that is unavailable to the scrutineer of surfaces. As Frye puts it, "Many who consider the structure of my view of literature repellent find useful parenthetic insights in me, but the insights would not be there unless the structure were there too" ("Reflections" 145).

This chapter will use Frye's literary theory to conjoin two kinds of cognitive criticism that are deliberately oriented to explanations that make essential, but not greedily reductive, use of cognitive research. On the one hand, there is the kind of criticism represented by Mark Turner (*Reading*), David Bordwell ("Case," "Contemporary"), and Noël Carroll ("Prospects"), who demur from both isolated textual "readings" and sweeping self-ratifying annexations of texts and theories by "grand theory" to focus on "middle-level" topics and problems specific to the arts. These critics aim to describe the commonplace background knowledge of audiences, and explain how it underpins their experience and interpretation of texts and films. On the other hand, there is the kind of criticism represented by Reuven Tsur, who distinguishes cognitive poetics from cognitive linguistics by the former's focus on explaining specifically poetic "effects" ("Aspects" 279–81). Yeshayahu Shen ("Cognitive Constraints," "Metaphor") makes a related distinction between approaches to the nature of poetic (especially figurative) structures. Contrary to approaches that highlight the creativity and novelty of poetic discourse, his approach highlights the need of such discourse to conform to cognitive constraints in order to be communicable. Poetic discourse must both conform to, and interfere with, cognitive processes (cf. Semino and Steen). Indeed, for Gibbs Jr., the "paradox of metaphor" everywhere, not just in literature, is that it is "creative, novel, culturally sensitive, and allows us to transcend the mundane while also being rooted in pervasive patterns of bodily experience common to all people" ("Metaphor" 5). As I will show, Frye's approach examines the special structures and processes specific to literature, but does so by comparing and contrasting literary cognition with non-literary cognition.

Frye's work evokes a vast horizon of implication in a "grand theory" way. Such ambition has an honourable pedigree. In the early part of his career, a number of influential scholars, under the aegis of anthropology and comparative religion, were studying large-scale symbolic cultural models, including cosmologies, that integrated myths, symbols, and rituals. Frye's particular focus was on "the identity of mythology and literature, and the way in which the structures of myth, along with those of folktale, legend and related genres, continue to form the structures of literature" (WP xii).[4] His aim of describing what Jung called the "grammar of literary symbolism" – an aim that ultimately derived from Giambattista Vico – was shared by Robert Graves, Joseph Campbell, and others, and was influenced by Sir James Frazer, Oswald Spengler, and Ernst Cassirer. These thinkers believed that such a grammar was the basis of all artistic thought and expression. Some believed it also shaped culture more generally, including philosophy, science, and everyday life. Frye thought of this search for a "coordinating principle" for criticism as seeking something analogous to the principle of evolution in biology, which, beginning with the "assumption of total coherence" in the subject, could then treat wholes (species/literature) as parts of individuals (organisms/works) (Salusinszky, "Towards" 237). The totality that Frye first referred to as a "language of poetry" or "grammar" of symbolism he later reconceived as an "order of words," then a verbal or literary universe (233).

Frye struggled all his life to work out a "total form" of such a grammar (Dolzani, "Introduction" xix). Total forms are in questionable taste at the moment, and so I will approach them tangentially rather than directly. Occupying a middle level, I will argue that cultural cognitive models exist that are larger, more plentiful, and more coherent than has yet been recognized, that they are grounded in natural perceptual and conceptual structures, and that they have important roles in cultural thought and experience. The focus shifts to the principles behind specific total forms, as some of Frye's reflections do:

> All my critical career has been haunted by the possibility of working out a schematology, i.e., a grammar of poetic language. I don't mean here just the stuff in FS [*Fearful Symmetry*] & AC [*Anatomy of Criticism*] & elsewhere, but the kind of diagrammatic basis of poetry that haunts the occultists & others. Whenever I finish a big job I seem to return to this ... In other words, once again I have a hope of reviving or making precise and detailed suggestions about – let's say the diagrammatic basis of schematology. (qtd. in Dolzani, "Book of the Dead" 23)

There are analogies of Frye's analogies in statements of the aims and ambitions of cognitive linguistics. Lakoff, comparing metaphoric dreaming to speech, writes, "Our metaphor system might be seen as part of a 'grammar of the unconscious' – a set of fixed, general principles that permit an open-ended range of possible dreams that are constructed dynamically in accordance with fixed principles" ("How Unconscious"). Fauconnier and Turner compare their theory of thought as "conceptual blending and integration" with evolutionary theory, and deny its reductiveness while they argue for its value in connecting presently disparate studies of universal human cognition and cultural particulars (e.g., qualitative social science with interpretive social science, in Turner, *Cognitive Dimensions* 11–12, 56–9; cf. Fauconnier and Turner, *The Way We Think* 91). Moreover, while Frye discusses the relation of metaphor to mathematics (AC 350–4), today's cognitive theorists have also found a major role for metaphor and other imaginative operations in the history and understanding of mathematics (Lakoff and Núñez; Fauconnier and Turner, *The Way We Think*).[5]

To turn to more specific parallel aims and principles, the aim of describing and explaining meaning by describing and explaining "structure" in language and literature is central to Frye and the conceptual party, in addition to its long history of scholarly attention. Frye's structural-totality approach reacted against both an extreme documentary historicism that dissolved individual texts in a welter of "objective" contextual detail, and the extreme ahistoricism of New Critical indifference to text-extrinsic details. His postulates are also idiosyncratic relative to the structuralist and post-structuralist tenets dominant through his later career, but I think this helped him avoid the excesses that contributed to their declines. Frye acknowledges an affinity with structuralism, the movement that came to analyse so many fields according to an idea of "a kind of structural unconscious," distinct from subjectivity and intention, that governs semiological expressions of all kinds (Ricoeur, *Rule* 319). He sympathized with the "direction" of structuralism toward interrelating different subjects non-imperialistically (SM x), but did not follow its specific principles. He speaks of structures of narrative and imagery rather than of conceptual binary oppositions. As a result, he did not contract the problems that plagued structuralist linguistics and its posterity, and was unaffected by its eclipse under the Chomskyan revolution in linguistics.

In a related way, Fauconnier and Turner see the twentieth century as the "age of the triumph of form" in "mathematics, physics, music, the arts, and the social sciences," in which knowledge reduces to "a matter of essential formal structures and their transformations" (*The Way We Think* 3). But form is not substance, and they seek "the human power to construct meaning" that lies behind form in the conceptual processes that constitute identity, integration, and imagination (6). Some cognitive critics try to recuperate, in a cognitive vein, the insights of earlier critics who examined the role of literary structure and form in relation to knowledge and experience. For example, both Spolsky ("Cognitive Literary") and Steen and Gavins admire Culler's efforts to characterize "literary competence" in structuralist terms, and the latter allude to precedents in Czech Structuralism, Russian Formalism, and semiotics (5–8). Indeed, while Culler's notion of "literary competence" in *Structuralist Poetics* is based on an analogy with Chomsky's approach to "linguistic competence" – i.e., the ability to understand an unlimited number of grammatically correct sentences (any number of literary texts, on Culler's analogy) – his account of that competence as consisting in knowledge of literary conventions, and his characterization of those conventions, are strongly influenced by Frye. Recall as well that Frye's original title for the *Anatomy* was *Structural Poetics*.[6]

Going farther back, both Frygean and cognitive poetics have significant family resemblances to Aristotle's *Rhetoric* and *Poetics*, which had an analytical focus on the relation of the structure of narrative plots to audience knowledge and response. Speaking of the cognitive study of art, language, and literature in relation to rhetoric, Turner declares that "if Aristotle were alive today he would be studying this research and revising his work accordingly" ("Cognitive Study" 10). Ellen Spolsky places Frye, along with other major scholars of structure, in this tradition:

> The claim that the ultimate goal of literary theory is to tell a story about the human mind can be traced back to Aristotle and, in modern criticism, to Northrop Frye. In his *Anatomy of Criticism* (1957), Frye claimed that the generic forms of literary works have a psychological reality that is separable from what he dismissed as "the history of taste." Literature, he assumed, displays the structure of the mind, the same claim Claude Lévi-Strauss had made for the material culture of Brazilian peoples in *Tristes Tropiques* (1955) and that Noam Chomsky was making for syntax in *Syntactic Structures* (1957). Whatever empirical data are studied, syntax or poems, face painting or pottery, the goal is ideologically humanist: the proper study of humankind is the human mind. ("Darwin and Derrida" 47)

The present study also moves along these lines, and participates in such efforts at recuperation in a cognitive key of critics with formalist-structuralist leanings. This aspect of the project offers something against the charge that cognitive approaches downplay their historical roots and affiliations (Richardson and Steen accept this critique from Adler and Gross) by noting possible common sources for ideas about spatial structure in metaphor and its bodily basis.[7] It will also bring into focus consensus, contention, and yet-uncharted regions of contact between Frye and cognitive poeticians.

As for post-structuralism, Hamilton overstates in saying that "post-structuralism seems inevitably post-Frye: he appears to belong to an earlier tradition, the assumptions, premises, and values of which have become alien" (*Anatomy* 7). It is true that Frye has been rebuked for sitting out the apotheosis of theory. For example, Leroy Searle says, bizarrely, that "the way that theory [Frye's *Anatomy*] was put together, while it now seems parochial, relied almost exclusively on work done in departments of literature" ("Afterword" 856). He continues:

> Frye's recommendation of "naïve induction," to try to find in literature alone an account of literary meaning, now appears not only naïve but precritical. One simply cannot proceed in ignorance of logic and philosophy, innocent of linguistics, isolated from intellectual history and

> anthropological learning and reflection, just as one cannot presume to be immune to practical and political considerations in reading and writing of any form. (858)

Searle may not be accusing Frye of ignorance of philosophy, linguistics, intellectual history, and anthropology (it is hard to imagine how anyone who has read Frye could lay this charge), but may instead be arguing that readers (presumably only professional readers) need these things to analyse literary meaning. There is considerable irony in the fact that, in sticking with his simple categories of myth and metaphor, Frye has turned out to be more prescient about meaning than those who pushed the assumptions of Saussurean structuralism into all the post-structuralist paradoxes of sliding and disintegrating signification. (I will examine the connections and contrasts among a spectrum of these views of thought and meaning in more detail in later chapters.)[8]

There may then be a further irony in an attempt to relate those simple categories to a movement in cognitive science and linguistics, especially given my earlier cautions about the pitfalls of connecting disciplines. However, cognitive science has repeatedly found that apparently simple elements of everyday life can turn out, at deeper levels of analysis, to be enormously complex. Speaking is simple for us; language is complex. Seeing is simple for us; vision is complex. Moving across a room is simple for us; such movement is complex. As long as we are careful about how we connect myth and metaphor with the sciences of mind, the simple with the complex, we may be rewarded with clarification of both.

The cognitive critics I consider in this chapter share further specific similarities of aims, assumptions, and principles with Frye. Like Frye, the conceptual party generally seeks to disclose how conventional metaphors and models underlie thought, language, and literature. The conceptual theory of metaphor was born in George Lakoff and Mark Johnson's book *Metaphors We Live By* (1980), and soon developed rapidly in several directions. Johnson's *The Body in the Mind* (1987) developed the implications of "image schemas," which were the central conceptual structures underlying metaphor that the earlier book had discovered.[9] In the same year, Lakoff's *Women, Fire, and Dangerous Things* worked out an extensive theory of thought (categories and concepts in particular) in terms of "idealized cognitive models," which are often metaphorical and image-schematic. Turner's *Death Is the Mother of Beauty* (1987) deals more directly with literature, and examines poetic metaphor in terms of models that derive from conceptual metaphors that use source domains of generation and kinship. Lakoff and Turner's *More Than Cool Reason* (1989) is probably the most important and influential book on cognitive approaches to poetic metaphor to date. It analyses how generic schemas behind metaphor enter into metaphoric elaboration, composition, and coherence (chapter 2); how a text conveys a global effect as a whole statement that builds on local metaphors (chapter 3); and how large cognitive and cultural models, such as the Chain of Being, frame metaphors and establish hierarchical and analogical relations among their elements (chapter 4). Turner's *Reading Minds* (1991), subtitled "The Study of English in the Age of Cognitive Science," focuses on the conventional unconscious conceptual patterns embedded in everyday language as the foundation of all special use of language and concepts in literary art.[10]

Lakoff, Johnson, Turner, and others persist in this general strategy of inferring relatively stable cognitive models underlying language, while expanding it by connecting it with other fields and topics. Frye also seeks larger patterns, or larger applications of patterns, and often observes structural analogies across multiple specific models, which Lakoff and Johnson do not generally concern themselves with. Frye's *Words with Power* describes a vast composite metaphor: literary cosmology is the metaphorical structuring of the target domain of consciousness by a variety of scalar source domains (151). Also unlike Lakoff and Johnson, Frye discusses what Talmy ("Fictive Motion") calls simultaneous "discrepant representations" of fictional and literal cognition: "Just as myth says both 'This happened' and 'This can hardly have happened in precisely this way,' so metaphor with the 'is' predicate says explicitly 'A is B' (e.g., 'Joseph is a fruitful bough,' Genesis 49:22), and conveys implicitly the sense 'A is quite obviously not B, and nobody but a fool would imagine that Joseph really was,' etc." (72).[11] Talmy's approach relates to conceptual metaphor theory (268–9): fictivity covers "metaphor" in other sensory modes (e.g., vision), as well as Gestalt pattern-completion phenomena that are marginally metaphorical, if at all (e.g., closure of a factive C-shape into a fictive circle). While Fauconnier and Turner's later work on conceptual blending (e.g., *The Way We Think*) takes a different approach from those of both Lakoff and Talmy and instead examines the processes and principles by which metaphors and other conceptual elements transform and combine in online meaning constructions, it also similarly stresses that blends remain connected to their input spaces, so that conceptual work, including "deblending," can be done anywhere in the network. The focus is on the extended context of metaphor and its interpretation, rather than on the established one-way mapping across domains.

I now turn (to use the rhetorical figure that Frye dubs the "topotropism" [AC 336]) to a more detailed comparison and integration of the theories of metaphor and thought of the two parties.

Agenda of Comparison and Integration

There are seven principal points of agreement on thought and meaning in language and literature between Frye and conceptual metaphor theorists Lakoff, Johnson, and Turner. These include:

1 Two linked processes are basic to conceptualization: first, sequentially scanning something occurring in time; second, "summarizing" such processes in a "spatial" way.
2 Metaphor is conceptual, not solely linguistic, as diverse linguistic expressions have an underlying systematicity.
3 Metaphoric conceptualization relies largely on the spatial (image-schematic) structure of concepts.
4 Image-schematic metaphoric structure is pervasive in thought and meaning, from micro-levels in meanings of words (e.g., in etymology, and connectives such as "in," "and," "on," "over," "through," etc.), sentences, and rhetorical figures, to macro-levels in cultural models, literary imagery and narrative, reason, philosophical systems, and cosmologies.
5 The basis for image schemas is the human body's experience of interaction with a spatial environment (its overall structure, and the entities in it).
6 Meaning and interpretation (linguistic and literary) require linking texts with a context of metaphors and models conventional in language and culture.
7 A text's power of "resonance" derives from the coherence of its metaphoric structure with such structures of knowledge, and with their grounding in experience.

Despite few direct connections between these approaches, they are highly congruent in that they all give prominence to the structure of conventional metaphoric models that underpin specific acts of meaning.

The two parties are divided by large differences of scholarly focus and style. Frye's work, rooted in traditional humanistic scholarship, is more concerned with religion, cultural history, the relation of culture to individual and social life, and the details of individual authors and texts than is the work of Lakoff, Johnson, and Turner.[12] Frye also does not deeply engage with their concerns with technical linguistic and scientific matters such as syntax, logic, mathematics, the origins of language, or the relation of culture to neuroscience and evolution.[13] However, both sides at least touch on the specialties of the other.

There are also differences of detail within the common ground:

- Frye's insights into conceptual systematicity in metaphoric models appear often, but are incidental to his explicit theory of metaphor, which concentrates on the psychological experience of "identification."
- The conceptual party is more consistently and thoroughly schematic about perception, conception, and language, whereas Frye sees meaning as more conventional and contextual. For him, the meaning of the word "in" is determined by context, and does not have a basic (physical "container") meaning (GC 59). Lakoff and Johnson argue that there is one word and one emergent concept for "in" for various uses, but the image-schematic conceptualization of it is basic, and non-physical extensions are metaphorical (*Metaphors* 59–60).
- In literary and cultural metaphor, both propose that a fundamental organizing vertical "axis" metaphor grounds cultural developments like the Chain of Being. But Frye sees kernel concrete images (e.g., Jacob's ladder) as primary (WP 158), organizing schematic images as verbal developments (e.g., "the scale, or measurement by degrees") (164–7), and theories (e.g., the hierarchical cosmology) as later rationalizations (158, 167–70). Lakoff and Turner treat schematic metaphor (e.g., the metaphors of quantity and quality in terms of a VERTICAL SCALE) as primary, cognitive models (e.g., the Great Chain) as built out of them, and concrete images as filling in metaphors and models (*More*, chapter 5).
- The conceptual party postulates conceptual parts and relations and processes – source and target, image schemas, figure versus ground, scanning and summarizing, mapping, etc. – and so can investigate the details and principles of how composition of elements (linguistic and literary) works. Frye's patterns generalize rudimentary

metaphoric structure to cover several examples, and so he regards his patterns as contexts, not essences. This enables him to observe structural analogies across multiple specific models, which the conceptual party overlooks (e.g., Freudian psychology and Marxist politics both invert the Great Chain's traditional top-down flow of causation and value).

- Frye agrees that fundamental concepts and beliefs are metaphorical, but celebrates self-consciously mythical and metaphoric "vision" as a shareable alternative to stock response and divisive "positions." The conceptual party argues that poetic metaphor goes beyond and even questions ordinary metaphor (*More* 67–72), but stresses how metaphor structures automatic everyday thought.
- Lakoff and Johnson say individuals have multiple worldviews (*Philosophy* 511). Frye recognizes openness, plurality, and fluidity within and across models, mythologies, and the individuals who hold them, but tends to talk in terms of single mythologies or worldviews for individuals and cultures.

Conceptual Metaphor Theory: Image-Schematic Mappings in Language, Reason, and Philosophy

A "schema" is an unconscious, simplified "cognitive model of some aspect of the world, which we use in understanding and in reasoning about it" (Lakoff and Turner, *More* 65). For example, journeys have necessary components, such as travellers, starting and end points, a path, and optional components, such as obstacles or a vehicle (61). Cognitive science can now describe in interesting detail the schemas that shape both *per*ception and *con*ception. For example, Lakoff and Turner provide some parameters for generic-level schemas:

- Basic ontological categories: entity, state, event, action, situation, and so on.
- Aspects of beings: attributes, behaviour, and so on.
- Event shape: instantaneous or extended; single or repeated; completed or open-ended; preserving, creating, or destroying entities; cyclic or not, that is, with or without fixed stages that end where they begin.
- Causal relations: enabling, resulting in, bringing about, creating, destroying, and so on.

- Image-schemas: bounded regions, paths, forces, links, and so on.
- Modalities: ability, necessity, possibility, obligation, and so on. (81)[14]

Systematic structure exists in and across metaphors, because they are mappings of schemas across conceptual domains. The basic metaphor LIFE IS A JOURNEY maps elements and relations from the source domain of travel to the target domain of life:

- The person leading a life is a traveller.
- His purposes are destinations.
- The means for achieving those purposes are routes.
- Difficulties in life are impediments to travel.
- Counsellors are guides.
- Progress is the distance travelled.
- Things you gauge your progress by are landmarks.
- Choices in life are crossroads.
- Material resources and talents are provisions. (3–4)

Partial uses and novel extensions of basic metaphors are all related, so readers grasp them easily. The opening lines of Dante's *Inferno*, "Midway along the journey of our life / I woke to find myself in a dark wood, / for I had wandered off from the straight path" (67) are related to Robert Frost's poem about taking the road less travelled by, to injunctions to stop and smell the roses, and even to the Volkswagen slogan, "On the road of life, there are passengers, and there are drivers." These expressions focus on different aspects of source and target, but they nonetheless all draw on the experience of journeying and knowledge of how it can connect with life.

Spatial-relations concepts are central to everyday thinking about concrete experience, and are an indispensable source for metaphorical structuring of higher concepts, and image schemas are part of the internal structure of elementary spatial relations (Lakoff and Johnson, *Philosophy* 31):

> A bounded space with an interior and an exterior is an ... extremely skeletal and schematic image. Sometimes we map this image-schema onto other images, such as our relatively rich image of a house ... or the outline of a country on a map. But we can also map [it] onto abstract target domains that themselves do not inherently contain images, such as

> wakefulness, alertness, and living ... When we understand a scene, we naturally structure it in terms of such elementary image-schemas. Prepositions are the means English has for expressing these schematic spatial relations ... [which also] structure abstract domains, as in "in love," "out of power," and so on. (Lakoff and Turner, *More* 97–8)

Johnson describes image schemas as "recurring, dynamic pattern[s] of our perceptual interactions and motor programs that give ... coherence and structure to our experience," which consist of "a small number of parts and relations, by virtue of which they can structure indefinitely many perceptions, images, and events" (Johnson, *Body* xiv, 29). They are "pervasive, well-defined, and full of sufficient internal structure to constrain our understanding and reasoning" (126).[15]

Image schemas underpin the most important property of metaphor: the projection of inferential structure to the target domain. For example, the image schema of BALANCE involves "a symmetrical arrangement of forces relative to an axis" (97). Correspondingly, the logic of balance has three important properties: symmetry, transitivity, and reflexivity. That is, "A balances B if and only if B balances A ... If A balances B, and B balances C, then A balances C ... A balances A" (97). Metaphorical projections inherit such inferential structure, which puts image schemas at the root of reason, both practical and formal. That is, image schemas create structures to reason with in any number of abstract domains (cf. Lakoff and Johnson, *Philosophy* 30–6, 544–6, on the inferential logics of image schemas and how they structure the syllogisms of formal logic). Balance is used metaphorically in thinking about mathematics (in equations such as X = Y), justice and law (punishments should fit crimes, people should have equal rights), and even diet (not too much of this or that).

Metaphor also defines the structure and overall coherence of philosophical concepts and systems: "First ... all philosophical theories, no matter what they may claim about themselves, are necessarily metaphoric in nature. Second ... the metaphorical thought is ineliminable: It is metaphoric thought that defines the metaphysics and unifies the logic of each philosophical theory. Third, this is simply a consequence of the fact that philosophical theories make use of the same conceptual resources that make up ordinary thought" (Lakoff and Johnson, *Philosophy* 345). Ordinary thought ultimately rests on metaphor, and philosophy ultimately rests on ordinary thought.

Frye's Literary Theory

Cognitive Processes

Approaches to literature and language are often "cognitive" in that they are informed by ideas about thought. This is especially true of Frye, who from his earliest work bases the fundamentals of his theory of culture primarily on postulated imaginative operations. Take a dozen or so of these fundamentals. His stated goal is "the systematic study of the formal causes of art" (AC 29) – meaning the imagined form of the work the artist aims to fulfil, as opposed to efficient, final, and material causes. Basic premises about the reading and writing imagination include two cooperating aspects of attention ("centripetal" and "centrifugal") and two cooperating aspects of literary response (literary experience as perceiving "movement" and literary knowledge as "static" conceptualization). Among basic techniques, literary stories descend from myths about gods, which are "ready-made metaphors" that identify an aspect of personality with nature. Hence literary myth and metaphor assume "a relation between human consciousness and its natural environment" that "outrages" the common sense based on separation of subject and object (WP 71), and literary stories are ultimately about losing and regaining this identity (121). Literary history evolves according to quasi-Freudian psychological principles: symbolic *condensation* (as in, e.g., tree god metaphors) in myth undergoes *displacement* toward "plausibility" – a more mind-centred term than "realism" (as in, e.g., characters associated with forests) (AC 51–2; cf. 136–40). Genre typology proceeds in several related dimensions. "Radicals of presentation," the basic conceptions of writer-audience relations, lead to the major divisions of *epos*, prose fiction, drama, and lyric (245–7ff.). Radicals of aural and visual design lead to the main tendencies and forms of lyric (babble-*melos*-charm and doodle-*opsis*-riddle) (275–80). Permutations of radicals of the author's approach to their content (personal versus intellectual) and characters (introverted and subjective versus extroverted and objective) lead to the major formal tendencies of prose fiction (novel, romance, confession, and anatomy) (308). This cognitive orientation appears in the interpretation of the broadest questions about the external relations of culture and criticism. Literature's relation to thought and language motivates the study of "conceptual rhetoric" in reason and philosophy (*Anatomy*'s conclusion concentrates on the spatial-conceptual metaphors linking logic to rhetoric) (326–37). Literature relates to society as part of its "mythology," a collection of stories that is, more than nature, the primary human environment – a "verbal universe." The theological universe with its heaven and hell translates into the levels of "the range of human mentality" (WP 175), so that stories of ascent and descent are finally about human consciousness (151) and literature's purpose is as an ultimate technique of meditation (28, 96). As Frye put it in an earlier essay: "The arts, including literature, might just conceivably be what they have always been taken to be, possible techniques of meditation, in the strictest sense of the word, ways of cultivating, focussing, and ordering one's mental processes, on a basis of symbol rather than concept" (SM 117).

It is curious that there has been relatively little discussion of Frye's theory of metaphor, or how it relates to his ideas about spatial thinking, given the essentially mentalistic approach to and considerable importance of both. But there are a number of possible reasons for this. First, when Frye discusses metaphor he stresses the relation of its "A is B" form, an identification of two distinct things, to a special kind of experience of empathic identification that overcomes the distinction between subject and object (e.g., WP 71–2). Second, he does not strongly connect this view of metaphor with his observations about metaphoric structure in conceptual thought (with heavy reliance on spatial connectives such as "on," "in," "depend," etc. [AC 335–7]), and in conceptual systems (e.g., psychoanalytic "hydraulic metaphors of drives and channels and blocks and cathects" [SM 71]). Third, his discussions of mental spatialization arise more in the context of narrative than metaphor. So studies of Frye's spatial thinking tend to skirt the issue of its usefulness and accuracy for criticism (e.g., Salusinszky, "Art of Memory"; Ayre, "Geometry," "Chart"). However, because Frye always aimed to "afford glimpses of interconnecting structural principles of literature that are actually connected with literature and the experience of studying it" (WP xxii), my point is not just that he or his literary subjects use image schemas – which is only trivially true if the conceptual party's idea that image schemas are ubiquitous is correct – but that he explicitly and persistently identifies, attends to, and analyses such schemas for their structuring role in culture, and that they do play something akin to the role Frye suggested.

Let us, then, take a closer look at Frye's story about this verbal imagination. When examining a verbal structure, "our attention is going in two directions at once," "centrifugally" gathering the conventional referential meanings of the words and "centripetally" interconnecting them to one another in their immediate context (WP 3). Centripetal attention builds up centrifugal meanings into a discourse-internal "structure" that is a gestalt sense of the whole. The principle echoes familiar sentence-level distinctions, like Frege's reference and sense, or semantics and syntax (GC 238n, 58). However, the "organizing effort of the mind is primary. Mere unfamiliarity with the referents, which can be overcome by further study, is secondary" (58). This primary meaning is metaphorical in a broad sense – most clearly in cases of "implicit metaphor" that are "produced by the juxtaposition of images only" without any explicit A-is-B grammatical form, as in Ezra Pound's poem "In a Station of the Metro" ("The apparition of these faces in the crowd / Petals on a wet, black bough") (GC 61, 56).

On the scale of whole narratives, there are two analogous stages in reading. First, the reader follows the narrative to completion; second, the reader responds with "a kind of *Gestalt* of simultaneous understanding, where we try to take in the entire significance of what we have read or listened to" (WP 69). The first response is associated with time and hearing; the second, with visual-spatial analogies, which "accounts for the word 'structure' as a critical term, where an entire work of literature is characterized in a spatial metaphor derived from architecture" (70).[16] We may "see" jokes, resolutions of mysteries, symbols, and thematic points. When a verbal structure is "reread often enough to be possessed, it 'freezes'" (GC 62). Thus, imaginative narratives are metaphorical in two senses: "If we 'freeze' the Bible into a simultaneous unit, it becomes a single, gigantic, complex metaphor, first by tautology, in the sense in which all verbal structures are metaphorical by juxtaposition, and second, in a more specific sense of containing a structure of significantly repeated images" (63–4). Frye's distinction also differentiates literary from non-literary language. Both operations apply simultaneously in all reading, but for the former, the "final direction of attention is inward" because literary texts "do not pretend to describe or assert," yet are not tautological either (AC 74). The process operates in larger contexts, too: a culture's traditional stories tend to stick together into a canonical structure that defines a worldview: "If we 'freeze' an entire mythology, it turns into a cosmology" (GC 76). Something similar happens with literary canons, which are the main descendants of religious mythologies. In the *Anatomy*'s "Polemical Introduction," the point is related to T.S. Eliot's notion of an "ideal order" implied in the literary monuments of the past (AC 16–19). Frye, though, develops the order as cultural mythology, not aesthetic pantheon.

There are nuances to how Frye developed and applied this basic idea. In *Words with Power*, he registers a few cautionary notes about how he spoke of this quasi-spatial seeing in earlier books. In the *Anatomy*, he spoke of it as a "thematic stasis" and identified it with Aristotle's term *dianoia* ("meaning" or "thought"), but noted that this *dianoia* "is the narrative looked at as a kind of still photograph: it should not be regarded as thought in the sense of a translation into discursive language" (WP 70). In the *Anatomy*'s reciprocating phrase (using Aristotle's *mythos* for plot), "the *mythos* is the *dianoia* in movement; the *dianoia* is the *mythos* in stasis" (AC 83). Producing this mental structure (and shifting from process to structure) appears to be partly automatic, but the ability can be developed with study. Yet with complex works there is no final and complete vision of the total structure. The response "is not simply to *the* whole *of* it, but to *a* whole *in* it: we have a vision of meaning or *dianoia* whenever any simultaneous apprehension is possible" (AC 78). Later in *Words with Power*, Frye recognizes that the two-stage distinction is a theoretical expedient. Yet the two kinds of perspective are psychologically real, however much we may and should assimilate them in practice (WP 74–5). In other late work, he favours the traditional term *anagnorisis* (understood to mean discovery or recognition [e.g., AC 187]) over "structure" (MM 6); and sees this simultaneous envisioning of narrative as connected to "peak experiences" or "moments of ecstatic union" (17).

Considering important parallels in cognitive research can fine-tune the idea of these complementary mental processes. Ronald Langacker defines the contrast between sequential and summary scanning (*Concept* 22, 78–9), and correlates it with distinctions in grammatical categories. These processes support other key aspects of cognitive linguistic theory, but the details of how they relate to image schemas and metaphor have not been much explored. Alan Cienki observes:

> Almost all image schemas ... can be realized in either a static or dynamic fashion. Most can represent a state of being as well as a process, e.g., we experience the PATH image schema in a dynamic way as we are moving, going from somewhere to somewhere else, and as a static *thing*, the spatial route that we have traversed or that we can traverse ... thus we can process a complex scene as a 'single configuration all facets of which are conceived as coexistent and simultaneously available' or as a series of states, successively transforming one into another (Langacker 1987: 145). The same dichotomy is found in metaphorical extensions. ("Some Properties" 6)

Thus the PATH image schema structures our knowledge of specific routes to and from familiar places, and we use that knowledge in our actual travels, and in informing other people (by language or drawing) how we got somewhere or how they can get there. Metaphorically, we can think of our paths through life or some event as processes or things, perhaps with some overall shape. The similarity to Frye's centripetal/centrifugal distinction is clear in certain formulations – e.g., "once the entire scene has been scanned, all facets of it are simultaneously available and cohere as a single gestalt," and in certain analogies – e.g., studying a photograph versus watching a motion picture (Langacker, *Concept* 78, 79). On the experiential quality and value of these forms of cognition, compare cognitive linguist Leonard Talmy's remarks on "ception" – a neologism meant to include both perception and conception:

> Cognitive dynamism is so much more the normal mode that the cognizing of staticism is often regarded as a special and valued achievement. Thus an individual who suddenly ceives all the components of a conceptual domain as concurrently copresent in a static pattern of interrelationships is said to have an 'aha' experience, while an individual who ceives a succession of one consequent event after another through time as a simultaneous static pattern of relationships is sometimes thought to have had a visionary experience. ("Fictive Motion" 271)

Thus the static spatial perception is important for the aesthetic-imaginative experience of resonance, but we must show how the image-schematic structure of metaphors in a text makes that possible.

Archetypes, Anagogy, and Literary Cosmology

Having gained a sense of the processes of literary apprehension – the dynamics of centripetal and centrifugal attention – we may now move into Frye's archetypal and anagogic forms of comparative contextual criticism. The "Theory of Symbols" in *Anatomy* distinguishes five phases of meaning that each specify a symbol's centrifugal relations and its increasingly inclusive contexts of centripetal relations – and thereby also its increasing resonance for the reader. Literal and descriptive phases deal with symbols like "cat" as (Saussurean) signs that designate referents, and as "motifs" that connect with and play roles in immediate contexts of syntax and discourse. The formal phase deals with symbols as images and poems as patterns of recurring images. Here, centripetal meaning links one image to another within the whole poem, and this internal structure of connections defines the form that organizes the content – which in turn is defined by the poem's centrifugal or referential relation to the world.

I gloss Frye's archetypal phase, a little glibly, by setting out the ligaments that interconnect a set of key "C" words: convention fosters communication, which fosters cultural community. A symbol is conventional when it is used in analogous ways in various works. This helps it to communicate within its culture and advance the poem's role in society as the "focus of a community." An archetype is a communicable symbolic unit that "connects one poem with another and thereby helps to unify and integrate our literary experience" (AC 99), prompting and guiding the creation of *categories* of types of characters, images, narrative formulas, ideas, genres, modes, traditions, and even "literature" as a coherent totality. Archetypal criticism concerns "literature as a social fact and as a mode of communication. By the study of conventions and genres, it attempts to fit poems into the body of poetry as a whole" (99). The word "fit" may be unfortunate here, as it evokes the cliché of the critic as pigeonholer; it is far more important that poetry is thought of as a whole body that conditions the reading of individual poems. Literary integration of this kind (by writers and readers) can build on some unity in physical nature – for example, the sea – or can be acquired by education – for example, studying pastoral symbolism to grasp the cultural resonance of Milton's "Lycidas" (99–100) (this example will become increasingly consequential in what follows). Frye concludes by stressing the cognitive basis of archetypal criticism:

> If we do not accept the archetypal or conventional element in the imagery that links one poem with another, it is impossible to get any systematic mental training out of the reading of literature alone. *But if we add to our desire to know literature a desire to know how we know it, we shall find that expanding images into conventional archetypes of literature is a process that takes place unconsciously in all our reading.* (100; my emphasis)

The stakes are high, as the alternative to total structure is incoherence:

> If there is no total structure of literature, and no intelligible form to criticism as a whole, then there is no such thing as an archetype ... But every student of literature has, whether consciously or not, picked up thousands

> of resemblances, analogies, and parallels in his reading where there is no question of direct transmission. If there are no archetypes, then these must be merely private associations, and the connections among them must be arbitrary and fanciful. But if criticism makes sense, and literature makes sense, then the mental processes of the cultivated reader may be found to make sense too. (qtd. in Hamilton, *Anatomy* 109)[17]

The archetypal perspective sees literature as an imitation of an order of nature as a whole, so it focuses on universal human symbols (e.g., food and drink, the quest or journey, light and darkness, sexual fulfilment). It infers from analogical interconnections among images, conventions, and genres that they are parts of a whole.

The anagogic perspective proceeds to a "real structure" for that whole, a "total form" that creates a "self-contained literary universe" out of the "aggregate of existing literary works" (AC 118). It is "apocalyptic" in recognizing only the limits of imagination and desire, not nature: it sees the subjective as containing the objective, nature within an infinite, eternal, omnipotent person (119).

Incidentally, this idea is less fuzzy than it sounds at first. The best-known remark about anagogy is Ezra Pound's memorably discouraging line about Dante's theory of meaning: "Anagogical? Hell's bells, '*nobody*' knows what THAT is!" (17). But Frye anchors his account of anagogy in fairly definite conceptions – though these conceptions are non-literal, and taxing to the imagination: "By an apocalypse I mean primarily the imaginative conception of the whole of nature as the content of an infinite and eternal living body which, if not human, is closer to being human than to being inanimate"; "a world of total metaphor, in which everything is potentially identical with everything else, as though it were all inside a single infinite body" (119, 136). His archetypal and anagogic readings of Milton's "Lycidas" help solidify what these conceptions imply. An overall form in a pattern of plot and imagery – the genre of pastoral elegy – connects to specific and general parallels in poetry, culture, society, and religious life (myth, ritual, doctrine) (99–100, 121–2). The former perspective finds "a whole liberal education simply by picking up one conventional poem and following its archetypes as they stretch out into the rest of literature," while anagogy focuses on idealized and paradoxical relations, uniting the archetypes of Lycidas's various divine roles in the figure of Christ (100, 121–2). The distinction between archetypal and anagogic levels may not be entirely clear, but, tentatively, in the archetypal perspective imagination is democratic, based in and contributing to society and common experience, while in the anagogic perspective imagination is akin to an absolute monarch, doing as it pleases and making the world follow it.

The god is the central image of anagogy and scripture is its primary form. But "encyclopedic" epics like those of Dante and Milton are related to these as "definitive myths, or complete organizations of archetypes" experienced as complete human worlds. Frye's affirmation of total structure both derives from and supports the idea of a "center" of literary experience, which is attested to by a "feeling":

> In the greatest moments of Dante and Shakespeare, in, say *The Tempest* or the climax of the *Purgatorio*, we have a feeling of converging significance, the feeling that here we are close to seeing what our whole literary experience has been about, the feeling that we have moved into the still center of the order of words. (117)

Encyclopedic epics operate as principles of cultural unification and resonance, seeming "applicable to, or [having] analogous connections with, every part of the literary universe" (120–1). This makes the anagogic perspective and response potentially omnipresent:

> The sense of the infinitely varied unity of poetry may come ... implicitly from any poem. Thus the center of the literary universe is whatever poem we happen to be reading. One step further, and the poem appears as a microcosm of all literature, an individual manifestation of the total order of words. (121)

Thus this centre is not, and does not belong to, any particular property or pattern of poetry. It results from, and so indicates, some total form, but is not part of it. The total form is conceptual, inferred from literary experience; the centre is the experience of relating the individual poem to these largest contexts, which are constructed in and projected from the mind of the properly responsive reader.[18]

Frye goes on to say that "anagogically, then, the symbol is a monad, all symbols being united in a single infinite and eternal verbal symbol which is, as *dianoia*, the Logos, and, as *mythos*, total creative act" (121). Reading the remark in terms of imaginative conceptualization rather than metaphysics may allay reservations about the air of ultimate synthesis here. It is possible to conceptualize a monad as a single part that contains a whole, and as "infinite and eternal" – for example, in Whitehead's sense that "everything is everywhere at once" (SM 292), in that all particular heres and nows epitomize all others because they embody the categories of space and time that are the conditions of any possible experience of them. These conceptions do not posit transcendental or idealistic realms that literature occupies or creates, but rather patterns of mapping developed in the process of comparative reading, which furnish contexts for more fully understanding individual works. Without them, readers could not understand WHOLE IS PART mappings in concepts like the microcosm, "concrete universal" symbols, or lines such as Blake's "To see a world in a grain of sand." Lakoff and Turner's GENERIC IS SPECIFIC mapping is intended to capture an aspect of such imagining, whereby readers understand specific situations in terms of the generic structure of other specific situations, as with widely applicable proverbs such as "when the cat's away, the mice will play" (*More*, chapter 4, especially 160–6).[19]

The interconnection of archetypal and anagogic contexts and responses is indispensable to Frye's central concept of "literary cosmology." To open his "theory of myths" (the theoretical core of "Archetypal Criticism"), he observes the strong appeal of certain features and kinds of models for cosmological themes:

> It has long been noticed that the Ptolemaic universe provides a better framework of symbolism, with all the identities, associations, and correspondences that symbolism demands, than the Copernican one does. Perhaps it not only provides a framework of poetic symbols but *is* one, or at any rate becomes one after it loses its validity as science, just as Classical mythology became purely poetic after its oracles had ceased. The same principle would account for the attraction of poets in the last century or two to occult systems of correspondences, and to such constructs as Yeats's *Vision* and Poe's *Eureka*.
>
> The conception of a heaven above, a hell beneath, and a cyclical cosmos or order of nature in between forms the ground plan, *mutatis mutandis*, of both Dante and Milton. (AC 161)

Thus "symmetrical cosmology may be a branch of myth" and "like myth, a structural principle of poetry ... Perhaps, then, this whole pseudo-scientific world of three spirits, four humors, five elements, seven planets, nine spheres, twelve zodiacal signs, and so on, belongs in fact, as it does in practice, to the grammar of literary imagery" (161). Frye considerably broadens the studies of Lewis, Tillyard, and others.

While these studies contextualize texts in a traditional overarching cosmological "background," Frye specifies a *generic* poetic cosmology and its productive *principles*: a schematic world-system that enables mappings across different levels and kinds of images. Dante's *Commedia* teaches "a grammar of the imagination," as he says elsewhere (qtd. in Denham, *Religious* 248). This broadened view of cosmological scaffolding applies to literature of many times and places and is thus a valuable instrument for comparative study. The four-level cosmology recurs throughout Frye's writings, and frames topics as diverse as individual works, writers, genres, periods, and traditions. Frye examines how such frameworks develop and how they relate to ethical and political values and beliefs. The cosmology is essential to his most celebrated insights: for example, his principle that "there are two fundamental movements of narrative: a cyclical movement within the order of nature, and a dialectical movement from that order into the apocalyptic world above" (161–2) (elsewhere he relates these to analogy and identity[20]); and his consequent identification of four pregeneric narrative structures, the archetypal *mythoi,* defined in terms of "movements" across the parts of the cosmological model (161–2). I will return to this cosmology below.

Frye's essays on the cosmologies of individual writers often examine them not as created *ex nihilo* but as revisions of or alternatives to this traditional one, as he learned from Blake that the phrase "private mythology" made no sense (SM 108). Frye's later work emphasizes the existence of a greater original symmetry hidden behind the Christian framework. Earlier gods might ascend from below, but Christianity viewed them as demons and their home as hell (WP 230, 276). A related insight appears in his argument that the Romantics finalized a revolution in the cosmological model, locating divinity not at the upper and outer limit of human reality, but as a force buried within and held down from above by oppressive worldly forces (inner and outer) (238ff.). Hence Frye's *Words with Power* presents the overall cosmology in terms of ascents and descents of higher and lower love and wisdom.[21]

Parallels: Metaphor in Culture

Expanding on parallels six and seven, I can specify five further interrelated principles linking these two approaches to metaphor in culture:

- a culture's metaphors interconnect, forming systems;
- the broadest system is a world or cosmos;

- that world is personal, charged with forces and values;
- such systems are organized by body-based orientational metaphors; and
- literary power comes from a work's resonance with these systems.

The principle of taking spatial (especially orientational) schemas as the basis of meaning is a key example of a point Frye suggested in rough outline in 1957, which cognitive science has since fleshed out. Under the heading "The Rhetoric of Non-Literary Prose," Frye discusses the links among grammar, rhetoric, and logic. He claims that there must be ideogrammatic "inner structures" or "middle grounds" that allow the assimilation of language to rational thought (whether between two languages or two speakers), and that these structures must themselves be symbolic (not "dictionaries"). He concludes that "the ideogram, in short, is a metaphor" (AC 334). After noting the failure of attempts to reduce grammar to logic and vice versa, he presents his version of rhetoric's link with logic:

> A great number of prepositions are spatial metaphors, most of them derived from the orientation of the human body. Every use of "up," "down," "besides," "on the other hand," "under" implies a subconscious diagram in the argument, whatever it is ... Very often a "structure" or "system" of thought can be reduced to a diagrammatic pattern – in fact both words are to some extent synonyms of diagram ... All division and categorization, the use of chapters, the topotropism ... signalled by "let us now turn to" or "reverting to the point made earlier," the sense of what "fits" the argument, the feeling that one point is "central" and another peripheral, has some kind of geometrical basis ... I question whether it is really possible to make B depend on A without in some measure hanging it on, or involve B with A without in some measure wrapping them up. (AC 335–6)

After the publication of the *Anatomy*, and rejecting the Jungian label that comes with any interest in "archetypes," Frye reformulates literary power in terms of resonance through the archetype-anagogy-cosmology bridge:

> For centuries the theory of music included a good deal of cosmological speculation, and the symmetrical grammar of classical music ... makes it something of a mandala of the ear. We hear the resonance of this mandala of possibilities in every piece of music we listen to. Occasionally we feel

> that what we are listening to epitomizes, so to speak, our whole musical experience with special clarity: our profoundest response ... [is] something like "This is the voice of music" – this is what music is all about. Such a sense of authority ... comes mainly from the resonance of all our aural experience within that piece of music ... The classic or masterpiece is a source of such a response that won't go away ...
>
> *Anatomy of Criticism* presents a vision of literature as forming a total schematic order, interconnected by recurring or conventional myths and metaphors, which I call archetypes ... I am providing a kind of resonance for literary experience, a third dimension, so to speak, in which the work we are experiencing draws strength and power from everything else we have read or may still read ... [T]he strength and power do not stop with the work out there, but pass into us. (SM 118–19)

Words with Power is "something of a successor" to the *Anatomy* (WP xii). Again, secular Western literature is intelligible overall because it presents a coherent human cosmos, which the Bible indicates or symbolizes: it is "a condensed and unified epitome of this poetic universe," a microcosm (xx–xxii, 121, 149–50). But this cosmos is "to be studied not simply as a map but as a world of powerful conflicting forces" (xxii). Frye generalizes "literary cosmology" to all schematic conceptual systems, but here he is more specific about their major structures. The *Anatomy*'s ideas about subconscious mental diagrams based on bodily orientation persist through to *Words with Power*, where Frye wonders whether whole metaphysical systems

> may not be growing out of a personal metaphor. We often run into diagrammatic illustrations, like the divided line in Plato's *Republic*, and other diagrams are implied by the connectives used. Some things are higher and other things lower; on the one hand we have this, on the other hand that; some data are inside us and others outside. Metaphorical connectives of this kind suggest the orientation of a human body in space. (13)

He urges critics to "look into some of these indecently naked formal systems that won't quite do: the cosmologies, for example, constructed out of the metaphors that lift us up or bring us down, that oppose one hand to the other, look in or out, go forward or back" (149ff.).[22]

Words with Power also modifies *Anatomy*'s argument, and drops the terms "archetype" and "anagogy" but maintains focus on the context of "total form." First, Frye analyses literature in terms of three "factors of the poetic": a narrative of losing and regaining identity, a pattern of imagery that creates an argument that separates a world of metaphorical unity from its demonic opposite, and a rhetoric of example and illustration (WP 121). Second, Frye thematically specifies the central cosmic pillar: "We may say, with many qualifications, that images of ascent are connected with the intensifying of consciousness, and images of descent with the reinforcing of it by other forms of awareness, such as fantasy or dream" (151). Third, he distinguishes between "the set of images that form the metaphorical kernels of the vision," and the "hierarchical cosmology" of nature as a structure or system, which derives from it (158–9), and is primarily ideological rather than poetic ("in the foreground of these cosmologies are the structures and ideologies of social authority that they do so much to rationalize" [170]). Its three aspects are more fully articulated as the cosmological chain, the quasi-scientific Ptolemaic cosmos, and Frye's preferred four-level theological version (166–70). Fourth, he argues that literary imagery and structure derive from four "primary concerns" that are based in the body but develop spiritual aspects: "The concern to make and create, the concern to love, the concern to sustain oneself and assimilate the environment, with its metaphorical kernel of food, and the concern to escape from slavery and restraint" (139). Further, building on the idea that following a narrative is closely related to a journey, he links his earlier observation of diagrammatic skeletons underlying conceptual systems with the quasi-visual "'thematic stasis' or simultaneous apprehension" prompted by the end of a narrative movement, and the specific vertical structure of the diagram: "As there is no more narrative to keep us moving ahead, our perspective shifts to an up-and-down vertical pattern. Out of this emerges the central metaphor of the *axis mundi*, a vertical line running from the top to the bottom of the cosmos" (120, 151).

Similarly, the conceptual party suggests that image schemas are rarely experienced as independent entities. They also stress that spatial connectives (especially orientational ones) play a role in organizing groups of metaphors, and that schemas interconnect in patterns of force to structure individual human worlds:

> By virtue of such superimpositions our world begins to take shape as a highly structured, value-laden, and personalized realm in which we feel the pull of our desires, pursue our ends, cope with our frustrations, and

> celebrate our joys. Much of the structure, value, and purposiveness we take for granted as built into our world consists chiefly of interwoven and superimposed schemata. (Johnson, *Body* 125–6)

Guiding this interweaving is a class of metaphors that

> does not structure one concept in terms of another but instead organizes a whole system of concepts with respect to one another ... [M]ost of them have to do with spatial orientation: up-down, in-out, front-back, on-off, deep-shallow, central-peripheral. These spatial orientations arise from the fact that we have bodies of the sort we have and that they function as they do in our physical environment. (Lakoff and Johnson, *Metaphors* 14)

Hence, metaphorically, happy, conscious, health and life, control or force, more, good, and reason are UP, whereas sad, unconscious, sickness and death, lack of control or force, less, bad, and emotion are DOWN (15–17). Metaphors that manifest these relations cohere with the deepest values of a culture. They are not a collection of separate cases, nor the result of mere convention. Metaphors that use the other spatial relations pairs as listed have a roughly positive-negative charge (cf. Krzeszowski, "Axiological"). So "coherence among metaphors is a major source of the power of poetry," and the resonance of a work depends on the coherence of its metaphors – with each other, with their grounding experiences, and with the culture's metaphoric system (Lakoff and Turner, *More* 56–89). As to the forces of these metaphoric worlds, I will now suggest that image schemas are the main elements of the literary cosmos, and are superimposed and interwoven to organize that cosmos (as with other metaphor systems) and its attendant tradition of narrative and imagery.

Image-Schematic Metaphor in Literature

Johnson's survey of image schemas explores their "pervasiveness in our experience," their internal structure, and their "range of metaphorical elaborations ... in our understanding of more abstract domains" (*Body* 117). He covers some of the very patterns that Frye analyses in terms of concrete image "kernels," schematic structure, ranges of metaphors based on structural variations, and how they interconnect. Let us survey some of these, building from the simple to complex.

Path

Johnson identifies typical characteristics that follow from PATH structure and are often projected in metaphor. Motion along a path from one point to another means "you have passed through all the intermediate points"; because humans have purposes in traversing paths, they tend to impose directionality on them and move *from* point A *toward* point B; they also impose temporal dimensions, so that further points along the path are reached later in time (114).

Physical journeys embody paths, and of course many stories involve a journey of some kind. The "quest" journey departs from a familiar point, such as "home," and heads toward a distant, exotic place, confronting perilous obstacles along the way, in order to find some special person, place, or thing. Frye's discussions are much denser and richer than a sketch that emphasizes schematic qualities shows. The *Anatomy* elaborates in considerable detail on the quest-romance's mythological and historical roots, various forms, and analogies with ritual and dream (AC 186–96). But it is the recognition of the schematic form that underpins those rich analogies. *Words with Power* discusses the journey's metaphoric connection with following a narrative, and then with the idea of a "way of life." The journey has variant forms in straight versus divergent and narrow versus broad ways, "the choice-of-Hercules or Y journey" that produces a haunting "road not taken," the interrupted journey, the involuntary journey, the meandering romantic journey of continual discovery, and quests that become cycles or spirals. Jesus's "I am the way" explodes the metaphor, of "the effort to go there in order to arrive here," because the goal of the quest, Jesus himself, is already present (WP 90–6).

Frye does not specifically say that the journey/quest can map onto any action whatever (and action in general), by instantiating the PATH image schema, as Lakoff and Johnson do with their analysis of the metaphor ACTIONS ARE MOVEMENTS (*Philosophy* 187–94). But he does note that "the word 'way' is a good example of the extent to which language is built up on a series of metaphorical analogies," as it can mean "a method or manner of procedure, but method and manner imply some sequential repetition, and the repetition brings us to the metaphorical kernel of a road or path," with its related meanings in straight, winding, or funny "ways" to do something, and so on (WP 91).[23]

Cycle

The action that ends by returning to some original state is another great organizing pattern in literature. It is said to be based on the important cycles in nature, such as days, months, seasons of the year, and stages of life. Also cyclical are Frye's model of cultural history (*Anatomy*, Essay 1), his four seasonal archetypal *mythoi* (Essay 3), and his maps of genres (Essay 4). Conceptualizing a CYCLE involves symbolizing an event as a PATH configured such that the SOURCE is also the GOAL (cf. Cienki, "Some Properties" 12). Cyclical journeys, even if fictional, must describe physical paths (e.g., leaving home then returning), but many other literary cycles need not. Natural cycles, actions with little motion, and narration itself may have qualities that are only metaphorically cyclical. Like Frye, Johnson represents a CYCLE as a circular motion, but does not stress the relation of circle to CYCLE. His many examples, natural (bodily and environmental) and conventional (various elements of clocks and schedules), show that human cycles are multiple and overlap, and may harmonize or clash (*Body* 119–21). Cycles are primarily temporal, and separable from spatial motion, though these often co-occur (e.g., going to work by the same route every morning at the same time, coming home by the same route every evening at the same time).

Axis/Scale

For Johnson, the SCALE image schema, the concept of a vertical axis, is the basis for all the metaphors that take UP as meaning more of some quantity or quality, and DOWN as meaning less. Quantitatively, we can add or take away from groups of objects or amounts of substances (making them go up or down). Qualitatively, "we experience objects and events as having certain degrees of intensity" like brightness, heat, force, and feeling (*Body* 122). In general, we experience the world "partly in terms of *more, less,* and *the same*" (122) and this abstract sense of amount is the basis of the schema. A SCALE can be symbolized as an ascending PATH. But unlike PATHS, SCALES imply a fixed directionality, a cumulative character, and a normative character (122–3).

For Frye, the "vertical line running from the top to the bottom of the cosmos" (WP 151) is a metaphor of a scale of human value or desire. It does not exist in nature, and hence appears to be based on the body's vertical orientation. This *axis mundi* is the most important schema in his work. To justify his "total form" approach, he demonstrates this line's pervasive and coherent role in literature and culture. It is essential to defining patterns of ascent, descent, arc, and spiral. Some essays also suggest that the *axis mundi* organizes narratives and genres by functioning as a continuum: groups of specific images can be ordered along it into a whole, which defines their locations and the relations among them (e.g., SM 160–7, on antimasque and masque characters experiencing levels of being from chaos to divine cosmos by physical movement or metamorphosis, and SM 162, on the similar alchemical symbolism of upward transformation of the soul from original sin to original identity in terms of transformation of substances).

Lakoff and Turner similarly recognize a "highly articulated version" of the Great Chain of Being, based on the SCALE and still existing through a wide range of world cultures, "as a contemporary unconscious cultural model indispensable to our understanding of ourselves, our world, and our language" (*More* 167). They analyse the component conceptual metaphors, common sense theories, and communicative principles that define several versions of it. Though they do not discuss movement along the chain, they examine analogical links across levels, as in proverbs – when, for example, animals are compared to people ("when the cat's away, the mice will play"), or sense is compared to thought ("blind blames the ditch"). The chain metaphor is applicable to our knowledge of everything it contains, and so "it allows us to comprehend general human character traits in terms of well-understood nonhuman attributes; and, conversely, it allows us to comprehend less well-understood aspects of the nature of animals and objects in terms of better-understood human characteristics" (172).

Much more could be said about how these thinkers use these and other schemas. SPLITTING is also important for Frye, as part of the fundamental narrative pattern of dialectical movement toward separating opposed worlds. CONTAINER manipulations are characteristic of his thought and rhetoric. For example, the frequent use of "interpenetration," "suppose we turned this explanation inside out" (GC 64), and similar locutions. They are also important in various kinds of literary patterns. Translating image-schematic Biblical expressions has far-reaching implications: the kingdom of God is *entos hymon*, which could be translated as "within you" or "among you," but *entos* as "within" you is more psychological, whereas "among" you is more social (54–5). The account of the psychological derangement Adam and Eve undergo in *Paradise Lost* superimposes force vectors as "drives" onto containers as selves:

> When appetite is perverted into passion, the drives of sex and hunger are perverted into lust and greed. Passion operates in the mind as though it were an external force ... The distinction between lust and greed is that lust is a vice turned outward and affecting other people; greed is a vice that turns inward and affects oneself. (RE 72–4)[24]

We now bump up against a central issue for extended literary discourse with its complex imagery: how simple image schemas interconnect into more complex constructions.

Sine Waves and Narrative Arcs

For Johnson, circles represent temporal cycles whose end state is the same as their initial state; but the "climactic structure" of the experience of cycles, their "character of build-up and release," is best represented by a "sine wave with its periodic 'rise' and 'fall'" (*Body* 119–20).[25] The *axis* schema also allows Frye to describe action in terms of patterns of movement between high and low points. It is essential to his understanding not only of ascent (*anabasis*) and descent (*catabasis*) narratives (e.g., SeS chapters 4 and 5, and WP chapters 5–8), but also of "cyclical" and other actions. The *Anatomy* distinguishes upper and lower halves of the natural cycle, and then associates the upper with romance, the lower with "realism" or experience, and movements down and up with tragedy and comedy (AC 162). The Bible's narrative structure is a "manic-depressive chart" that repeatedly takes its protagonists from experiences analogous to heaven to those analogous to hell and back again (GC 169–71). Overall, since it leads toward a "deliverance," the Bible has a "U-shape," which "recurs in literature as the standard shape of comedy, where a series of misfortunes and misunderstandings brings the action to a threateningly low point, after which some fortunate twist in the plot sends the conclusion up to a happy ending" (169). By contrast, "the inverted U is the typical shape of tragedy ... it rises to a point of 'peripety' or reversal of action, then plunges downward to a 'catastrophe,' a word which contains the figure of 'turning down'" (176). Hence comic and tragic "arcs" are halves of Johnson's sine wave.

Much hangs on the validity of characterizing complex actions in such schematic terms. Johnson's account of cyclic experiences already assumes this extra dimension of actions – everyday actions of varying duration and complexity – characterized simultaneously according to ontological structure (i.e., participants, roles, relations, and basic actions) and to patterns of intensity and value (i.e., build-up and release). His relatively simple sine wave can apply to various integrated personal experiences in the world (e.g., a kick, jump, throw, etc., but also sex, music, a party, etc.), but it is already an example of superimposed and interwoven schemas. Frye's sine waves and other patterns apply to much more extensive and complex patterns of literary narrative, so the question is about the legitimacy of seeing the latter in terms of the former. However, such reading is itself an integrated personal experience, and traditional notions of story "movement"; "flow"; "arc"; and conflict, tension, rising action, climax, and denouement imply that the "structure" of the work is inseparable from the emotional force-dynamic structure inspired in the reader. It is also not uncommon to frame large-scale experience in such terms (e.g., periods in life, or in histories of various kinds). As a result, I see no obstacle in principle to developing this connection.

Spirals

Spiral movements interweave in a highly integrated single image several major image schemas and at least four orientation-direction vectors: FORWARD along a PATH, UPWARD along a SCALE, in a cycle around a sequence of parallel sets of stages, INWARD toward a CENTRE, and possibly through nested CONTAINERS. Frye notes that simple upward movement is closely linked to

> the immensely long tradition in ritual and literature of ziggurat imagery, where the theme is the climbing of a tower or a mountain representing the hierarchies of being. This latter is as old an archetype as civilization affords: it is the basis of Dante's *Purgatorio*, and is going strong as ever in Yeats, Eliot, and Ezra Pound, whose "Dioce" goes back to Herodotus and his description of the original towers of Ecbatana and Babylon ... In narrative poetry the sequence usually goes up some kind of spiral climb. (SM 162–3)[26]

This pattern best shows the importance of coherently interconnected image schemas in forming distinctly cultural archetypes that (a) cohere with a wide range of other patterns of image and narrative, (b) cohere with a range of basic, major conventional metaphors, and therefore (c) recall, resonate with, and integrate one's total literary experience, but (d) have no plausible basis in ordinary experience, and seem to derive instead from the imaginative/aesthetic impulse to integrate multiple metaphoric images as fully as possible. Hence the conceptual party does not recognize the spiral or ziggurat as an image-schematic compound or grouping, and the image marks the distinctive purview of culture.

Circular Diagrams

Frye describes some overall narrative movements with a clock-like cyclical pattern of descent and return, mainly in deeply traditional (not necessarily conservative) writings: Homer (AC 318–19), the Bible (GC 174–6), Milton (RE 18–21), and Eliot (TSE 77–9). Frye also famously proposes that his four *mythoi* (romance, tragedy, irony, and comedy), as they correspond to the four stages of the romance quest, are aspects of a "central unifying myth" (AC 192). Frye's diagrams recall mandala images and the hypothetical "monomyth" that he and many others sketch.[27] These diagrams integrate "sine wave" narrative patterns (with their assumed axis) with the cycle as return to source. The circular maps of *mythoi* phases and genres use different (non-sequential) spatial metaphors: the circle is a categorial spectrum, where similarity is proximity, contrast is opposition, and extremes are cardinal points.

The Poetic Cosmos

Consider an economical statement of Frye's "literary cosmology" principle:

> From the beginning the poetic imagination has inhabited a middle earth. Above it is the sky with whatever it reveals or conceals: below it is a mysterious place of birth and death from whence animals and plants proceed and to which they return. There are therefore four primary narrative movements in literature. These are, first, the descent from a higher world; second, the descent to a lower world; third, the ascent from a lower world; and, fourth, the ascent to a higher world. All stories in literature are complications of, or metaphorical derivations from, these four narrative radicals.
>
> Explicitly for the first eighteen centuries of the Christian era, and implicitly after and long before that, these patterns of ascent and descent have been spread over a mythological universe consisting of four main levels, two above our own, and one below it. The highest level is heaven,

> the place of the presence of God ... Level two is the earthly paradise or Garden of Eden, where man lived before the fall. The associations of the word "fall" suggest that Eden is to be thought of as the highest point in the world, as it is geographically in Dante. Level three is the world of ordinary experience we now live in. Animals and plants seem to be well adjusted to this world, but man, though born in it, is not of it: his natural home is level two, where God intended him to live. Level four is the demonic world or hell, in Christianity not part of the order of nature but an autonomous growth, usually placed below ground. (SeS 97–8)

This cosmology's organizing structures are orientational image schemas that (a) supply major structure by linking many regions of the cosmos, (b) interconnect coherently, and (c) enter into general metaphors of value. Its chief metaphor is a SCALE of imaginative or spiritual desire, projected onto an imagined world. I use Frye's word "desire" because it suggests a broader context wherein the physical, intellectual, emotional, moral, aesthetic, and spiritual dimensions the SCALE implies are related to one another. As briefly mentioned, Krzeszowski shows that many other image schemas, especially orientational ones with opposing poles (e.g., IN-OUT, FRONT-BACK, etc.), also have a roughly positive-negative charge, which is fairly stable across contexts of use, including metaphors. He calls his image-schematic parameter PLUS-MINUS, and suggests that good and bad are the most general of axiological concepts, as they are "least context sensitive" and have the "largest scope of application." These concepts can emerge from "practically all preconceptual image schemata and refer to values at all levels of the axiological hierarchy" ("Axiological" 326). (Krzeszowski means a hierarchy of abstraction, from basic bodily experience to more complex actions to linguistic expressions, etymologies, and metaphors [310–11].) But Frye's desire is more concrete and personal, and also includes good and bad in a broader sense, beyond the basic moral implications of those terms.

However, in Frye's cosmology, it is difficult to untangle even fundamental metaphoric images such as the SCALE from others. Instead, they are compound: sub-worlds within the cosmos are ordered as regions distinguished by boundaries but linked as vertical levels. When a story informed by the cosmos introduces an agent who moves and perceives and acts, the world becomes a setting for scenes, and some key principles of metaphoric narrative fall out. The metaphors ACTIONS ARE MOTIONS and STATES ARE LOCATIONS become available:

movements within the cosmos afford, but do not determine, certain intuitive meanings and values (e.g., movement forward is progress beyond some prior state; movement upward is change to some superior state). Further, specific images participate in or echo its structure (e.g., the ziggurat).[28] Just as interconnected and superimposed image schemas give coherence to experience, so narrative and imagery based on them give coherence and resonance to the experience of symbolic worlds.

To push his analysis to achieve the broadest meaningful generality, Frye focuses on the role of such central structures in creating coherences *across* works, and other areas of culture. However, he recognizes that his quite general model functions as scaffolding, and that many other metaphors and myths find places within it. As a result, it should be possible to examine how organizing structures beyond the *axis mundi* are integrated in that model and used in literature. For example, Frye's "The Times of the Signs" contrasts the metaphoric values implied by Ptolemy's geocentric cosmology with those of Copernicus's heliocentric cosmology (SM 66–96). "The Drunken Boat" shows how another dimension of bodily orientation, the IN-OUT schema, has a structural role in the poetic cosmos that interacts with its UP-DOWN structure (StS 200–17). The interaction is revealed in the shift in Romantic cosmologies from looking outward and upward for the divine to looking inward and downward (cf. Ekberg, "Mental" esp. 84–6). *Words with Power* returns to the point and discusses cosmological inversions in Blake, Rousseau, Marx, Freud, Darwin, and others (172–4; 239–52). At present, though, I want to examine how the central version of Frye's model used in Dante's *Divine Comedy* tends toward a maximally coherent integration of relatively few image-schematic metaphors, which greatly intensifies the work's conceptual and emotional resonance. The first step is to determine how to assess metaphorical coherence.

Metaphoric and Image-Schematic Conceptual Coherence

Lakoff and Johnson propose that the coherence of two or more metaphors depends on the abstract topological (image-schematic) structure of the (source and target) concepts they involve. This kind of topological structure determines the imagery and inference that the metaphors can support, so when metaphors share concepts with such structure in common, they are coherent by sharing entailments of imagery and logic, and hence also by sharing superordinate categories. A culture's fundamental values cohere with the metaphorical structure of its fundamental concepts (e.g., good is UP, however a culture interprets good); and some metaphors cohere because their source domains share larger categories, though they differ in details (e.g., LOVE can be a JOURNEY by car or boat; TIME PASSES US whether we move or time moves) (*Metaphors*, chapters 5, 9).

The coherent structuring of experience is the basis of metaphoric coherence. For example, various events can be categorized as arguments because they are experienced as having the same kinds of participants, parts, stages, linear sequence, causation, and purpose. A metaphor can further map war onto argument because the concepts share such categories of abstract event-structure (chapter 15). Different metaphors for the same target focus on different aspects of it. For example, ARGUMENT AS JOURNEY focuses on the argument's process or goal. It entails that the journey defines a path, and the path defines a surface, hence the argument defines a surface. ARGUMENT AS CONTAINER or AS BUILDING focus on content or structure, respectively. The three source domains of these metaphors – JOURNEY, CONTAINER, and BUILDING – share a "content-defining surface," but in their images surface defines content in different ways. None of the metaphors defines an image that is fully consistent with the target or the other sources, but all are partially coherent (chapters 16, 17).

Some other scholars identify details that suggest Lakoff and Johnson exaggerate the coherence of metaphoric systems. Grady, Taub, and Morgan ("Primitive") and Kevin Moore ("Deixis") are sceptical about metaphor systems and about duality. Grady et al. argue that the metaphor DIFFICULTIES ARE BURDENS need not be understood as part of ACTIONS ARE MOTIONS (on the basis that burdens are impediments to motion), because it is directly grounded in experience, and examples do not always mention motion (e.g., "He's *weighed down* by lots of assignments") ("Primitive" 183). From such examples, Grady develops his distinction between *primary* (or primitive) metaphor and *complex* (or compound) metaphor. Primary metaphors are directly grounded in "primary scenes" where domains are co-experienced simultaneously (or conflated, to use Christopher Johnson's term) because of some causal relationship between them. For example, AFFECTION IS WARMTH is primary because warmth is commonly co-experienced with affection and love, as in the primary scene of loved ones holding one another. Complex or compound metaphors are grounded in primary metaphors (Lakoff and Johnson, *Philosophy*, chapters 4, 5). For example, LOVE IS A FIRE is based not on any natural connection between love and fires, but by adding knowledge of fire and love to AFFECTION IS WARMTH (and perhaps LOVE IS HEAT), so that love can be seen as something that burns brightly at first, and cools and fades over time. *Philosophy in the Flesh* develops Lakoff and Johnson's earlier claim that there are two main versions of a single underlying TIME PASSES US metaphor, which are inconsistent but coherent. MOVING OBSERVER ("we're approaching spring") and MOVING TIME ("spring is approaching") are "figure-ground reversals," and such "duality" is a general phenomenon (*Philosophy* 148–9, 194–200): many "event structure" metaphors have dual "location" and "object" versions (e.g., CAUSES ARE FORCES [199–200]). This example is also useful for defining the distinction between coherence and consistency: while the latter means "forming a single image," the former implies sharing abstract structure and thus major entailment(s) and a higher category (but not creating a single image) (Lakoff and Johnson, *Metaphors* 44). Coherence is more common than consistency.

Grady et al. and Moore properly emphasize the need to specify as precisely as possible the details of mappings in order to individuate metaphors and determine their interconnections, and both refer to grounding scenarios (such as Grady's "primary scenes") for this purpose. However, neither directly addresses how the mappings that emerge from their interpretations of linguistic evidence relate to one another or to the larger metaphoric conceptual system. Moore proposes an additional FRONT-BACK MOVING TIME mapping and argues that it is not a figure-ground reversal of the MOVING OBSERVER mapping because it arises from a distinct grounding scenario that judges the metaphoric meanings of "ahead" and "following" by reference to directionality of motion, and therefore requires no observer at all. He does not deny that MOVING OBSERVER exists or that it is a figure-ground reversal of ego-centred MOVING TIME. He says his mapping is "compatible" and "presumably related" to the others, but does not say how ("Deixis" 156, 157). Grady et al. grant that DIFFICULTIES ARE BURDENS is "*compatible* with metaphors for action as motion" but question "whether they should properly be understood as *instances* of such metaphors" ("Primitive" 180). They claim that both are primitives, and so they do not consider that a mutually motivating part-whole relation may exist between mappings. It is possible for both primary metaphors to occur in a single experiential gestalt that provides a grounding scenario for both of them, even though burdens are optional parts in relation to motions. Although burdens are directly embodied difficulties, they are also impediments to action generally: for example, carrying something somewhere is a scenario that grounds both metaphors. Similarly, Grady et al. argue that the metaphoric meanings of "stand" as "cease" versus as "continue" must be products not of contrasting versions ("branches" or "duals") of the same event structure, but of distinct primitives, ACTION IS MOTION and ACTION IS LOCATION ("Primitive" 183). They do not consider that the latter mapping implies a compound of two aspects of the former. With "stand" as "cease," standing is simply stopping a motion (ACTIONS ARE MOTIONS). But "stand" as "continue" assumes that performing an action can be a continuing state, so starting the action is moving (ACTIONS ARE MOTIONS) into a location (STATES ARE LOCATIONS) where the action proceeds, and continuing the action is stopping and staying in that state-location. In any case, these fine-grained analyses provide excellent bases on which to address questions of how metaphors hang together in the conceptual system.

Alan Cienki deals with one aspect of these questions by examining the properties and operations of two major classes of groupings of image schemas. First, there are "co-experienced gestalt groupings (groups which co-occur in our experience and in metaphorical extensions, especially in spatial and force-dynamic combinations)" (Cienki, "Some Properties" 4). As an example, he notes a common gestalt of CENTRE-PERIPHERY, NEAR-FAR, SCALE, and FORCE:

> In our bodily experience, we are centers of force, sources of movement and action. While on one hand each of us is subjected to many external forces on a daily basis (literally and metaphorically), the individual is also a starting point of vectors of force, which can be exerted outward from the body, and which typically decrease in intensity the further out they extend (hence their scalar nature). (8)

The lesson here is that "analyses which concern the metaphorical extension of any individual image schema need to take into account what other image schemas commonly co-occur with it, and consider what roles they may play in the metaphorical extension" (8). For example, metaphors of social force include the interplay of several aspects of this gestalt, in a sentence like the following: "Local peer pressure is stronger than the impact of global media because it is closer to individuals and more encompassing, but it can only counter media pressures to conform to roles and images within an immediate circle." Cienki's point relates metaphorical coherence to experiential grounding at a different level than "domain conflation." Second, there are "categories which share significant common properties (but whose image schemas are not necessarily co-experienced)" (4). This means that "more specific" image schemas inherit properties from "more general" ones under which they can be classified (e.g., LINKING and SPLITTING are both PROCESSES; ATTRACTION and COMPULSION are both FORCES) (9–13). The former class of groupings is most important for analysing the coherence of complex metaphors in literary depictions of experience, which often draw on image-schematic coherence in actual experience. Indeed, Cienki's insight about the importance of co-occurring gestalts of image schemas, and how the gestalt structure may carry over from bodily experience into metaphorical extensions of those image schemas, will have considerable bearing on my analyses of Frye's and Dante's literary cosmologies.

Lakoff and Turner consider how metaphors combine into coherent new wholes that apply to a range of concrete source domains. Combining two metaphors, for instance LIFE IS LIGHT and LIFE IS HEAT, implies a more general composite metaphor of life as a waxing and waning cycle of light and heat, which then "gets filled out with specific instances" of other source domains that structure the target domain in analogous ways, such as a day, a year, a flame, and a fire (*More* 88). Thinking from the other direction, models or commonplace theories for a target domain (life, time, the universe, etc.) can structure it in a way that "constrains the choice of source-domain structure" (87). The model of life as a cycle of not being alive, being alive, and being dead therefore naturally fits source domains of day, year, flame, fire, precious possession, and fluid, which have a cycle of not existing, existing, and disappearing.

This research indicates a cluster of related issues that should be considered in analysing metaphorical coherence. First, image-schematic thought is not necessarily tied to metaphor. Thus, second, metaphoric thought may draw on conventional mapping structures, but without being locked in to specific source domains (whether basic or complex): it can proceed by extracting and manipulating image schemas from perceptual and conceptual experience, and gradually adjusting and rematching them to structure in both source and target domains. Third, as image schemas arise from experiential gestalts, the latter determine many aspects of metaphorical coherence. The experiential gestalts of grounding scenarios determine the structure of primary metaphors, and hence their possibilities for coherence with other metaphors. Experiential gestalts determine how image schemas form groupings, and those gestalt groupings can affect the metaphorical extension of any particular image schema. Furthermore, the general experiential gestalt of the body in its canonical orientation determines the general positive/negative polarities of image schemas, which also inform their metaphorical extensions (Krzeszowski, "Axiological"). However, fourth, they do not absolutely determine coherence in specific uses of metaphor. In Fauconnier and Turner's "conceptual blending theory," metaphoric mappings may structure "input spaces," but may be modified during projection into the blend space, where they combine with other material in the "online" construction of thought and discourse. Hence the analysis of coherence turns from the question of shared abstract structure and entailments to the question of how a set of sometimes competing "optimality principles" are balanced differently in different blends.[29]

Lakoff and Johnson note that coherence depends on abstractness: abstract only coheres with abstract. But as specific concepts instantiate more abstract ones, we must also consider how abstract can connect with abstract through levels of specificity. This too is especially important with literary texts. There are four such levels: *specific* (this journey), *basic* (journeys), *image-schematic* (motion along a PATH), and *abstract* (event). In order to cohere, metaphors must have common structure at some level in both source and target. We can discern this common structure across specific metaphors by viewing source or target or both in more abstract terms. Those with most shared structure across levels are most coherent. For example, LOVE IS LIGHT and LOVE IS HEAT are highly coherent because they share a basic target, image-schematic source structure (e.g., both radiate), abstract source category (both are natural forces), and some experiential grounding for both source and mapping (both often co-occur and are valued positively). In short, there are the following kinds of coherence across metaphors:

- an image-schematic source with variants of an abstract target (many GOODS are UP)
- variants of an image-schematic source with an abstract target (many UPS are GOOD) (including duality: variants of TIME MOVES)
- variants of a basic source with an abstract target (many JOURNEYS of LIFE)
- variant image-schematic sources (from various basic sources) with a basic target (PATH and CONTAINER can both be ARGUMENT)
- variant sources and targets of a basic metaphor with those of an abstract metaphor (many EVENTS are many ACTIONS)

I am most concerned with forms of coherence relevant to compound metaphors. Coherence across elements at the same level is especially important, since elements must connect at the same level in order to combine. Image schemas are prominent in this regard, since they are often the basis of the source-target connection in individual metaphors and of the connection across sources in compound metaphors. Since the coherence of image schema groupings can be assessed in itself, the coherence in compound metaphors can be assessed by considering kinds of coherence on their source sides:

- among individual superimposed image schemas (IN is CENTRAL)
- between image schemas and more abstract categories (MERGING and SPLITTING are PROCESSES)

We can go on to consider how such source compounds cohere with the target side:

- across individual image schemas in the compound (IN and CENTRAL are both GOOD)
- between individual image schema plus-minus values and their grounded values (UP-DOWN are GOOD-BAD)
- between groupings in source compounds and in experiential gestalts, in terms of both image-schematic structure and their associated axiologies

Lakoff and Turner write that: "Complex metaphors grip us partly because they awake in us the experience and knowledge that form the grounding of those metaphors, partly because they make the coherence of that experience and knowledge resonate, and partly because they lead us to form new coherences in what we know and experience" (*More* 89). They speak of the power of metaphor "to reveal comprehensive hidden meanings to us, to allow us to find meanings beyond the surface, to interpret texts as wholes, and to make sense of patterns of events" (159). It is now time to consider how the various metaphors used in Dante's compound cosmos, in virtue of being coherently connected (according to the forms of coherence just stated), resonate with one another and with grounding experience, and reveal new patterns in existing knowledge.

2 Spatial and Spiritual Orders: Metaphoric Coherence in Dante's and Frye's Cosmologies

Among all things, however disparate,
there reigns an order, and this gives the form
that makes the universe resemble God ...

and in this order all created things,
according to their bent, maintain their place,
disposed in proper distance from their Source;

therefore, they move, all to a different port,
across the vast ocean of being, and each
endowed with its own instinct as its guide.

This is what carries fire toward the moon,
this is the moving force in mortal hearts,
this is what binds the earth and makes it one ...

Dante, *Paradise* 4

... and as the soul within your living dust
diffuses through your body's different parts,
adapted to its various faculties,

just so does this Intelligence unfold
its bounty which the stars have multiplied
while turning ever in its unity ...

Dante, *Paradise* 22

In seeking to understand metaphorical coherence, we must also consider how the specific discourse context affects our analysis. Dante compounds many metaphors in the storyworld of a literary narrative (storyworlds, as I noted, are mental models of the events and worlds depicted by narratives). Spatial modelling is an essential part of narrative processing, as stories prompt readers to "spatialize storyworlds into evolving configurations of participants, objects, and places" (Herman 263). Such a storyworld is ostensibly consistent in Lakoff and Johnson's sense – that is, in the sense of forming a single image (as the cosmological diagrams that often accompany Dante's text suggest). However, that is not the same thing as, and does not guarantee, metaphoric coherence or consistency. We will judge the latter not only among the set of conceptual mappings Dante draws on, but also in terms of how he adapts them to this specifically narrative context.[1] The interplay of narrative and metaphor has not been studied as it deserves to be.[2] Vico proposed long ago that "every metaphor is a fable in brief" because the best metaphors of the first poets "attributed to bodies the being of animate substances, with capacities measured by their own, namely sense and passion, and in this way made fables of them" (qtd. in Schaeffer 94). Frye developed the point: "Every metaphor, however casual, is ready to embark on a journey toward the myth" because it is "an embodiment of myth. Reversing this principle, metaphors are the exfoliation of myths" (qtd. in Denham, *Religious* 72). For the conceptual party, the same schema (e.g., for a journey) structures both static concepts and dynamic events, and thus both metaphor and story. But I ultimately want to consider a level of structure that falls in between the level of the cognitive unconscious (the collection of conventional metaphors a reader brings to the text) and the level of Dante's specific narrative articulation of metaphor – that is, Frye's level of "literary cosmology," which views Dante's creation as filling in a more abstract but still complex metaphoric model.

I am not trying to insist on maximal coherence, in the manner of the stereotypical New Critic who sees a triumphant reconciliation or harmonization of tensions of imagery and theme in every literary work. Instead, I emphasize how metaphoric coherence relates to literary meaning, understanding and experience by supporting the assimilation of conventions to one another and their resonance with one another. I am trying to figure out how much coherence there is in the text, because a sense of coherence is part of the experience of and response to art. (This chapter studies this phenomenon by looking at the text in detail, but it might also be possible to approach it by examining actual reader processing: what coherences do readers find, and how do they sort out potential incoherences?)

I am concerned with the major "organizing" metaphors of Dante's *Comedy* – those that define the structure of the setting and action, and hence remain operative in the background throughout. (Obviously images that are solely part of the narrator's rhetoric may clash with one another and with the imagery inherent in the narrative world – e.g., the various source domains used in Dante's epic similes). To see how those metaphors fit together, I will concentrate on coherence at the image-schematic level. I begin with a sketch of Dante's cosmological model.

Setting: Orientational and Locational Structure

The world of Dante's *Comedy* is richly detailed; much of it is traditional to medieval thought, a certain amount of it is Dante's own invention, and both of these immediate sources draw on a mix of further sources. The main structures tend to come from Biblical and classical mythology, theology, and science, while some of the residents and other elements also derive from history and literature. According to Dante's Ptolemaic model, the central spherical earth is surrounded by nine concentric hollow globes made of a transparent crystalline substance. Each of the first seven spheres has a "luminous body" – one of the seven planets – fixed in it. Beyond is the "*Stellatum*" of the "fixed" stars, then "the First Movable or *Primum Mobilę*" (Lewis, *Discarded* 96).[3] This arrangement adds IN-OUT and CENTRE-PERIPHERY orientational schemas to Frye's model, and gives them structural roles analogous to the *axis mundi*. Dante specifies a range of these orientational and spatial elements within sub-worlds (see accompanying chart).

Coherence and Consistency

Traditional cosmologies are potentially fully consistent, despite some tensions among cosmological goals (e.g., of representing experience, answering cosmic questions, and maximizing human intelligibility). Frye's model is consistent, partly because its simplified plan omits much of the structure that more specific cosmologies include. For example, it says little about absolute temporal and spatial limits. Dante's sub-worlds of Purgatory and Inferno are each visually consistent, but Paradise is not (hence nor is the cosmos as a whole) because of a basic

Orientational Structure	Cosmic Region: Paradise	Purgatory	Earth	Inferno
Location on Cosmic Scale	Top	Upper Middle	Lower Middle	Bottom
Centre	God	Earthly Paradise	Purgatory (surface) / Inferno (interior)	Satan
Periphery (point of entry)	Earthly Paradise	Mountain Base (Earth / First Terrace)	Sphere of the Moon / Sphere of Air	Inferno Mouth (Earth / First Circle)
Top	God	Earthly Paradise	Mt. Purgatory Base / First Terrace	Earth / First Circle
Bottom	Earthly Paradise	Earth / First Terrace	Inferno Mouth / First Circle	Satan
Containers Defining Regions / Levels	Spheres	Terraces		Circles
Innermost Region	Empyrean	Earthly Paradise	Purgatory / Inferno	Ninth Circle
Outermost Region	Sphere of the Moon	First Terrace	Sphere of Air	First Circle

conflict over assigning human or divine standpoints the absolute "centre." But again, visual consistency does not guarantee metaphoric consistency or coherence.

Coherence and Clashes

Across Image Schemas in Cosmos and Sub-worlds

Within the basic plans of the cosmos and sub-worlds, orientational schemas are generally superimposed so as to maximize coherence. As a result, their poles tend to converge and there is a single location in each sub-world indicated, or led to, by all of them: the CENTRE-INSIDE-BOTTOM of Inferno, and the CENTRE-INSIDE-TOP of Purgatory and Paradise. We can partially resolve clashes across sub-worlds by finding more general categories for the clashing elements: in this case, TOP (of

Purgatory and Paradise) and BOTTOM (of Inferno) are both endpoints of a SCALE. As well, the PERIPHERY-SCALE-CENTRE pattern corresponds to a PATH that leads from a SOURCE location to a GOAL.

Across Metaphoric Target Values in Cosmos and Sub-worlds
All orientational dimensions define the same scale of value, divided into regions: in Purgatory, and in the whole cosmos, CENTRAL, UP, and IN are all desirable. We can resolve apparent clashes in the way these metaphors are projected onto sub-worlds, by finding superordinate categories to include these metaphoric projections as subcategories. Inferno shows that CENTRAL is not simply desirable. But there is a more general target: CENTRAL is most valued in the sense of most powerful and important in that region. This restricts the clash to a lower level of specificity, rather than removing it.

There are also more specific coherences across and within sub-worlds: different specific source images embody the same abstract mapping by filling the same orientational and locational roles (e.g., circles, terraces, and spheres all define hierarchized regions).

To supplement Frye's stress on *axis mundi* imagery, I will examine how imagery related to the CONTAINER structure of cosmic regions works as a literary organizing principle. Krzeszowski notes the "contradictory values" of being in and leaving a CONTAINER: inside, we are sheltered but constrained; outside, we are free but exposed to danger. He suggests that the archetypes of "paradise lost" and "return" in mythology and religion are grounded in such experiences, especially that of being born. (Except for the image-schematic details, this association is commonplace.) Additionally, PLUS-MINUS is not systematically correlated with IN-OUT; rather, there is a dynamism and a "dialectical struggle" of values ("Axiological" 315–7).

One could consider the metaphoric implications of the extent, limits, and points of entrance and egress for various cosmic regions, and following Cienki's injunction to attend to commonly co-experienced image schemas, also configurations of internal and external forces, centres, and peripheries. Tillyard's *Elizabethan World Picture* (1979 [1943]), Lewis's *Discarded Image* (1964), and Hammil's *Celestial Journey and the Harmony of the Spheres* (1980) discuss the celestial spheres in literature. The gestalt of a bounded region also metaphorically extends to abstract concepts. The myth of celestial spheres seems to lie behind the expression "sphere of influence," and there are also the related ideas of "personal space," moral "transgression," ideas of consciousness expansion, concentration, etc. There are highly significant manipulations of aspects of the CONTAINER schema throughout *Paradise*. Dante thematizes relations among the spheres; fields of vision; bodies; and physical and mental movements of entering and exiting, expansion, and contraction.

Such relations also enter into wordplay, especially in the many neologisms that use "in"-type prefixes. A few from *Paradise* alone: "m'intuassi" and "t'inmii" as "inme" and "inyou" (114n); "m'inventro" as "enwombing me" (255n); "inlei" as "insiding" (268n); "'mparadisa" as "imparadised" (334n); "s'interna" as something like "trinity" or "trinitize" (339n); "s'invii" as "insight" from "inire," "to enter" (396n); and "s'indova" as "conform" (399n). These also relate to the use of ordinary "in-" words and the complex imagery of in and out movements.

In literature more generally, repeated incidents of exiting and/or entering build into overall patterns of movement, for example, toward an ultimate boundary or outside, or ultimate centre or inner sanctum. (I know of no terms for such patterns comparable to *anabasis* and *catabasis* for ascent and descent stories.) Milton's Satan penetrates numerous barriers to break out of hell, and then crosses many more to break into Eden in disguise in order to destroy it from within by entering Eve's mind. There are also examples in more "realistic" earthly landscapes. Like Milton, Homer contrasts patterns of movements: the story of Odysseus's return home (*nostos*) requires his journey to the land of the dead at the edge of the world, Ocean Stream; followed by disguised penetration into his own house on Ithaca to kill the chief suitor and his followers in the locked dining hall where they have lodged in the heart of the family home (this pattern might also link to the destruction of Troy from within by Greeks hidden inside the Trojan horse). Dante presents Odysseus conventionally in *Inferno*, canto 26, as continually driven forward to experience and know all, and hence transgressing proper bounds (symbolized by the pillars of Hercules). In popular literature, *The Lord of the Rings'* Frodo and Sam sneak past all barriers to infiltrate Mount Doom, in the heart of Mordor, as its forces spread outward toward their homeland.

Agent Spatiality

Coherence and Clashes across Image Schemas

The range of possible locations, orientations, and movements by agents within this cosmology defines further structure, including two orientational dimensions not so far discussed: FRONT-BACK and LEFT-RIGHT.[4] (These dimensions include perceptual, not just bodily, orientation, i.e., looking upward, forward, etc.) These spatial factors correlate highly with one another. Within sub-worlds and the whole cosmos, any location, orientation, and/or movement relative to one schema will correspond to a certain location, orientation, and/or movement relative to many, and perhaps all, of the others. This is clearest in Purgatory's spiral climb: UPWARD movement is also INWARD, CENTRE-WARD, FORWARD, and RIGHTWARD.[5]

Coherence and Clashes across Metaphors

In the whole cosmos, it is generally but not absolutely true that locations, orientations, and movements UPWARD, INWARD, CENTRE-WARD, FORWARD, and RIGHTWARD are spiritually desirable, and their opposites undesirable. To be more precise about sub-worlds: this coherence holds throughout Purgatory; it holds in the latter part of Paradise, excepting the LEFT-RIGHT schema, which is ignored. It is significant that Dante places a single ruling figure at the anchor-point of each sub-world where the poles of its image schemas converge and its values are concentrated and maximized: Satan, Beatrice, and God.

However, once we include, in our consideration of the cosmos, agents with their own locations, orientations, and movements, the resulting increase in spatial complexity also increases the potential for both clashes and coherence among spatial schemas and metaphoric values. Even if the cosmos is metaphorically coherent, if a character is located at a height, but looks and turns and moves downward, this may indicate a clash of the character's metaphoric value with that of the cosmos. However, the example also shows the potential to depict greater psychological and dramatic complexity, if the writer can make the various schemas interact coherently. It would be natural to interpret the action just described as delineating a loss of some good – perhaps succumbing to some temptation, perhaps sacrificing one's position to help someone in a worse position.

Clashes and Resolutions in Dante's Cosmos, Sub-worlds, and Specific Scenes

There are image-schematic clashes in the large-scale structure of the cosmology, within sub-worlds, and in particular scenes that are not resolved when framed as subcategories of higher categories. Some are resolved by other means, and some are left unresolved.

Remarkably, there are two major image-schematic clashes in Dante's journey, which he highlights only to make a point of resolving them by "reframing" the local image-schematic (orientational) structure within a wider cosmological context and shifting from an earthly to a heavenly standard of orientational judgment. First, in the final canto of *Inferno* (canto 35), he passes through the base of hell to climb up toward Mount Purgatory and his descent is revealed to have been upward all along (relative to the whole cosmos, in which hell's mouth faces downward and its base upward). Second, in *Paradise* 27–8, when Dante passes into the Primum Mobile and sees how the Empyrean contains it, his movement from earth is revealed to have been not outward toward a boundary, but inward toward a centre all along. In both cases, the earlier orientations are not subcategories of the later; rather, the first orientational frame is cancelled or relativized to a lower level of reality, and the second takes precedence. Both cases also suggest that UP-DOWN takes precedence over IN-OUT and CENTRE-PERIPHERY as a metaphoric organizing structure. The vertical orientations and valuations of Inferno and (early) Paradise are continuous with those of the other sub-worlds and the cosmos; but this is not true of their CENTRE-PERIPHERY and IN-OUT orientations.

Both shifts make metaphoric sense. The first reframes the journey as one of increasing knowledge of sin rather than acquisition or performance of sin, which assists with moving upward toward goodness rather than downward into greater evil. The second reframes the journey as moving toward a heavenly centre, rather than away from an earthly one, and hence as learning a new sense of origins and boundaries for spiritual norms, rather than merely leaving behind an old one. Lewis detects "an unresolved discord between those elements in [medieval] religion which tended to an anthropocentric view and those in the Model which made man a marginal – almost ... a suburban – creature" (*Discarded* 51). Dante resolves it:

> Alanus ab Insulis compares the sum of things to a city. In the central castle, in the Empyrean, the Emperor sits enthroned. In the lower heavens live the angelic knighthood. We, on Earth, are 'outside the city wall'. How, we ask, can the Empyrean be the centre when it is not only on, but outside, the circumference of the whole universe? Because, as Dante was to say more clearly than anyone else, the spatial order is the opposite of the spiritual, and the material cosmos mirrors, hence reverses, the

> reality, so that what is truly the rim seems to us the hub ... We watch 'the spectacle of the celestial dance' from its outskirts ... The Medieval Model is, if we may use the word, anthropoperipheral. We are creatures of the Margin. (58)

Lovejoy provides a complementary mirror image for this point in his remark that "in the spatial sense the medieval world was literally diabolocentric" (*Great* 102). This resolving shift suggests coherence without consistency: it seems impossible to visualize the outer limit of the celestial spheres as simultaneously the centre of the universe. That would mean rearranging all the preceding sphere boundaries as organized from outermost to innermost, which clashes with the image of earth as the centre of the nested spheres that necessarily increase in size with their distance from earth. The same sphere cannot surround two different centres. Nor are there two sets of nested spheres that happen to meet at the points Dante crosses.[6]

The diagram Musa provides for the whole paradisal cosmos (*Paradise* 25) shows the purported correspondences between sets of spheres in their opposing arrangements (diabolocenric versus theocentric), but does not resolve the clash. Musa explains that the Empyrean is immaterial, while the world up to and including the Primum Mobile is material. This does little to resolve the clash, since the immaterial realm is still visualizable, at least symbolically, and has material relations with the material world (e.g., it surrounds, contains, and supplies energy to that world). Compare the impossible-to-visualize metaphor of God as a circle or sphere whose centre is everywhere and circumference nowhere. The implication of an omnipresence whose intensity is undiluted by space contradicts the idea that God's power diminishes as it descends or refracts through creation (see the section below on the force-dynamic structure of the setting).

Some lesser tensions within scenes, and between such scenes and their sub-worlds, are not resolved. The celestial rose that contains the souls of the saved and blessed in *Paradise* 30–2 is not wholly coherent with the established cosmological axiologies. It is structured like an amphitheatre and hence its centre is its lowest point (as in *Inferno*), whereas the holiest beings within the rose are in the highest and outermost rim. There is no effort to resolve the clash by image-schematic manipulation or reframing, but again the SCALE takes precedence over the CENTRE as an axiological principle. The rose glows with divine light reflected from above, and after viewing it, Dante looks upward to perceive God directly.

There are other examples. The temporary reversal of several patterns in *Paradise* 21, when Dante enters the sphere of Saturn, is another exception to the clear tendencies of the orientational axiologies. Beatrice cannot smile here, there is no music, and the environment becomes colder rather than warmer. The reason for this is that the good always implies a critique of the failure to pursue or attain it. This canto focuses on such critique, and on the power of good to correct, punish, or even destroy what fails it. Confronted with a power of good too great for his present state, Dante would be overwhelmed with its intense light, heat, and beauty. Further, in *Paradise* 26 (306ff.), Dante loses his sight but then regains it in purified form. There are also clashes between orientational and other traditional meanings of certain structures (rather than between the metaphoric meanings of two orientations): the inward-tending nested circles of hell indicate increasing evil, but not the circularity of perfection.

Numerous image-schematic metaphors can interact in specific scenes in much more complex ways. An example from canto 1 can suggest how the context of narrative discourse, with its actors and scenes constituting parts linked to other scenes in a larger story of a larger action, relates to the context of the background compound metaphoric storyworld.

The first canto of the poem focuses on the interaction of pilgrim-Dante's movement with his setting. In the middle of life's way (between source and goal), he strays from the straight, forward-leading road and enters a wood that obstructs both movement and vision. He tries to regain the road by ascending a hill, but three beasts block potential paths out, which forces him to turn backward and downward, into a valley and the cave that is the mouth of Inferno. These metaphoric details are as they are because Dante wants to link this scene with the larger background setting of metaphors recruited to structure the cosmos.

A closer look reveals some clashes and resolutions of clashes among metaphors. For example, when Dante takes steps upward but is deterred by the beast he sees, his steps show only that he wants and tries to improve his spiritual status, not that he does. The potential inference from the setting/source is qualified by the action context (he is immediately driven down, then progresses forward and upward by another route) and the context of the target (spiritual improvement cannot be gained directly or easily; there is no "shortcut"). Different parts of scenes foreground different metaphors that structure the background model; within a scene, these foregrounded elements may combine, clash, and resolve locally, apart from how they relate in the overall model.

Further Cosmological Metaphors and Coherences

The metaphoric coherences I have examined thus far are almost unavoidable for any writer who relies on some such cosmological model as this (whether it is regarded as real or fictional), because narrative almost always involves an agent's position, orientation, and movement in a setting. I come now to connections and coherences in Dantean metaphor groupings that are strongly motivated by common human bodily experience, but are less imperative for writers because they are less inherent in the nuts and bolts of narrative. I will sketch the intelligible interactions of these metaphor groupings, their mutually supporting meanings, and their coherence with experiential gestalts.

Setting: Force-Dynamic Structure and Other Sensory Modes

Elements within Dante's cosmos are also organized according to the spatial relations schema NEAR-FAR, and are governed by force-dynamics even prior to the projection of any mortal agent into the picture:

> The parts of the universe are hierarchically positioned in relation to God; those *most perfect* are closest to Him, and those *least perfect* are furthest away. Each part seeks by instinct its proper position in the hierarchy, moving in response to a kind of "attraction" or "desire" toward its destined place. (Musa, *Paradise* 15n)

Aspects of setting are not fully distinct from the forces of supernatural agents, for example, spirits are associated with heavenly bodies: "Each sphere, or something resident in each sphere, is a conscious and intellectual being" (Lewis, *Discarded* 115). Musa adds, "The combined force of these angelic intelligences over all the spheres is what is known in Dante's world as Nature" ("Introduction to the *Paradise*" x). In the universe, God is the sole source of energy, which all things receive according to their capacity – first the Primum Mobile, which in turn imparts it to lower spheres and their intelligences (x). Mutual love between God and nature draws things to their proper stations. However, humans with their immortal souls are, as in Frye's model, "between the realm of brute matter and the angels ... beckoned by the spheres which circle around and above ... reflecting God's creation" (x). Providence works through the operation of the spheres to bring the souls of the elect back to their original place with God (116n). Divine energy is metaphorically rendered mainly as movement and light, which diminish as they are reflected through the orders and degrees of creation, and then infuse organic and inorganic earthly elements. Demonic powers are associated with opposing forces of darkness, gravity or downward force, and immobility.

As for connections among metaphors here, two metaphorical mappings forge the links between love, light, and movement. LOVE IS LIGHT becomes reified in the cosmology when both the target emotion and the source LIGHT are understood via force-dynamic metaphors. Light is a "translucent substance" (277n) (perhaps decomposable into a force with substance) that proceeds from God. As a force, it enters and causes movement in substances (e.g., the spheres) and living things (growth in plants, self-motion in animals). Hence LIGHT is also LIFE (God is "Living Light" in one aspect [*Paradise* canto 13; see n41]; and we still use "spark of life," "glowing with life" etc.), and embodies God's love for his creation.

The metaphor of God or nature as artist illustrates how much Dante's model of the world as governed by conscious energy owes to gestalts of human bodily experience. Musa paraphrases St Thomas Aquinas's explanation to Dante in *Paradise*, canto 13:

> All creation – both immortal and mortal – reflects the Light of the Idea (the Son of the Trinity, or the Word). This Living Light streams forth from its Source (the Father or First Cause) throughout creation though itself remaining unseparated from its Source and from the Love (Holy Spirit) which binds the Trinity ... The basic material ... of these creations receives the Divine Light according to each one's varying capacity; this phenomenon explains the vast diversity within Creation ... Nature (second cause), the process of causation or distribution of light, is incapable of passing the light throughout creation without the light's attenuation. Therefore, Nature resembles the artist who conceives his idea but cannot execute it perfectly. (164–5n)

The causal chain of artistic creation shares structure with everyday actions, wherein we conceive an action plan (an idea we "see") and carry it out via (willed) actions that involve bodily perception and movement (force) (cf. Cienki's account, above, of image-schematic coherence in experiences of being centres of force). This gestalt coheres with the cosmological model of the divine idea/vision as a metaphorical light source that radiates directed energy with force, which causes motion of substances but diminishes with distance.

There is an important superordinate mapping here, which Kövecses claims governs all specific emotion metaphors: EMOTION IS A FORCE (*Metaphor* 17). God's love pulls his creation together and upward, and Satan's hatred pulls creation apart and downward. More generally, the human experience of the body, the feel of its form, and how it works seems to be a constant point of reference for explaining complexities of cosmological structure (see Barkan, *Nature's*). For example, Lewis reports that "the older view was that the Intelligence is 'in' the sphere as the soul is 'in' the body" (*Discarded* 115). Musa likewise remarks that "in the same way that the soul distributes its power throughout the body, where it becomes differentiated according to the nature of the receiving part or faculty, the undifferentiated power of God, when it is distributed through the spheres, becomes differentiated in the stars and planets as it combines with the qualities inherent in them" (*Paradise* 31n).[7]

The finer-grained physical structure of this world includes other vertically scaled properties. The four elements of the "Mundus" are layered from heaviest to lightest: earth, water, air, then fire (Lewis, *Discarded* 95). Hence I add to the scale of the spiritually undesirable to desirable the opposed qualities of a scale of mass (heavy to light), which implies a scale of density (dense to rarefied) (naturally associated with a scale of substance types, solid-liquid-gaseous), a scale of temperature (cold to hot), a scale of light (dark to light), and a scale of transparency (opaque to transparent). These scales are highly coherent with with one another, in that they co-occur in experience and interact in understood, predictable ways (i.e., their degrees of intensity increase and decrease together). Dante magnifies this correlation. Imagine a generic substance in a spatial environment organized by light and heat that increase upward and decrease downward. According to experiences of the effects of temperature and light on substances, as we proceed upward we expect the environment to become brighter, hotter, less solid, lighter, more rarefied, and more transparent; and as we proceed downward, we expect it to become darker, colder, more solid, heavier, denser, and more opaque.

Intriguing evidence bears on how the Dantean cosmos builds on and resonates with general psychological principles that guide mental modelling of the real world. Gibbs and Colston suggest that people may internalize a complex unified model of the environment that – like

Dante's metaphoric storyworld – is integrated through mappings of image-schematic structure across various perceptual modes (not simply by internalization of the real world, externalization of bodily experience, or gestalt processes) ("Cognitive" 362). First, an "internalized representation of physical momentum" affects conceptualization across auditory, kinesthetic, and visual modes. That this "representational momentum" includes gravity effects suggests more general "internalized environmental constraints" on conceptualization (357–9). Second, even young children demonstrate synaesthetic mappings across such domains. Indeed, synaesthesia "may rest on a universal understanding of cross-modal equivalence ... people do make systematic connections between dimensions of specific modalities, for example, soft and low-pitched sounds are associated with dim or dark colors" (363).[8] This is of considerable interest not only to the study of Dante's storyworld, but also to the study of how the grounding of metaphors in bodily experiences relate to metaphoric narratives.

This idea relates to an anthropological context with David Bordwell's citation of Robin Horton's claim that there is a "primary theory" of the physical world, largely defined by what the conceptual party calls image schemas, that "does not vary significantly from culture to culture" despite differences of emphasis ("Convention" 92). Such a model would have to be grounded in commonplace psychology, and would therefore have profound implications for the kinds of embodied cognitive scientific theories on which I have drawn. In the theory of primary metaphor, regardless of whether this "primary theory" world model forms before or after specific domain conflations, the two kinds of mappings would interact, and perhaps compete, in thought. In the study of literary and cultural cosmology, the model could help us to compare cosmologies across cultures and to work out their structure and operation in detail. It would give us a rudimentary standard shape to expect, against which elaborations and variations would stand out.

Action and Setting: Perception, Movement, and Force

Character agency makes metaphors of animate perception and force-dynamics available for interaction with the storyworld (with the physical setting, other characters, and the divine force dynamics). Perception interacts coherently with position and movement. As a protagonist can instantiate KNOWING IS SEEING, a journey's sequence of new visions (or new sense experience in general – touch, hearing, etc.) can delineate an education. Potential coherences multiply when elements of viewpoint and focus are included. To move upward is to become able to see and know more: both more of what is above, because it is closer and clearer, and more of what is below, because distance creates a wider perspective (perhaps on one's original location/state). Indeed, the upward-and-outward journey often includes a conventional thematic event: the *catascopia*, or vision of the earth as small and insignificant relative to the cosmos.[9] Metaphors of light and darkness can also become relevant to this kind of journey, since better light (i.e., larger, closer, brighter, more central, in front, and more directly focused on the object) affords better vision – though it can also be blinding. Love in Dante's world is a quasi-physical force, and in his characters it is a vector-like power of attraction and repulsion that links and draws them toward what they desire and pushes them away from what they fear or hate. As characters can control (to some extent) how their inner forces interact with outer ones, a central goal and duty in life is to organize them properly: to orient one's desire toward what is good, to strengthen good attractions, and move toward good objects; and to resist the pull of evil, stifle its attractions, and turn and move away from it. However, good and bad forces can interact complexly to represent complex reasoning: one may resist an attraction to goodness because of the frightening difficulty of the pursuit. (Recall Frye's image-schematic analysis of the complex psychology of Milton's Adam and Eve.) Character forces interact with those of the environments of the sub-worlds. Inferno is full of the pain of eternal coerced movement metaphorically suited to sins: there is frenzied movement driven by flies and hornets (canto 3), windstorms (canto 5), dogs (canto 13), fiery rain (cantos 14–15), etc. Residents of Purgatory constantly struggle against gravity and other impediments to climbing the mountain. They move extremely slowly (canto 3), or are forced to wait (canto 4), or carry great slabs of stone ("burdens" of sin) on their backs (cantos 10–12). Force and perception also interact. Dante is drawn toward the love he sees as radiance in higher beings, including Beatrice (*Paradise* 55, 169; 59n). On the other hand, Paolo and Francesca are stuck together in Inferno as punishment for succumbing to the attraction generated by vision and touch. Ignorant souls are dark and blind, unaware of God's love for them and of the proper object of their own love. God's punishment includes cutting off perception and communication between them. Again, this extends to interaction with cosmological energies. Those in Purgatory cannot move at night because the darkness of shadows afflicts their wills with impotence (canto 7).

In real-world experience, powers of action and perception interact coherently with each other and with the overall environment. Better perception generally means better action, and both are impeded by heaviness, cold, darkness, density, and opacity, and become easier and more effective with lightness, warmth, brightness, rarefaction, and transparency. In Dante, this contrast corresponds to DOWN versus UP. Spiritual progress becomes more difficult with descent and easier with ascent, because sin restricts freedom of thought, feeling, and movement, and finally freezes sinners irreversibly in their sins, while goodness continually enables such freedoms. Dante's travel up Purgatory gets progressively easier and faster (*Purgatory* 43), and ascent is easier and faster still through the spheres of Paradise, unimpeded by gravity (at times it is literally effortless, even unnoticed).[10] These interacting sources symbolize Dante's education. He gets stronger in action and perception as he goes. At first he is frequently diverted by curiosity about the sinners, and occasionally faints from shock, and Virgil or Beatrice often scold and pull him back to the path; gradually, he becomes a more imperturbable, vigorous, and dexterous traveller. His senses, especially his vision, also improve.

Coherence-Based Inference, Comprehensiveness, and Resonance

An important further kind of conceptual potential in metaphoric coherence has gone unnoticed by scholars. The details of the cosmos, considered as a compound source projected to a compound target, reveal that the projection of multiple but connected source domains to multiple but connected target domains licenses what we may call "coherence-based inferences." That is, there are intelligibly interconnected groupings of conceptual domains in both source (space, force-dynamics, perception) and target (intellect, emotion, ethics, aesthetics). Within each grouping, interconnections in experience are separable in thought, and there are no non-metaphorical connections across these sources and targets in experience. However, Dante's depiction of them as an interconnected whole leads to complex transfers of inferences. Two types of metaphoric projection arise only in such contexts: (1) each source domain can project to several or all target domains; and (2) connections within and across source domains can project connections within and across target domains. The first type applies in a limited way to relatively abstract structure to indicate connections across broadly-conceived target domains. For example, UPWARD movement tracks improvement not only in intellect, but also in emotion, ethics, and aesthetics. But some source domains are more broadly applicable than others: heat, for example, metaphorically applies to emotion much more than to the other target concepts mentioned. The second type elaborates on the details of such correlations by using correlations within and across source domains (which I will call intra-source and inter-source coherence based inference). Highlighting such further connections across source and target domains can suggest higher-level unified categories of experience. Consider an image-schematic example and a basic-level example.

Intra-Source Coherence-Based Inference

Some inferences follow from projecting interconnections within one source domain (e.g., movement) to interconnections within one target domain (e.g., spirituality). Pilgrim-Dante's movements embody simultaneously three orientational directions, in virtue of the sub-world's image-schematic coherence. In Paradise, when he moves UP along a SCALE, readers may infer that he also moves OUT of CONTAINERS and toward a PERIPHERY from a CENTRE. This is an inference about relations among source domain structures, not about targets. In itself it is not very informative, because it reveals nothing about what these movements mean. It becomes more meaningful when readers reconnect it to targets. Lakoff and Johnson argue that since different image-schematic structurings of the same concept focus on different aspects of it, different metaphors can combine or mix to focus on various aspects at once, and hence provide more comprehensive understanding. Overlapping image-schematic properties and entailments in various source domains correspond to shared metaphoric purposes. All these movements of Dante the pilgrim traverse a PATH, and so create distance from an original SOURCE and progress toward an opposing GOAL. All manifest the primary metaphor ACTIONS ARE MOTIONS, one of the structural metaphors of the cosmos. But each manifests a different aspect of its submapping, STATES ARE LOCATIONS (and the entailment that a change of location is a change of state). Their combination presents these distinct foci and purposes at once. Movement UP focuses on cumulative increase of a single homogeneous quality (since in terms of "horizontal" coordinates, it occurs in the same location without leaving its centre). Movement OUT focuses on boundaries that border other locations, and hence on incremental changes of state. Movement PERIPHERY-WARD focuses on variations within a single location/state, and hence on expansion from one sub-state to include a range of other sub-states. Each embodies a different kind of increase in some quality that defines an improvement in the mover's state. Therefore, as Dante passes each sphere, readers understand that he at once rises above his earlier states of spirituality (one continuous quality) and enters into a new sub-state (of some aspect of spirituality), which includes the former states and more besides.

Inter-Source Coherence-Based Inference

The sets of inferences described above convey a quite broad version of the target, but there are also more complex inferences about specific coherences among the targets based on specific coherences among the sources. If light means knowledge and heat means love, and heat and light increase correlatively (with ascent), then an increase in knowledge correlates with an increase in love. This suggests that love and knowledge are mutually enabling; each leads to the other. Indeed, for Dante they have an identical source and goal in God. (Goodness and "bliss" are also correlated.)

As with all metaphor, the projection of an inference does not guarantee its correctness or the justice of any particular application of it. The critique of "enlightenment" (e.g., by the Frankfurt School of cultural analysis) reveals a powerful example of potential error in Dante's metaphors. This critique attacks the assumption that cultural training in intellect and emotion – what Frye calls the educated imagination – is automatically morally elevating: the point is forcefully symbolized by the image (perhaps now a cultural stereotype) of the refined Nazi who weeps at classical symphonies. In fact, the sense of potential disconnect between cultural and moral "elevation" or "advance" has been around for at least two centuries. Raymond Williams, discussing the meanings of "culture," notes that Herder attacked European imperialism, and historians' assumption that the process of civilization or culture leads unilinearly to "the high and dominant point" of eighteenth century European culture, as if this end justified all the world's past deaths (*Keywords* 79).[11]

Although the interconnection of multiple sources and multiple targets is powerful in Dante, at other times he uses distinct sources to stress the sequentiality of spiritual development. Here it follows a definite one-way causal sequence (reflecting experiential sequences): the state of bliss of souls in heaven "is based upon the act of seeing God, / not loving Him which is the second step" (*Paradise* 333). The act of seeing God, which is a form of knowing, leads to love, which is a subsequent action of the will and which in turn leads to joy, which is the fulfillment of vision/knowledge and love/will (358n). Light precedes heat. But these operations are ultimately united in the same metaphorical image:

> light of the intellect, light full of love,
> love of the true good, full of ecstasy,
> ecstasy that transcends the sweetest joy. (353)

Light embodies intellect, love, goodness, and joyous ecstasy. The sequence does not disappear, but the single image of light-filled vision of an object summarizes the sequence as a single simultaneous compound of various interconnected aspects of image-schemas. The light *source* is intellect, its *content* is love, its *goal* is the good; and since it also *contains* ecstasy, the action of loving becomes its own fulfilled goal. Lakoff and Turner caution against the unwarranted assimilation of various metaphorical meanings – for example, lumping together the quite different metaphors that map a single source to distinct targets in LIFE IS FIRE and LOVE IS FIRE into "fire metaphors" (what they call the "Source-domain-only Error" [*More* 128]). But in Dante's case, and for many others, the writer makes a point of prompting the transfer of inferences by presenting complex relations across sources and targets and the mappings that connect them.

That a metaphoric compound can generate inferences about a target that are not supported by one source, but are supported by another or by some combination of them, shows that the complete metaphor system of a text or storyworld (if not of the whole cognitive unconscious) is more than the sum of its parts. Such inferences pertain to a generic target/topic that subsumes them as aspects of a whole – in decreasingly specific terms, as God and the Christian life, spirit and the spiritual life, virtue and the good life, or desire and the desirable life. The result is a coherent worldview that offers potentially profound insight as a schematology of intellect, emotion, morality, and aesthetics, but that is useless as scientific cosmology, biology, or physics.

Conclusions

Dante's Metaphoric Cosmology

At any given point in the Dantean character's experience, he is involved in a highly coherent network of many interconnected metaphors, with source domains in the most basic aspects of embodied experience, projected into a storyworld. This cosmological background defines the locations, orientations, forces, perceptions, and actions that structure the larger narrative, as well as its specific settings and scenes. This integrated metaphor system illustrates the significance of these elementary narrative features and patterns, and underlies much of the work's power.

Coherence and Resonance

A scene's or work's resonance arises from both internal (or textual) and external (or readerly) coherence: the more its metaphors cohere with one another and with salient metaphorical patterns in the reader's existing experience, the more it will resonate with them. In Dante's cosmos, the orientational schemas and sensory/perceptual structure of the cosmos are integrated in a way that substantially reflects, and therefore resonates with our everyday first-person bodily experiences of the human environment. Its locations, orientations, and directions, and their values, generally cohere together, as does the "me-first orientation" – the set of polarized orientational schemas (valuing UP, FRONT, HERE, NOW, etc. over their opposites) whose "conceptual point of reference" is the general experiential gestalt of "the canonical person, who functions in an upright position, maintains his/her balance, looks and moves forward, exists here and in the present, etc." (Cienki, "Some Properties" 5). In common understanding of substances, there is a rough hierarchy of types. Solids tend to be heavier, denser, and more opaque than liquids, which are more so than gases; hence gravity tends to arrange them in a scale from most solid up to most gaseous. Additionally, cold tends to solidify and heat to liquefy substances. Of course these correspondences are not absolute: the inside of the earth is hot and liquid, cold increases as we move up and out of the atmosphere, some solids float, and so on. But that is beside the point. The multidimensional coherence of this idealized environment helps to organize linguistic and poetic metaphor.[12] Dante's cosmos reflects this, and also the typical correspondences in experience among power of action, power of perception, and enabling environment (e.g., action improves with vision, which improves with environmental transparency).

We find coherences with our conceptual structure in Dante's reliance on many primary metaphors,[13] and of central metaphors for mind (MIND IS BODY) and emotion (EMOTION IS FORCE) – which enter into his metaphors for knowledge, learning, morality, and others. He interconnects these according to their correspondences in experience. His cosmos reflects the me-first orientation's general axiology of plus-minus values for image schemas, and so it resonates with the many metaphors that axiology motivates.

Further culturally specific systematic correspondences among these basic elements also provide opportunities for poetic connections across more specific elements in many domains. For example, medieval theory associated black bile, one of the four humours or substances of the human body, with a melancholic disposition; with earth, the dry and cold element; with the planet Saturn, its sphere, and the god Saturn; with cold and dry weather, including winter and the north; and with old age and death. Some of these connect in obvious ways to the DOWN end of the SCALE and its projection onto gravity in the cosmos. One could go on to conventional associations with Denmark, given its location and climate and its brooding Hamlet and Kierkegaard. These associations are all readily available to the poet writing about a "*descent into* melancholy" or in a modern idiom about "depression" or even "inertia," regardless of literal belief or disbelief in the associations.

Frye's Literary Theory

This analysis of Dante helps me propose a new version of Frye's "literary cosmology" thesis. It is plausible to think of important conceptual metaphors as structuring "archetypal" conventional images and stories of literature. Such mappings compose the poetic cosmos – the background world-model in which these stories and images unfold. Orientational schemas give the poetic cosmos overall organization, and are interwoven and superimposed for maximum coherence, guided by their interconnections in human experience. The poetic cosmos becomes a generic compound metaphor by association with human values – the "plus-minus parameter" of image schemas – and by specification and elaboration of sources and targets. Its properties of conceptual and emotional coherence and resonance are unique to metaphoric storyworlds.

Of course, such elements need not be metaphorized in all texts, or may only be metaphorized in particular parts of texts, and to a greater or lesser degree. Sometimes a cigar is just a cigar, and sometimes a mountain is just a mountain. Modifications and reversals of typical values and meanings are also possible. But singling out one such metaphor, or a group of them, for special attention is often the basis for particular scenes (e.g., stone slabs as "burdens" of the sin of pride "bringing low" the penitents in *Purgatory* 10–11). Additionally, the larger system is often drawn on to accentuate and contextualize such metaphors. For Frye, the essential point is that once picked up, this poetic cosmos is always available to the "educated imagination" of readers and writers, a semantic framework that is potentially – though not necessarily – applicable to all literature. However, since many of the metaphors I described in Dante are part of the everyday conceptual system, the reader need not be quite as "cultivated" as Frye suggests in order to feel literary resonance. Cultivation may mean becoming aware of them, how they interconnect, and their role in thought, language, and culture.

3 Family, City, and Body Politic: Metaphor and Framing in Social Thought

Metaphors, and senslesse and ambiguous words, are like *ignes fatui*; and reasoning upon them, is wandering amongst innumerable absurdities; and their end, contention, and sedition, or contempt.

Hobbes, *Leviathan* 116–17

... the nature and conditions of *ratio*, so far as *ratio* is verbal, are contained by *oratio*.

Frye, AC 337

... figures of speech are not the ornaments of language, but the elements of both language and thought.

Frye, StS 93–4

The foregoing chapters have sketched ways to connect Frye's literary theory with cognitive linguistic and literary theories, and have shown the advantages such connections offer to literary criticism and to the understanding of how metaphoric, imagistic, and narrative inferences interact in imaginative (aesthetic and moral) worldviews. This chapter moves on to consider how an integrated framework for cognitive-cultural poetics can also address the concerns of cultural studies by illuminating non-literary discourse. I now turn to an exploration of how aspects of literary cosmology supply and organize the metaphors and myths that structure moral-political worldview, ideology, and discourse. I found that Dante's cosmology was a version of Frye's general (Western) literary cosmology, but, so to speak, renovated (somewhat transformed) and decorated (further specified). In this chapter, I will find that metaphors and myths prominent in political thought and discourse also complexly relate to elements of Frye's literary cosmology. On the table in particular will be metaphors of the nation as a family and of the body politic, and myths of the loss and restoration of Paradise (the Fall and the Holy City). The family and body politic metaphors are, by virtue of their source domains, related to metaphors and metonymies of the universe and of the human race as a family and as a body. (Whereas a metaphor is a mapping across conceptual domains, a metonymy links an element of a domain with one or more other elements of the same domain. To think of all humans as a single human body is metonymy, because it links a whole with a part.) Moreover, human places of residence, such as homes, gardens, cities, and communities generally, are often seen as metaphorical (and metonymic) bodies and families. Hence the loss and regaining of Paradise (regarded as an ideal home for human life) can be seen as being expelled from, or welcomed into, a body or family. Here again metaphor borders on story and can even be seen to spawn it. Again, as Vico says, every metaphor is a fable in brief; and as Frye says, metaphors are the exfoliation of myths. Bringing into the picture the metaphor-structuring image schemas that have proven so central to the Frygean-cognitive conjunction, Paradise is also generally seen as UP, INSIDE, and CENTRAL, and the Fall accordingly as DOWN, OUT, and toward the PERIPHERY. Political thought and discourse combine and transform these elements and mappings in various ways. Frye's account of the social aspects of mythology and literary cosmology invites comparison with analyses in cognitive linguistics and cultural studies of the relations between meaning structures and social worldviews.

Mythology in the Making

In *The Critical Path*, Frye speaks of his long preoccupation with the question, "What is the total subject of study of which criticism forms part?" (14). Literary criticism "seemed to be part of two larger but undeveloped subjects. One was the unified criticism of all the arts," that is, "aesthetics"; the other was "some area of verbal expression which had not yet been defined," which he calls "mythology" (14). Toward a definition, Frye takes up Vico's account of "how a society, in its earliest phase, sets up a framework of mythology, out of which all its verbal culture grows, including its literature" (34). Early verbal culture includes a group of stories, some of which take on educational functions and canonical importance, that stick together to produce stable personal gods and heroes. Mythology "tends to become encyclopaedic, expanding into a total myth covering a society's view of its past, present, and future, its relation to its gods and its neighbours, its traditions, its social and religious duties, and its ultimate destiny"; it "comprises everything that it most concerns its society to know" (36). Images of accretion give way to an arboreal metaphor of gradual diversification:

> In origin, a myth of concern is largely undifferentiated: it has its roots in religion, but religion has also at that stage the function of *religio*, the binding together of the community in common acts and assumptions. Later, a myth of concern develops different social, political, legal, and literary branches. (36)

"Mythology" thus grows to mean "verbal culture" in general, and the modern critic's remit is consequently vastly broadened:

> His total subject embraces not merely literature, but the areas of concern which the mythical language of construction and belief enters and informs. These areas constitute the mythological subjects, and they include large parts of religion, philosophy, political theory, and the social sciences. (98)

Disciplinary partitions still discourage this kind of daunting and exhilarating charge, but interdisciplinary passages have opened up in places. Both cognitive linguistics and cultural studies have some jurisdiction here, with their overlapping themes: imagination, language, literature, culture, society, and ideology. However, they have little common ground when it comes to approach. Frye has enough in common with both, however, to help bring them into productive alignment: a mixed framework is possible, and probably necessary, for pursuing the "impossible project" of "the study of all the relations between all the elements in a whole way of life" (Nelson et al. 15). Here is a prognosis of my diagnosis. Cultural studies and new historicism produce compelling analyses of "applied mythology," the ways in which culture and language are mobilized for "concerned" social purposes. But they lean on shaky assumptions about how meaning works. Cognitive linguistics produces powerful analyses of how metaphor, narrative, and models shape everyday language and thought. However, it needs a richer view of the relation of language and ideology to literature and culture.

Frye can bridge these analyses, because his account of meaning in language and literature is interwoven with an account of their role in society and history, and both centre on an evolving overall mythology, or model of the human situation and destiny, built out of myth and metaphor. These frameworks can be compared where their overlaps converge on a common question: "social mythology," or *how cultural meaning creates political common sense*. My example will be the metaphors and myths behind concepts of liberalism and conservatism.

Cultural Studies: Code and Ideology

Introductions to cultural studies tend to observe that it grows out of "both a broad, anthropological and a more narrowly humanistic conception of culture." However, it departs from traditional forms of these because it arises from "analyses of modern industrial societies," and rejects "the exclusive equation of culture with high culture"; in fact, "all forms of cultural production need to be studied in relation to other cultural practices and to social and historical structures" (Nelson et al. 4). It continues to rethink the relation of culture to society, beyond the Marxist dogma that an economic/material base "ultimately determines" a mental superstructure or ideology. Three principles recur:

- Ideology (of dominant versus subordinate groups) is still the main issue in interpretation, although it is seen as neither wholly determined nor all-encompassing.
- Meaning is in the first place literal concepts; and cultural meaning is therefore the representation or encoding of literal concepts in symbols, myths, and images.
- The effect of this encoding is to make the cultural meaning – which is a debatable product of the dominance of a particular culture, class, or group at a given time and place in history – appear as normal, natural, universal, and eternal; commonsense, or "just a fact" (Barthes 124).[1]

Critics claim that these ideas are over-enthusiastic extensions to literature, culture, etc., of structuralist and semiological ideas about language:

- Meaning is arbitrary (i.e., our names for things are conventional, not natural).
- Meaning is defined by binary oppositions (originally a point about sounds and phonemes, extended to words and concepts).
- Meaning is sign-like: a use of symbol X to stand for concept Y.[2]

As I shall show, modern linguistics undermines all of these points.

In a classic example of cultural studies practice, Roland Barthes treats myth as "a type of speech" (109).[3] He writes that on a magazine cover, "a young Negro in a French uniform is saluting, with his eyes uplifted, probably fixed on a fold of the tricolour" (116). The whole situation depicted "is the *meaning* of the picture," the signifier. The signified is "French imperiality" (118ff.); or more fully, "that France is a great Empire, that all her sons, without any colour discrimination, faithfully serve under her flag, and that there is no better answer to the detractors of an alleged colonialism than the zeal shown by this Negro in serving his so-called oppressors" (116). The "presence of the signified through the signifier" is "signification" (116–17). In its own context, the signifier has a genuine meaning, value, and history: "The meaning is already complete, it postulates a kind of knowledge, a past, a memory, a comparative order of facts, ideas, decisions" (117). Thus, "a *complete* image would exclude myth ... myth prefers to work with poor, incomplete images, where the meaning is already relieved of its fat, and ready for a signification, such as caricatures, pastiches, symbols, etc." (127). Myth alienates that meaning by tearing the signifier out of its own context in a complex reality, making us forget that context by placing it in another, hollowing it out and turning it to other purposes such as propaganda, advertising, or entertainment – those of the myth's producers and consumers: "In the case of the soldier-Negro, for instance, what is got rid of is ... the contingent, historical, in one word: *fabricated*, quality of colonialism ... If I *state the fact* of French imperiality without explaining it, I am very near to finding that it is natural and *goes without saying*: I am reassured" (143).

That Barthes treats myth as *ordinary* discourse is a basic mistake, in Frye's view. As discussed above, the principal context for literary texts is literature, and literary discourse assumes and invites a kind of attention distinct from that called for by ordinary discourse: centripetal or coherence-oriented, as opposed to centrifugal or reference-oriented.[4] Barthes's "mythology" is Frye's "social" or "secondary" mythology (as I will show below). Barthes's example is not literature, but his analysis is off-target anyway because his view of ordinary discourse is also off-target and overlooks its literary dimensions.

Cognitive linguistics supports Frye's view of ordinary discourse. Lakoff and Johnson stress that meaning is generally *motivated*, in the sense that meanings are neither determined by nature nor wholly arbitrary, but rather have some understandable basis (see e.g., *Philosophy* 464–6). Turner points out that deconstruction wrongly extends Saussure's idea that phonemes are defined by contrasts with other phonemes to claim that lexemes (words, mainly) consist in traces of what they contrast with. This, says Turner, is "wrong on a grand scale": the "putative linguistics presupposed by the principle of the free play of signifiers has no serious basis in contemporary linguistics or cognitive science. If anything, the opposite seems to be true" (*Death* 6–7). In one of the founding essays of conceptual metaphor theory, Reddy observes how the "conduit metaphor" for communication distorts reality. The idea that meanings are put into words, which are sent to a receiver who then unpacks them, implies that communicative success should be automatic and only failures require explanation (295). Reddy's analysis undermines informational models of communication, including the ideas of encoding and decoding (306). The social implications are that people ignore their own large role in reconstructing meaning, blame senders for problems, and begin to think other people are stupid or insane (307–8). Fauconnier's studies of language as promptings for conceptual mappings also show that language is very different from codes (or truth-conditions) because it only sets a schematic stage for meaning to be built and negotiated locally in context by language users (*Mappings* 164). The complexity of the cognitive operations of meaning construction "far exceeds the overt information that a language form could carry" (187).

Thus semiology exaggerates the sense that meaning is a literal assertion that is contained in a "sign" or "code," packed up and sent by a speaker, and unpacked by an addressee. This carries the potential for significant distortion, as when the implications are taken up by analysts, that the sender aims solely at persuasion or dictation; thus the recipient should agree or disagree, submit or resist. Through this distortion, verbal culture is all "ideological struggle," propaganda, or even, because it is everwhere as a "way of life," blanket mental obfuscation and oppression, omnipresent but mysteriously sourceless. A response developed within cultural studies recognizing creative "resistance" by cultural consumers; this in turn snowballed into visions of omnipresent resistance – as one critic complained, "the discovery that washing your car on Sunday is a revolutionary event" (Morris 312).

Many cultural critics accept the kinds of assumptions I have sketched, but it is important to note that cultural and historicist criticism is not necessarily as reductive as it may seem from the Frygean point of view. It is not entirely ruled by deconstructive and ideological criticism, or what Frye called "sociological" approaches to literature, which he opposed, or at least was sometimes impatient with: "My opposition to sociological criticism is based on the principle that mythology is prior to ideology, the set of assumptions being always derived from a prior story ... Criticism often assumes that the ideology goes all the way" (qtd. in Adamson, "Treason" 76). This opposition was partly due to the fact that he associated sociological criticism with critics such as Barthes, who seems incapable of not taking ideas to the furthest extremes possible. For Barthes, the counter-intuitive, hyperbolic, paradoxical aphorism is the always-greener field on the other side of the fence of common sense. Mark Turner, describing how the basic assumptions of cognitive science are "widely rejected by literary theory," quotes Barthes's remarks in "The Death of the Author":

> Writing is that neutral, composite, oblique space where our subject slips away, the negative where all identity is lost, starting with the very identity of the body writing ... [T]he modern scriptor is born simultaneously with the text, is in no way equipped with a being preceding or exceeding the writing ... The reader is the space on which all the quotations that make up a writing are inscribed without any of them being lost; a text's unity lies not in its origin but in its destination. Yet this destination cannot any longer be personal: the reader is without history, biography, psychology. (qtd. in Turner, "Cognitive Science")

Turner also references Derrida's remark that there is nothing outside the text ("il n'y a pas de hors-texte") and Foucault's observation that "the human being is only a recent invention, a wrinkle in our knowledge that inevitably will be displaced as other wrinkles arise." Steven Pinker gives Barthes "the prize for the most extreme statement," for "man does not exist prior to language, either as a species or an individual" (qtd. in *Blank* 208). For other contenders, consider Jameson's remark that "history itself becomes the ultimate ground as well as the untrascendable limit of our understanding in general and our textual interpretations in particular" (*Political* 100); and Franco Moretti's unabashedly reductive "basic hypothesis," "let us say that the substantial function of literature is to secure consent. To make individuals feel 'at ease' in the world they happen to live in, to reconcile them in a pleasant and imperceptible way to its prevailing cultural norms" (*Signs* 27). These are leading figures in the field. Yet there is in the literature more plausible sociological criticism and various exceptions and qualifications to the ideas that cultural meaning is code-like in being arbitrary and message-governed, predominantly ideological, and inescapably constructive of and controlling over minds.[5]

For example, both Barthes and Hall recognize limits to semiotic "arbitrariness." Barthes qualifies that signs and myths are partially motivated by forms of *analogy* – that is, by analogy with other signs, by fitting into a structure (e.g., subject-predicate agreement in grammar), and by analogy with reality (the black soldier's salute with that of the French soldier) (126). But such formal analogies are created by history, are always partial, and choose from among other possible motivations: "I can very well give to French imperiality many other signifiers" (127). Hall's view is similar and is based on his own spin on the distinction between denotation and connotation. Denotation is taken to be the "literal meaning" of a sign, almost universally recognized, especially with visual signs (e.g., photographs); this gets confused with a natural and uncoded "literal transcription of 'reality' in language" (Hall, "Encoding" 96). Connotation implies less fixed associative meanings (96). In actual discourse, most signs combine both aspects (97). At the connotative level, there is "the active intervention of ideologies in and on discourse: here, the sign is open to new accentuations and, in Volosinov's terms, enters fully into the struggle over meanings – the class struggle in language" (97). The denotative meaning is not "outside ideology," but "its ideological value is strongly *fixed*" because its meaning is "apparently fixed in natural perception," naturalized (97).

Ideology is still "the central concept in cultural studies" (Storey, "Introduction" viii–ix). It has undergone considerable evolution and revision from its Marxist original, generally toward decreasing determinism.[6] For Storey, Hall's formulation from the early 1980s is "generally accepted as the dominant working definition within cultural studies ... meaning is always the result of an act of 'articulation' (an active process of production in use within specific social relations) ... The cultural field is defined by this struggle to articulate, disarticulate and rearticulate cultural texts and practices for particular ideologies, particular politics" (ix). Hall is less extreme than Barthes or Althusser on cultural construction of thought: "The cultural industries do have the power constantly to rework and reshape what they represent; and, by repetition and selection, to impose and implant such definitions of ourselves as fit more easily the descriptions of the dominant or preferred culture ... These definitions don't have the power to occupy our minds; they don't function on us as if we are blank screens ... [These effects] are neither all-powerful nor all-inclusive" ("Notes" 460).[7]

Elsewhere, when Hall goes over related ground and considers the specific issue of popular consent to ideologies that seem to go against popular interest (i.e., the popular support for "Thatcherism"), he stresses the limited rationality of such ideologies, rather than their irrationality, in a way that briefly comes close to Lakoff's account of the rationality of conceptual framing. This is worth quoting at some length, as Hall critiques the failure of Marxist – and particularly Althusserian – theorizing about ideology to explain contemporary political experience, and lays out some new avenues of approach:

> Ruling or dominant conceptions of the world do not directly prescribe the mental content of the illusions that supposedly fill the heads of the dominated classes. But the circle of dominant ideas *does* accumulate the symbolic power to map or classify the world for others; its classifications do acquire not only the constraining power of dominance over other modes of thought but also the inertial authority of habit and instinct. It becomes the horizon of the taken-for-granted: what the world is and how it works, for all practical purposes. Ruling ideas may dominate other conceptions of the social world by setting the limit to what will appear as rational, reasonable, credible, indeed sayable or thinkable, within the given vocabularies of motive and action available to us. Their dominance lies precisely in the power they have to contain within their limits, to frame within their circumference of thought, the reasoning and calculation of other social groups. ("Toad" 44)

Thus, crucially, the "discourses" of opposing political views are "ways of organizing, discursively, not false but real, or (for the epistemologically squeamish) real enough, interests and experiences. Both impose on the same contradictory elements alternative inferential logics" (46). Furthermore, what should be asked about a politically successful ideology "is not what is *false* about it but what about it is *true*. By 'true' I do not mean universally correct as a law of the universe but 'makes good sense,' which – leaving science to one side – is usually quite enough for ideology" (46). Unfortunately, Hall's suggestions as to how ideas and discourses make claims to be, and come to count as, true and real – that is, how mappings of the world and inferential logics are structured and connect to reality – are brief and somewhat obscure. In Hall's words, an ideological discourse

> combines ideological elements into a discursive chain in such a way that the logic or unity of the discourse depends on the subject addressed assuming a number of specific subject positions. The discourse can only be read or spoken unproblematically if it is enunciated from the imaginary position of knowledge of the self-reliant, self-interested, self-sufficient taxpayer – Possessive Individual Man (*sic*); or the 'concerned patriot'; or the subject passionately attached to individual liberty and passionately opposed to the incursion of liberty that occurs through the state; or the respectable housewife; or the native Briton. (49)

These "subject positions" sound like character types, social narrative roles that one might take on and perform. However, while the notion of subject position relates to knowledge, it is not analysed in terms of the structures of thought, action, and institution related to social narrative roles, so it ends up sounding entirely aesthetic in the irrational sense of being a matter of personal feeling and style. This is where Frye and cognitive literary study can contribute to the study of ideology in culture.

In any case, the Barthesian legacy includes some fascinating sociology and anthropology of high culture, pop culture, and everyday life; and acute studies of the uses of cultural forms to frame moral and political situations and arguments.[8]

Cognitive Linguistics and Culture: Metaphor and Framing

I noted earlier that cognitive linguistics is highly interdisciplinary and broad in scope – it shares these qualities with cultural studies, as well as with Frye. Its interest in worldview and common sense is a particularly important overlap with cultural studies.[9] Frye and the conceptual party agree that metaphor and myth are schematic, pervasive in language and thought, and grounded in bodily experience. To repeat a point worth repeating, Frye, discussing the literary basis of non-literary discourse, speaks of a "conceptual rhetoric" (AC 331ff.) and famously suggests that "the nature and conditions of *ratio*, so far as *ratio* is verbal, are contained by *oratio*" (337). Thus he later speaks of the need to train people to "think rhetorically, to visualize ... abstractions, to subordinate logic and sequence to the insights of metaphor and simile, to realize that figures of speech are not the ornaments of language, but the elements of both language and thought" (StS 93–4). Analogously, for Lakoff and his school, metaphors are in the first place conceptual mappings, or ways of understanding one thing in terms of another. Hence, meanings are motivated rather than arbitrary, often widespread or universal; and there are limits to the explanatory reach of ideology and social construction. Thus Lakoff calls for a "higher" or "real" rationality that recognizes the imaginative dimension of thought and language (*Whose* 15–17, 249–59; *Thinking* 39–41). In a similar spirit, Turner calls for a "cognitive rhetoric" that would link everyday thought and language to literature and criticism (*Reading* chapter 11).

In recent years, Lakoff has set up a progressive think-tank and published five remarkably influential cognitive studies of politics to alleviate his frustration at how liberals were being manoeuvred into accepting conservative background assumptions instead of arguing from their own turf.[10] According to Lakoff, these background assumptions are involved in *framing*, which is the name of the game of moral and political thought and persuasion. Frames are knowledge structures; they shape the way we see the world and act in it. Words are defined relative to frames, and they evoke those frames. Evoking a frame reinforces the frame in thought and memory. Since negating a frame also evokes and therefore reinforces it, Lakoff's advice is to "respond by reframing" (*Don't* 119). Consider the recent Republican mantra of "tax relief." In the frame for *relief*, there must be an affliction, an afflicted party, and a reliever who removes the affliction and is therefore a hero. Anyone trying to stop the hero is inevitably (also) a villain (*Don't* 3). When this is connected to "tax," it becomes a *metaphorical* frame (4): by offering tax relief, Republicans will rescue the electorate from financial torment. To oppose the idea in these terms is to side with the villain. You may have all the facts and figures in the world on your side; if you accept the wrong frame, you hide them all under your big black hat. As Lakoff puts it, "frames trump facts" (*Don't* 115; cf. 17, 37, 109–10): "If a strongly held frame doesn't fit the facts, the facts will be ignored and the frame will be kept" (37).

This is *not* to say that facts do not exist or matter. Indeed, a key difference from the cultural studies model of discourse is the insistence on the possibility and importance of *honest* and *accurate* framing. For Lakoff, "framing is normal. Every sentence we say is framed in some way. When we say what we believe, we are using frames that we think are relatively accurate" (*Don't* 100). Thus he can contrast honest and truthful framing with "spin" and "propaganda" as manipulative uses of frames (*Don't* 100–1). In cultural studies, these often seem distinctions without a difference. Social constructionism favours simply framing in support of what it considers the right values and politics (i.e., progressive or emancipatory) and against the wrong ones (i.e., conservative or reactionary).

There are different but interconnected levels of frames, including lexical frames, surface frames, issue-defining frames, and deep frames. Lexical frames are associated with particular words in their ordinary senses. Surface frames are built on lexical frames, and are associated with expressions (e.g., slogans like "tax relief" or "war on terror"). Surface frames both activate and depend on deep frames, which constitute worldviews or (e.g., political) philosophies and "define one's overall 'common sense'" (*Thinking* 28). Deep framing is "the framing of moral values and principles" (31). Issue-defining frames, however, "exist at an intermediate depth" between surface and deep frames (32). An issue-defining frame "characterizes the problem, assigns blame, and constrains the possible solutions. More important, issue-defining frames *block* relevant concerns if those concerns are outside of the frame" (31–2).

Lakoff's analysis of conservative and liberal deep frames begins with several puzzles. First, the language of the two sides "seemed to use virtually the same metaphors for morality but with different – almost opposite – priorities"; hence they "could seem to be talking about the same thing and yet reach opposite conclusions" (*Moral* 11–12). Also, typical sets of opinions seem at first glance random: "What does opposition to abortion have to do with opposition to environmentalism? What does either have to do with opposition to affirmative action or gun control or the minimum wage?" (12). The same goes for the liberal "cluster of opposing political stands" (12). The two sides are also split on what they like to talk about: discipline and toughness versus need and help; direct causes versus social causes (13). Lakoff's question is: how must liberals and conservatives think to produce these effects? His explanation is that the coherence of political worldviews is based on coherent moral worldviews, which in turn are based on two opposing models of what family life should be: the Strict Father and Nurturant Parent models, which are about "strictness and nurturance as ideals at all levels – from the family to morality to religion and, ultimately, to politics" (x).

The Strict Father model portrays a traditional nuclear family. The father is responsible for support and protection, and has authority to set and enforce rules for the children. The mother cares for the house and children, and supports the father. Children build character (self-discipline and self-reliance) by respecting and obeying their parents (33). In the Nurturant Parent model, parents share responsibility equally. Love, empathy, and nurturance are most important, and children become responsible, self-disciplined, and self-reliant through being cared for and caring for others. Parents support and protect, which requires strength and courage. Children's obedience comes from respect, not fear (33–4). These are idealized (and here, abbreviated) models of family life; most people have some version of both models, may have variations and combinations of them, and may apply different ones in different domains (156–61).

Strict Father priorities are moral strength, respect for authority, strict behavioural norms, and so on; Nurturant Parent priorities are empathy and helping those in need (34–5; cf. chapters 5 and 6). The principles of each model appear in the other, but with opposing priorities, which drastically changes their effects (35). In the Nurturant model, strength functions in the service of nurturance; and in the Strict model, empathy and nurturance are a means to the end of moral strength (e.g., as "a reward for obedience" [35, 101]). Lakoff goes on to analyse the models' contrasting reasoning on a wide range of policy issues (chapters 10 to 16).

But other or supplementary explanations for the political division are possible. For example, Steven Pinker sees views of human nature as the key factor.[11] He names the conservative versus liberal visions after literary genres, "tragic" versus "utopian." However, what Pinker downplays – the metaphoric and narrative aspects of these "visions" – Frye delves into directly.

Social Mythology and Framing

The Critical Path presents conservatism and liberalism first as elements of society constituted by myths of concern and freedom, and second as social views based on polarizing social myths: the social contract and the Utopia.

To begin, Frye describes a dialectic of concern and freedom at the core of society and social thought. Freedom grows out of concern but conflicts with it; the myth of freedom is "part of the myth of concern, but is a part that stresses the importance of the non-mythical elements in culture," which support "truth of correspondence" (such as logic and evidence) (44). The mental attitudes associated with truth of correspondence become social: objectivity, suspension of judgment, tolerance, and respect for the individual (44). It follows that, "the myth of freedom thus constitutes the 'liberal' element in society, as the myth of concern constitutes the conservative one" (45).

Literature is a totality or great code of all possibilities of concern, and thus provides a context for myths of concern, though it is not one itself. Social mythology is a poor substitute for the genuine mythology of literature, and steals its forms. At times Frye writes as if social mythology is junk mythology – parasitic, parodic, and wholly irredeemable:

> All around us is a society which demands that we adjust or come to terms with it, and what that society presents to us is a social mythology. Advertising, propaganda, the speeches of politicians, popular books and magazines, the clichés of rumour, all have their own kind of pastoral myths, quest myths, hero myths, sacrificial myths, and nothing will drive these shoddy constructs out of the mind except the genuine forms of the same thing. (StS 105)

In the light of Frye's views, then, Barthes's saluting soldier suggests a perverted myth of loyalty and sacrifice to a colonial occupier, demystifiable only by literary myths of devotion to some genuine (spiritual) authority. One thinks of myths of sacrifice for family and friends (e.g., Odysseus giving up the company of a goddess, and even her offer of immortality, to struggle back to his wife and son), or for a divinity who cares for and protects the individual and the community, perhaps even to the point of dying for them. In *The Critical Path*, social mythology has lost some of its tarnish and gained a little lustre. A mythology need not be closed but may be open. An open mythology allows a progressive education in forms of social mythology, from early clichés geared toward civil obedience, to later forms that may confirm, question, or outgrow the initial ones. For example, we may come to see democracy rather than capitalism as the real American myth of concern (136–8).

Conservatism and liberalism as social views are based on concerned versions of the two myths that polarize social mythology, the social contract, and the Utopia (158):

> There are two social conceptions so deeply rooted in our experience that they can be presented only as myths. One is the social contract, the myth which attempts to explain the nature of the conditioning we accept by getting born. The other is the Utopia, the myth of an ideal social contract. Both these myths have religious affiliations: the contract is connected with the alienation myth of the Fall of Man, and the Utopia with the transcendence myth of the City of God. The overtones of the social contract myth are ironic, sometimes tragic. (SM 36)[12]

Conservative and liberal views side with the social contract and the Utopia respectively, and understand the development of individual human lives (socially, as well as personally) in relation to them. The conservative's "development is a matter of growing organically out of the roots of his social context," whose fundamental institutions civilize and give significance to life; whereas "to try to reject what one is already committed to can only lead to confusion and chaos, both in one's own life and in society" (SM 36). The radical feels that "maturity and development ... are a matter of becoming aware of our conditioning, and, in becoming aware, of making a choice between presented and discovered loyalties" (37). The conservative favours commitment, while the radical favours detachment followed by new commitment: "The end of commitment and engagement is the community: the end of detachment, then, is clearly the individual" (39). Both tend to rationalize rather than recognize anomalies and absurdities in their chosen society (CP 160–2).

But how exactly do these myths induce moral and political values? Interestingly, Lakoff examines how arguments and stories can interpenetrate, as "arguments have implicit story elements – heroes, victims, villains, crimes, rewards, punishments" (*Thinking* 137), and vice versa: stories have implicit argument elements. Indeed, frames themselves have a narrative structure. The concept was developed in part from sociologist Erving Goffman's analysis of how people grasp social situations and institutions in terms of the "life is a play" metaphor: people know how to act in hospitals, restaurants, banks, courts, parties, etc., because they know all of their conventional roles, settings, props, and scenes, and their internal logic and order.[13] As I have mentioned, there are different interconnected levels of framing. Lakoff shines a light on the interrelations between story frames and argument frames, and shows how the former help to focus the emotional, personal, and evaluative aspects of the latter. The story evokes and shapes emotions and judgments that relate to characters and their experiences. Good arguments include conflicts of heroes and villains because those elements "help transform a set of values, principles, beliefs, and statistics into stories with a beginning, a middle, and an end. Isolated political issues have little appeal. As stories, they begin to connect with a deeper understanding of personal and national identity" (124). Moreover, stories do not just heighten interest but actually mould arguments: "They require moral values and fundamental principles to identify heroes, villains, and victims. They require issue-defining frames to tell just what the offenses, rescues, and forms of justice are ... In short, narratives give arguments a trajectory that both compels an audience and guides their understanding of the issue itself" (130–1). Thus, a common background in political arguments is a kind of fairy tale – or in Frye's terms, romance myth. The fairy tale-like story of the USA rescuing Kuwait from Iraq guides understanding by carrying inferences about emotional moral values. Hence there appear to be seeds of major genres (or myths) in various arguments – and even within the phrase "tax relief," which also evokes a conventional scenario with roles of victim, villain, and hero.[14]

In Lakoff's terms, the basic story/argument elements of Frye's models are the abstract "characters" of society and the individual, and their relations. To merge Frye's broader discussion with Lakoff's analytical terms: Frye presents contrasting narrative models of the individual developing or maturing as a function of her attachment to and/or detachment from existing or ideal societies. These models have role-defining moral values. The conservative sees existing society as good: to break from it to pursue a utopian mirage would be a crime, and would be punished by social and personal chaos (making them both victims as well as villains). In the conservative's view, heroism means defending social institutions, which is rewarded with order and fulfillment. The liberal sees existing institutions as partly or potentially unjust, defined by villains harming victims. In this view, it is heroic to try to redress such crimes by rejecting the social status quo to build the ideal or at least improved society, which is itself the hero's reward.

Lakoff highlights some genre structures (e.g., fairy tale, "American stories") and how they interact with argument frames. He also remarks on how some basic narrative types relate to basic narrative roles:

> Our most basic roles in narratives are hero, villain, victim, and helper. And some of our basic narrative forms are self-defense (villain hurts

> hero-victim), rescue (hero, with helpers, fights and wins over villain), overcoming obstacles (hero as victim of circumstance who surmounts difficulties), and achieving potential (hero has special potential and, through discipline and fortitude, achieves it). (*Thinking* 124)

His later study, *The Political Mind*, expands on these ideas about narrative thinking in greater detail. Lakoff concentrates on how the situation and event structures of frames and scripts become simple stories via binding with properly narrative roles of hero, victim, helper, and villain, and thereby acquire the extra structure of moral and emotional evaluations of roles and events (*Political Mind* 33, 22–3). These simple story structures combine to form the complex stories of literature and lives and oft-repeated "deep narratives" (22, 24). He shows how they function as frames ("pick one and it will hide the other"), and how they can frame personal identity and political thought (31ff.).

Yet Frye's work reveals serious shortcomings in Lakoff's account of narrative. Lakoff catalogues some other types of "deep narratives" and their variants, such as rescue, rags-to-riches, reinvention of self, woman's lot, redemption, and others (24, 29, 30, 35). He also considers cultural prototype roles and stereotypes (chapter 9). However, he discusses only simple story types and structures of roles and relations, and his selection of types seems more random than systematic. He cannot explain why we have the types we do, nor their deeper commonalities, oppositions, etc. Nor does he fit them into a more encompassing system or link them with the major literary genres. He overlooks the power and importance of, for example, tragedy, which often lacks straightforward heroes, villains, and victims, and of complex literary texts, which are often similarly ambiguous. He shows little interest in narratology, even cognitive versions, even some developed by his colleagues. (Propp is the only narratologist he cites, which partly accounts for the prominence of the "fairy tale" structure.) There are also more specific problems: he does not explore in depth how narratives link surface frames with worldview deep frames (ch. 17, esp. 234–9) and their "background assumptions" such as "life is difficult" and "the world is fundamentally dangerous" (*Moral* 65). Such an assumption is neither a metaphor nor a model, but it is, or is part of, a quite broad and abstract narrative frame. It specifies qualities of a large-scale action (life) and situation (the world), and so implies or constrains scenes and settings. The broader and more integrated vision of the framing spectrum that comes from these considerations suggests how central genres are to thinking, values, feeling, action, and identity, and how rich the potential may be of linking genre studies like Frye's with language studies like Lakoff's. Frye begins with some simple roles, such as *alazon* and *eiron*, respectively the deceiver or self-deceiver and the self-deprecator (figures who pretend to be more and less than they are). However, he elaborates these roles in connection with supporting roles, the societies that form around or against the roles, more specific roles and plots (e.g., lovers in the love story, monster and hero in the quest), and variant forms of *alazon/eiron* relation (the four mythoi) and the thematic worlds they imply. His models are far richer, more adequate to literary narrative, and more deeply connected to mythologies and worldviews.

There remain large questions about the details of the possible interconnections among the theories of Frye, cultural studies, and Lakoff, and about where mixing frameworks might lead. Lakoff's studies paint an important part, but not the whole picture, of the political contrast. From the present perspective there are two major points to register. First, Frye shows that conceptual structures other than metaphor are necessary to understand that contrast: the "deep frames" of conservative and liberal worldviews must be understood in terms of conventional narrative patterns – myths and genres. Second, narrative and metaphor (both types and specific instances) interact constantly in thought and discourse. My next step, then, will be to consider ways to develop and refine the integrated framework I have proposed, by examining some of those metaphor-narrative interactions in discourse, in the example of two founding documents of modern conservatism and liberalism, Hobbes's *Leviathan* and Rousseau's *Social Contract*. This will reveal some of the ways in which Lakoff's investment in family metaphors needs correction and supplementation, and will add a few additional key ingredients, focused on the body politic, to the potent mixes of metaphors that define liberalism and conservatism.[15]

Myth and Metaphor Interaction in Political Discourse: Hobbes and Rousseau

Both Hobbes's *Leviathan* and Rousseau's *Social Contract* yield to both Lakoff's and Frye's analyses (as well as Pinker's). These decisive texts include all three keys to political meaning: Lakoff's metaphors of the family, Frye's tragic and comic social myths of social contract and Utopia, and theories of human nature (though these often appear in the guise of story and metaphor). Yet the concept of the "social contract" or "social pact" is certainly more central for both Hobbes and Rousseau than the occasional discussions of the family as a model for government; and what is more, in both books the metaphor of the body politic is far more important than that of the family. Finally, metonymy also plays an essential role in distinguishing the two versions of the body politic metaphor, and hence the contrasting social visions.

For both the Ur-conservative and the Ur-liberal, the social contract or pact is that agreement, and act of agreement, that takes humanity out of a state of nature into a civilized state. By that step, one loses natural freedom, but is also freed from the "war of all against all" in the state of nature. One gains justice, moral freedom, ownership over possessions, etc. This agreement, seen as a thing, is a metaphor; seen as an act, it is a metaphorical story. In fact, the body politic figure is a key player in the social contract myth: in both texts, the contract is the act that creates the body. Moreover, in order for readers to understand these texts, they must understand how metaphors and stories interact, and in order for critics to understand readers' understanding, they must analyse the same phenomenon in more detail. Indeed, in actual discourse, both literary and non-literary, metaphor and narrative structures (and other structures and mappings, such as metonymy) interact regularly, and often in ways central to the story or conceptual argument. Again, if metaphors are fables in brief (Vico), or embodiments or exfoliations of myth (Frye), it is somewhat strange that this connection has not been much discussed. In the following foray into Hobbes and Rousseau, I will pay particular heed to how the story of the creation of the social contract interacts with metaphors of body politic and nation as family, and with stories of the Fall from Paradise and restoration of the Holy City (as per Frye's sense of their significance).

The first thing we hear from Hobbes's *Leviathan* is an account of the mapping between the body and the state: "For by Art is created that great LEVIATHAN called a COMMON-WEALTH, or STATE, (in latine CIVITAS) which is but an Artificiall Man ... in which, the *Soveraignty* is an Artificiall *Soul*, as giving life and motion to the whole body," which continues in considerable detail, and includes officials as joints, reward and punishment as nerves, wealth as strength, and more (81). The family metaphor for the state, on the other hand, appears rarely and later on (to be examined below), where it is contrasted unfavourably with the body politic metaphor.

As noted, the social contract is the act that creates the body. We begin to see what this giant form is made of when we approach more closely. In the introduction to *Leviathan*, where the body politic analogy is set out explicitly, the analogy culminates in a reference to this mythical act: "Lastly, the *Pacts* and *Covenants*, by which the parts of this Body Politique were at first made, set together, and united, resemble that *Fiat*, or the *Let us make man*, pronounced by God in the Creation" (81–2). The Genesis allusion repeats the equation of state-creation with person-creation. It also backs up some aspects of Frye's analysis, but here the social contract is compared to the creation of man rather than his Fall. This is a serious difference, as creation precedes the sin of Adam and Eve and the subsequent divine wrath, and pre- and post-lapsarian humanity live in very different kinds of societies. Yet elsewhere, Frye connects creation and the Fall tightly (e.g., GC 109–10: because God could only have made a model world, the world we live in now must be the result of a "fall"; the Fall myth is "inseparable" from the creation myth). In any case, Hobbes does not develop the Genesis resemblance in detail, though he does later return to his hypothetical story in a prominent place. In "Of the Causes, Generation, and Definition of Common-wealth," the chapter that opens Part II, he discusses the need for "the terrour of some Power" in society to counteract the natural human passions that lead to war, and thus achieve the purpose of commonwealths, "preservation, and ... a more contented life thereby" (223). Hobbes eventually concludes that "the only way to erect such a Common Power as may be able to defend them from the invasion of Forraigners, and the injuries of one another ... is, to conferre all their power and strength upon one Man, or upon one Assembly of men" (227). Here the "or" states alternatives less than it states an equivalence: the metonymy of one man standing for the assembly, or perhaps containing the assembly (the part containing the whole). Moreover, the retrospective story seems both prescriptive and descriptive: both what people in such a situation ought to do, and what society must have done in the past. Hobbes gives the action more specificity, and it shifts from hypothetical ("as if") to historical ("this done") as individual actions of contract create the unification that constitutes the body politic:

> As if every man should say to every man, *I Authorise and give up my Right of Governing my selfe, to this Man, or to this Assembly of men, on this condition, that thou give up thy Right to him, and Authorise all his Actions in like manner.* This done, the Multitude so united in one Person, is called a COMMON-WEALTH, in latine CIVITAS. This is the Generation of that great LEVIATHAN, or rather (to speake more reverently) of that *Mortall God*, to which wee owe under the *Immortall God*, our peace and defence. (227)

Again, the metaphors of giant and "generation" lead into Biblical and religious references. What is created is several things at once: the literal common-wealth, the city that is metonymic for the commonwealth (from *civitas*), and the metaphors for the commonwealth as a divine sea monster (Leviathan), and as God (perhaps Christ, a god who was also mortal). The emphasis is on the unification of multiple bodies into one larger body, and the unification of mortals into something divine. For Frye, this social pact is a fall in that individuals give up their individuality as they are, in a sense, devoured by the leviathan they create. According to *The Great Code*, the Bible sees the world as leviathanic, a general condition with several aspects: "All of us are born, and live our natural lives, within the leviathan's belly. In the political aspect of the leviathan, we live in subjection to secular powers that may become at any time actively hostile to everything except their own aggressiveness" (190). Citizens suffer the fate of fish food. But the pact is also a restoration, as partakers regain contact with God via an act that is both joining the "Mortall God" (and according to Christianity the mortal god is the son of the immortal one) and entering the Holy City – presumably the *civitas dei*. For Hobbes, whether this event is demonic or apocalyptic, Fall or restoration, depends on how "reverently" one wants to think of it. The body politic permeates the text and reappears again and again in numerous, sometimes rather baroque, elaborations.

The family metaphor appears most significantly in the same chapter opening Part II, as Hobbes discusses the power needed to push people to keep natural passions in abeyance and follow the laws of social morality, which he calls "Lawes of Nature" (223). On the way to his conclusion about the generation of Leviathan, Hobbes argues that familial groups, and their principles of behaviour, are not sufficient to restrain passions and enforce those social laws, as they in fact contradict them. First, "in all places, where men have lived by small Families, to robbe and spoyle one another, has been a Trade," and the only laws observed are those of honour, that is "to abstain from cruelty" (224). This brief quasi-historical narrative leads to the metaphor, which carries the familial principle over to governments: "As small Familyes did then; so now do Cities and Kingdomes which are but greater Families (for their own security) enlarge their Dominions" (224). A few pages later, Hobbes uses a variation of this metaphor to describe one of the ways by which sovereign power is attained. It is the way of "naturall force; as when a man maketh his children, to submit themselves, and their children to his government, as being able to destroy them if they refuse" (228).

Another example of natural force, listed immediately after the family way, is war. The second way to attain sovereignty is voluntary agreement to submit to some man or assembly. So in fact Hobbes treats the family model for sovereign power as contrasting with, more primitive than, and implicitly inferior to the body politic model of that power, which defines the social contract. The former is a "Common-wealth by *Acquisition*" and the latter a "politicall Common-wealth or Common-wealth by *Institution*" (228). Family government is a step up from the individualistic state of nature but a step down from the orderly commonwealth of the body politic.

The family metaphor recurs when Hobbes treats the commonwealth by acquisition in greater detail. Indeed, it appears in the title of chapter 20, "*Of Dominion* PATERNALL, *and* DESPOTICAL" (251). The issue is how dominion is acquired. Hobbes argues that paternal right of dominion by generation is not derived from the generation itself but from the child's consent, because two parents are involved in generation and the child cannot be equally subject to both. Moreover, dominion is not to men only, because men are not necessarily superior to women in strength or prudence. In commonwealths, the controversy is decided by civil law (usually in favour of the father, as most commonwealths were erected by fathers). In the state of nature, however, there is only inclination and no law, so parents determine dominion of the child by contract (and presumably arrive at some agreement on their own). If there is no contract, dominion is with the mother, because in nature only the mother's declaration can identify the father. There is also a general principle that everyone should promise obedience to the person with the power to save or destroy them, as preservation is the end for which one person is subject to another. Thus the infant is obliged to obey its mother, as it owes its (continued) life mainly to her (and someone can gain dominion over an infant by saving its life). Hobbes specifies chains of dominion for several variations of family relations (from parents to children and grandchildren; and among monarchs), such that each is subject to all above them, but the highest in the chain has most authority. Ultimately, Hobbes concludes that both paternal and despotical dominion produce the same rights and consequences as sovereignty by institution, as sovereignty is absolute in all cases (256). From this, he concludes that in terms of rights of sovereignty, a great family is "a little Monarchy" if it is not part of a commonwealth (257). But he immediately stresses that families are not commonwealths, unless they are powerful enough to engage in war. Thus even in these apparently straightforward relations of paternal dominion there are elements of contract (consent, agreement), nature, and brute power (the power to save/destroy life). One has the impression here that Hobbes is thinking of the family in terms of politics, rather than vice-versa; and this politicized view of the family is then applied to politics per se. His view of the family is reminiscent of the Strict Father model, but his occasional developments of the analogy rely on those non-familial elements and end up foregrounding the social pact that establishes the sovereign. It seems that the logic of the family metaphor downplays what for him are central factors in political thinking: consent, agreement, and the threat of war.[16]

The nation as family metaphor gets better billing and is more central in Rousseau's argument. Book I, chapter II, begins: "The oldest of all societies, and the only natural one, is that of the family ... It can thus be said that the family is the first model of political societies: The father corresponds to the ruler, the children to the people; and all, having been born free and equal, give up their freedom only for their own advantage" (9). Thus the family also participates in the social contract myth. However, there is a difference between family and state in the emotional relationship that is the basis of the power relation: "In the family, the father's love for his children rewards him for the care he gives them, while in the state, the pleasure of commanding takes the place of love, which the ruler does not feel for his people" (9).The chapter ends in a rather virtuoso fashion, in terms of its rhetoric, as once again Rousseau nicely choreographs several metaphors together. He speaks of a "King Adam" who "was the sovereign of the world ... as long as he was its only inhabitant" (10). As per Frye, the Genesis myth is added to the contract myth, along with the idea of royalty; as per Lakoff, family government is also added to this complex: Rousseau speaks of his own descent from "Emperor Noah, father of three great monarchs who divided the world among themselves" (10). But with King Adam, loss of royal status comes with loss of solitude – that is, with creation of family and society – and in this situation the focus shifts toward the climactic Fall of the Genesis myth: "Adam was the sovereign of the world as Robinson Crusoe was of his island, as long as he was its only inhabitant; and the advantage of that empire was that the monarch was secure on his throne, with no rebellions, wars, or conspirators to fear" (10). The "king" of Paradise is also a castaway on a desert island, a solipsistic kind of body politic doomed to lose its position of sole power.[17]

Rousseau presents the family metaphor as quite limited in its scope of application. He focuses on the insecurity and instability of the family community – inevitably riven with conflict and destined to pass away (to future descendants) over time. The metaphor fades from view by the beginning of the hypothetical story of the contract, in Book I, chapter 6, "The Social Pact." As in Hobbes, the metaphorical social body begins at the climax of the contract story, as "in place of the individual persons of the contracting parties, the act of association immediately creates a collective, artificial body, composed of as many members as the assembly has voters, and the same act gives this body its unity, its collective self, its life, and its will. Such a public person, formed by the union of all other persons, was formerly called a *city*, and is now known as a *republic* or a *body politic*" (17–8). This creation story sets the stage for further stories, as the personification of the state provides an actor whose actions can embody those of the state.

The passage also brings to the fore a striking convergence: both Hobbes and Rousseau also seem to connect the body politic with the city and even the Holy City (*civitas dei*). The physical spatial arrangement of the body is more significant than at first appears; and the collective man (as on Hobbes's title page) seems to be a realization not only of the metonymic identification of the sovereign with the people, but of the metaphor of the commonwealth or city as body, occupying a certain area of land. This would suggest that the act of creating the body by the social contract is also the act of founding a city; which founding act is (at least ideally) a utopian achievement.

Both Hobbes and Rousseau proceed to use this pact-built body and its metaphorical story as a basis for examining the relative rights and duties of subjects or citizens to the sovereign and to each other. The difference in their views seems to be a result of the difference in the relative power, responsibility, and authority they assign to the parts of the artificial body politic: the individuals who comprise it and its sovereign. Both say that the body politic is essentially infallible because it has been voluntarily formed by all individuals. As Rousseau says, in words that could give comfort to tyrants or mobs depending on how they are taken: "Merely by virtue of existing, the sovereign is always what it should be" (19). But each takes a different view of where in this situation the authoritative will lies: in the people or the ruler. And the view they take of the locus of authority derives from the stage in the causal sequence of the action at which they locate the essential roots of authority.

For Hobbes, it is the sovereign empowered by that action who is sacrosanct; he identifies with the perspective of the Leviathan: "Because the Right of bearing the Person of them all, is given to him they make

Soveraigne, by Covenant onely of one to another, and not of him to any of them; there can happen no breach of Covenant on the part of the Soveraigne; and consequently none of his Subjects, by any pretence of forfeiture, can be freed from his Subjection" (230). He explains that "he which is made Soveraigne maketh no Covenant with his Subject beforehand" because he would have to covenant either with the whole or with every individual, and the whole does not exist before the covenant, and any individual pacts prior to the ruler gaining the sovereignty are superseded by the social pact (230). Moreover, "because every Subject is by this Institution Author of all the Actions, and Judgments of the Soveraigne Instituted; it followes, that whatsoever he doth, it can be no injury to any of his Subjects; nor ought he to be by any of them accused of Injustice" (232). Hobbes often repeats this paradox: since subjects create the social pact, or agree to it by remaining in it, the sovereign body politic can do no wrong and cannot be destroyed. One does not have to peer too deeply into this political theory to discern, behind or beneath it, so to speak, the contours of the theological notion of God as omniscient, omnipotent, omnipresent, and immortal.

The political theory also has a conceptual-rhetorical aspect, which turns on part-whole relations. In short, by the act of agreement, each part transfers its identity entirely to the new whole, and so cannot in any way (or with any legitimacy) go against that whole, on pain of logical contradiction and physical non-existence. What is clearly missing from this view is the recognition that the act of creation of this social pact is a fiction and a metaphor: the point that the sovereign is not literally identical to the collection of his subjects, and that an assent to have laws and a ruler does not constitute ongoing assent to everything the ruler does. Of course, real social life, including the processes of authority-constitution and assent to collective decisions, is far messier than these doctrines would have it. Incidentally, this idea of every subject being, by this institution, author of all of the sovereign's acts, also has hints of the idea, related to the above-mentioned sense of theology suffusing politics, of God being in everyone, everywhere, always (more abstractly, the part participating causally in the whole).

For Rousseau, the "original contract" by which the body politic comes into existence is sacrosanct. He identifies with the perspective of the contributing individuals: "Since the body politic or sovereign draws its being only from the sanctity of the contract, it can never obligate itself, even to an outsider, to do anything contrary to that original agreement, such as alienating some portion of itself, or placing itself under the authority of another sovereign. To violate the agreement by which it exists would be to annihilate itself, and that which is nothing can do nothing" (19). Subjects can still do wrong, however, so there is still what is now called the "free rider" problem: that "each individual can, as a man, have a private will different from or even contrary to the general will which he has as a citizen" and "may want to enjoy the rights of a citizen without fulfilling the duties of a subject" (19). This problem clashes with the body politic metaphor's assumption of parts absorbed into a harmonious whole, and to recognize and explicate the problem, Rousseau switches to other, related metaphors of health and mechanical functioning. He describes the problem in terms of a disease, "an injustice that would bring about the ruin of the body politic if it were to spread," and describes his solution as "essential to the functioning of the political machine" (19, 20). He says the pact includes the tacit stipulation – rather Orwellian-sounding to modern ears – that "anyone who refuses to obey the general will shall be compelled to do so by the whole body," that is, "he shall be forced to be free" (21).

In Book II, discussing sovereignty and law, Rousseau elaborates the keystone concept of the general will. He argues against identifying the sovereign with the ruler, and in support of identifying the sovereign with the people, or more precisely, with the general will, which is inalienable, indivisible, unerring, and has absolute power over its members, including the right of life and death (chapters I–V). (Again, the figure of a godlike being hovers in the background.) Like Hobbes, Rousseau argues by the logic – the metaphoric and image-schematic logic, or conceptual rhetoric – of a whole that takes precedence over its parts. For Rousseau, however, that prevailing whole is the general will, not the ruler. First, "only the general will can direct the forces of the state in such a way as to achieve the goal for which it was instituted, namely, the common good" (24). Hence, in agreement with Hobbes, "sovereignty, being only the exercise of the general will, can never be alienated," but in contradiction of Hobbes, "the sovereign, which is only a collective being, can be represented only by itself; power can be transferred, but will cannot" (24). Second, Rousseau argues for the indivisibility of the general will by analogy with the indivisibility of a body. Only the will of the whole people is general, and, when declared, it is "an act of sovereignty and constitutes law" (25). Otherwise it is but the will of a part, and an act of administration or decree. Other political theorists (anticipating Frankenstein) "make the sovereign a fantastic being put together from various bits and pieces; it is as if they composed a man of several bodies" (25). To mistake "mere manifestations" of the sovereign body for "parts" of it leads to failure to see that "all the rights taken for parts of it are subordinate to it," and hence to confusion over the "respective rights of kings and peoples" – as when Grotius "spares no effort to strip peoples of all their rights and bestow them on kings as artfully as possible" (26).

Ultimately, the two theorists' opposing but complementary senses of the part-whole relations of people and ruler in the constitution of the body politic leads to their opposing but complementary political views, with their complementary benefits and dangers. Hobbes's celebration of the ruler as the embodiment of the body politic only avoids the injustice of traditional tyranny by what is essentially wordplay. Rousseau's favouring of the people, or the general will, as the embodiment of that body, leads to a more democratic vision, but one vulnerable to the "tyranny of the majority," as the term "general will" is another kind of wordplay, a placeholder or blank cheque that can be identified with the will of neither the actual people nor the actual rulers.

It is something of a surprise, and a significant surprise, to find that both Hobbes and Rousseau acknowledge the imaginative or fictional quality of their social contract myths. Hobbes writes of his "war of all against all" state of nature: "It may peradventure be thought, there was never such a time, nor condition of warre as this; and I believe it was never generally so, over all the world" (187). But he counters that people live this way now (the savages of America); that civil wars can illustrate how things would be with no "common Power to feare"; and that sovereign powers are always "in the state and posture of Gladiators" (187). To clarify the nature of the pact by which one man rules and represents the many, Hobbes also devotes the final chapter of Part I to the nature of fictional representations (217–22). Rousseau says that "as a general rule, the most instructive part of the annals of a people, namely, the story of its origin as a people, is the part we know least about. The causes that bring about the rise and fall of empires are still demonstrated to us every day by experience, but since no peoples are being formed in our time, we have little more than conjectures to explain how they were formed in the past" (91). He, too, goes on to investigate this nonetheless, in the example of Rome.

From the vantage afforded by a comparison of the arguments of Hobbes and Rousseau, it is now evident that in the actual texts ushering in founding moments of liberalism and conservatism, both sides use all of the conceptual structures I have examined: family metaphors, body politic metaphors, and primarily fictional stories of losing and regaining Paradise (the Fall/the Holy City). The texts suggest that the body politic is the most important of these structures. What distinguishes the reasoning of the two writers from one another most clearly is how exactly they manipulate the body politic metaphor in the story of the creation of that body. More precisely, the difference has to do with how they construe the causal sequence of the narrative (i.e., the cause of the constitution of the whole); with variant image-schematic interrelations of part and whole; and with how the elements of the story map onto persons and things in the real world – the who or what with which the writers identify that whole that takes precedence over the parts.

Bodies Politic: A New Anatomy

My analysis makes it seem likely that varieties of the body politic metaphor and the social contract myth are additional bases of liberal/conservative models. Frye and Lakoff both show that it is a favourite trope of power to present particular actions of particular people who hold power at particular times and places as the unified actions of whole collective bodies. The favourite frame in which to cast those actions is that of heroic romance or fairy tale. There is ample linguistic and textual evidence that these structures still exist; the enthusiasm for them (or at least the unconscious use of them) seems to flow unabated. There are "heads" of groups (e.g., states, departments, or committees), groups are "bodies," and those who belong to them are "members" (e.g., of parliaments, congresses, or committees). There are also numerous metaphors of social personification and action: societies "speak," "listen," "watch," "sleep," and "wake," and have "heartlands," "voices," "spirits," "souls," and "wills." They may "fight with" or "reach out to" one another, "snub," "flatter," or "negotiate," and one may "welcome" another when the latter "visits," and so on. Their connection with Biblical creation and Fall may be neither necessary nor commonplace today. But Frye is surely right about the continuing power of the "royal metaphor" that identifies an individual with its class. In social terms, a head of state becomes the unified people and the nation in individual form, and this, along with lingering potential connections with the idea and aura of a divine monarchy, may make the sovereign "either the most attractive of icons or the most dangerous of idols" (GC 87–8). In democracies today, whether the head of state seems icon or idol probably depends on whether or not one voted for him or her.

The body metaphor as such does not distinguish liberal from conservative views, since both sides use it. We can, however, recognize a new aspect of the distinction by combining my point about the primacy of the body politic with a development of Lakoff's ideas. First, Lakoff never examines his concepts of "strictness" and "nurturance" beyond their manifestation in his family models, yet they seem to apply even more broadly than he indicates (as psychological types, for example). Strictness and nurturance can be understood in bodily terms, as they seem to be metaphorically based on the contrast between muscular tension and relaxation. We all experience this contrast every day, but the rigidity associated with tension and the flexibility associated with relaxation can translate into entire bodily postures, and concepts of "posture," "stance," "attitude," and "disposition" also apply metaphorically to whole worldviews. "Government," moreover, is often related to bodily muscular control, as in "self-government" and in the practice of parents who "govern" children and train them to be independent by physical constraint and guidance, in the first place of their bodies. This suggests that there are contrasting models of the body as a moral ideal – simply put, strong versus flexible – and consequently contrasting versions of the body politic metaphor. Establishing contrasting types of body postures and even whole bodies can lead to establishing contrasting types of bodily action, and that in turn can link moral-political metaphors with moral-political story types. In an intriguing study, Pierre Bourdieu notes that posture may reflect and convey a whole personal attitude, covering physical values as well as moral and social ones. Discussing the moral and political struggle over the "legitimate definition of sporting practice" and the "*legitimate use of the body*" (344) generally, he suggests these struggles may present "*invariant* features" in

> the recurrent opposition between two antagonistic philosophies of the body, a more ascetic one ... [that] emphasizes culture, *antiphysis*, the counter-natural, straightening, rectitude, effort, and another, more hedonistic one which privileges nature, *physis*, reducing culture to the body, physical culture to a sort of "laisser-faire" ... as *expression corporelle* ("physical expression" – "anti-gymnastics") does nowadays, teaching its devotees to unlearn the superfluous disciplines and restraints imposed, among other things, by ordinary gymnastics. (345)

He later says that "a postural norm such as uprightness ('stand up straight') has, like a direct gaze or a close haircut, the function of symbolizing a whole set of moral 'virtues' – rectitude, straightforwardness, dignity (face to face confrontation as a demand for respect) – and also physical ones – vigour, strength, health" (351).

These remarks suggest that simple metaphoric terms and images associated with the political contrast may be based on the contrast of bodily postures or conditions. The same kinds of postures can evoke both positive and negative connotations: liberals are seen as "open," "flexible," "tolerant," "inclusive," "broad," "relaxed," "giving," and "warm," but also as "soft,""weak,""pliant,""loose,""messy,""yielding," "melting," and "coddling"; while conservatives are seen as "strong," "tough," "solid," "firm," "stable," "orderly," "clear," "reserved," "restrained," and "rigorous," but also as "closed," "narrow," "rigid," "(up)tight," "hard," and "cold". This bodily contrast also to an important extent fits, as Lakoff's and Frye's (and also Pinker's) analyses do not, the etymological meanings of "liberal" ("free in bestowing, unrestrained, free from prejudice") and "conservative" ("preserves safely"). An analysis that can go some way toward accounting for the etymologies of the words has an advantage over those that cannot. Moreover, these qualities relate to metaphorical actions associated with liberal and conservative attitudes to society – as holding onto or standing by (or with) existing society and values, or letting go, moving forward, making progress, and reaching for something new. Hence other kinds of political thought and discourse should reveal in more depth how this bodily contrast matches and interacts with Lakoff's contrasting family types and Frye's contrasting myth types.

Conclusions

As in other chapters, I end this one with the sense I have presented a brief exploration of multiple structures, and there is much more to discover about how and how far they all fit and work together. Cultural studies continually challenges us to be suspicious of our beliefs and other conceptual structures (even the hypothetical ones), to discover in what ways they are constructed out of materials, and for purposes, that are specific to local historical socio-cultural contexts and informed by ideological values and interests – and then passed off as normal, natural, universal, and inevitable. Nonetheless, although we should suspect and look for interested social constructions in thought and discourse, it hardly follows that everything we think (and can think) is so constructed, including every appeal to reality, reason, and truth. Frye's and Lakoff's ways of linking bodily experience, common-sense social knowledge, linguistic knowledge, and cultural knowledge are far more supple, powerful, and true to experience than those suggested by Barthes, Hall, and others. They will refine, rather than dislodge, the kind of cultural critique of rhetoric and symbolism carried out in all of these frameworks: they indicate that we see by these structures, but they hide certain things from us as they reveal others. *Anatomy of Criticism, The Critical Path,* and Frye's other studies are pre-eminently rich and suggestive analyses of these structures in literature, culture, and society. He recognized that "myths of concern, democratic, Marxist, or what not, are ... founded on visions of human life with a generic literary shape" (CP 128). He also recognized that these myths are descended from scriptural and ritual forms, where they are often integrated in an overall form. If we want to understand how culture, society, literature, language, and common sense interconnect, we will have to make a place at the table for Frye, and take a fresh look at his work.

Given Frye's commitment to the autonomy of culture and to the detachment of criticism and the university from any myth of concern, it is difficult to imagine him putting his grasp of mythology to work for a party or a movement (although his social-democratic political sympathies are evident enough). Frye proposes reintegrating conservative and liberal myths at the imaginative level, to envision people assimilating their social traditions in order to grow through them toward social progress via disciplined individuality (SM 39–40). But while Lakoff and cultural critics may be more openly partisan than Frye, their studies too help alert us to our social-mythological conditioning, and so also "liberate the language of concern" (CP 166) and return us to literature – the "laboratory of myths" (SM 44) and the "great code of concern" (CP 128) – having won some of the imaginative freedom that gives glimpses of a "concern behind concern" (103).

4 Pastorals with Power: Universal Nature and the Cultural History of Genre

Pastoral ... an elaborately conventional poem expressing an urban poet's nostalgic image of the peace and simplicity of the life of shepherds and other rural folk in an idealized natural setting. The conventions that hundreds of later poets imitated from Vergil's imitation of Theocritus include a shepherd reclining under a spreading beech and meditating the rural muse, or piping as though he would ne'er grow old, or engaging in a friendly singing contest, or expressing his good or bad fortune with a lovely mistress, or grieving over the death of a fellow shepherd. From this last type developed the *pastoral elegy*, which persisted long after the other traditional types had ceased to be written ... Classical poets often described the pastoral life in terms of the mythical golden age; later Christian pastoralists combined allusions to the golden age and to the Garden of Eden, and also exploited the symbolism of "shepherd" (the ecclesiastical or parish "pastor," the Good Shepherd) to give many pastoral poems a Christian range of reference.

M.H. Abrams, *A Glossary of Literary Terms*, 1981 (127–8)

In ["Lycidas"] there is no nature, for there is no truth; there is no art, for there is nothing new. Its form is that of a pastoral – easy, vulgar, and therefore disgusting: whatever images it can supply are long ago exhausted; and its inherent improbability always forces dissatisfaction on the mind ... We know that they never drove a field, and that they had no flocks to batten; and though it be allowed that the representation may be allegorical, the true meaning is so uncertain and remote that it is never sought because it cannot be known when it is found.

Among the flocks and copses and flowers appear the heathen deities, Jove and Phoebus, Neptune and Aeolus, with a long train of mythological imagery, such as a College easily supplies. Nothing can less display knowledge or less exercise invention than to tell how a shepherd has lost his companion and must now feed his flocks alone, without any judge of his skill in piping; and how one god asks another god what is become of Lycidas, and how neither god can tell. He who thus grieves will excite no sympathy; he who thus praises will confer no honour.

This poem has yet a grosser fault. With these trifling fictions are mingled the most awful and sacred truths, such as ought never to be polluted with such irreverent combinations. The shepherd likewise is now a feeder of sheep, and afterwards an ecclesiastical pastor, a superintendent of a Christian flock. Such equivocations are always unskilful; but here they are indecent, and at least approach to impiety, of which, however, I believe the writer not to have been conscious.

Samuel Johnson, *Milton*, 1779–81 (450–1)

What are the cultural conditions under which "Lycidas" can be called "damaging" and removed from the syllabus? At the very least, surely diverse resources should be available to any generation as it moves through history. And after a decade in which thousands of young men have died prematurely in the course of the AIDS epidemic and thousands of other young men have mourned them, "Lycidas" is quite probably a resource as rich and useful as many that could be named ... cultural studies cannot be used to denigrate a whole class of cultural objects, though it can certainly indict the uses to which those objects have been put.

Cary Nelson, Paula A. Treichler, and Lawrence Grossberg,
"Cultural Studies: An Introduction" in *Cultural Studies*, 1992 (13)

Literary genres can lead long and curious lives. The above remarks on the pastoral genre illustrate three attitudes registering its changing place in cultural knowledge and experience over history. Pastoral, let us confess, is a little weird. Even in the first quotation, from a popular glossary of literary terms, one gets the sense of weariness with an artificial form exhausted long ago by mass production. In the second quotation there is a stronger sense of familiarity breeding contempt, as the genre had begun to lose its vogue when Samuel Johnson penned his well-known complaint on the deadness of the horse Milton insisted on flogging in "Lycidas." Johnson bemoans pastoral as so formulaic, outworn, and artificial that it actually undermines the purposes for which it is used, whether grieving, praising, or both. The third passage floats the possibility of recovering an old poem in a new context, for a new purpose, against the assumptions of some cultural critics that earlier literature is forever hopelessly stuck in the tangle of its ideological roots, and thus possibly even "damaging." (Presumably, it is damaging as a form of brainwashing or soul washing – except that this corruption is highly contagious, as it is borne by words and its antisocial sequelae could also cause collateral harm to others.) On the contrary, it is more possible that the poem's strange combination of the distant and the familiar may give it a power to help readers see and respond to the mixed strangeness and familiarity of a new situation. That these remarks are all about the same genre (and some about the same text), yet use and respond to it with such different shadings of attitude, illustrates something of the possible interplay of continuity and change in a culture. Perhaps I should place cautionary scare quotes around "a culture," as recent accounts of culture emphasize its multiplicity (and may forgo the singular for plurals) and evoke the variety, change, and intertwining of forms and uses of forms across communities and histories.

There are sociologies of literature and culture, less seduced than Barthes by the *jouissance* of the provocative exaggeration, that are plausible and important, and have influenced the study of literary history. I have in mind the new historicism, which is the dominant approach to such issues today. New historicism grew out of and rejected New Criticism, which focused on the internal structure and meaning of the individual canonical text, and the accompanying (at least attributed) ideas: that literature exists in an autonomous realm of aesthetic experience distinct from texts' histories of production and reception, and that that realm gives writers and readers access to universal and timeless human ideas and values. New historicism also rejects analogous ideas in "old" historicism, structuralism, and to some extent post-structuralism. Instead, it focuses on how literary production and reception, including everything thought of as "aesthetic," are implicated in (local) relations of power. Different communities and individuals construct literary categories differently and constantly revise them over time. Thus a pastoral poem will mean different things to, and create different effects in, different audiences (and different parts of a single audience), with no limit to the degree of difference, so there is no reason to think that what Milton's "Lycidas" says to us (or our various usses) has anything in common with what it meant to earlier readers, or even its author.[1]

However, despite its disavowal of efforts to ascertain universal elements in human culture, new historicism has a longstanding, somewhat conflicted concern with the transhistorical: it runs up against "a need to formulate ... new ways to understand the vitally important dialectic of cultural persistence and change" (Greenblatt, "Cultural" 2). Cognitive literary studies, by contrast, is enthusiastically concerned with universal aspects of human minds and culture, partly for the intellectual reasons outlined in the introduction (to discover what is common and stable in order to recognize what is particular and varying), but partly also I think as a form of self-knowledge. The dictum that "nothing human is alien" speaks to many people beyond as well as within the academy, as it expresses the desire to understand ourselves by getting to know others; to locate ourselves, so to speak, on the map of all possible human experience and variation. It relates to the intuition that we may see ourselves more clearly by distinguishing what we share with the rest of our species from what we have acquired through the cultural forces of language, education, history, custom, ideology, and mythology. This desire may foster certain illusions, but so too does the desire to deny the humanly universal.[2]

This chapter will show, first, how Frye has been wrongly lumped in with the New Critical views enunciated above; and second, how Frye's actual analyses of cultural history take account of the questions new historicism raises, and can critique and correct its approach to them. In making this second point, I will again show how Frye's view creates possibilities for a synthesis of cognitive and historicist views of the history of literary meaning in culture; that is, how it corrects both due to the particular way in which it connects them. The historicist view neglects the many kinds of relevance that literature can have to all of its readers, and focuses too exclusively on certain social-political functions for certain readers in the original context of literary production (and sometimes in contexts of reception). The cognitivist view, with its emphasis on the general and universal, can illuminate factors of stability and continuity in literary production and reception, and thus can help explain the communicability of literature. But it can also miss a number of things, even (other) general principles, by isolating factors and texts from one another in certain ways. It can miss the interplay and interconnection of (partly independent) universal factors (this relates to my point in chapter 2 that conceptual metaphor theory slights the interplay of conceptual metaphors with one another in extended thought and discourse). It can also miss the relation of universals to the historical development of literature. Frye identifies important ways in which general principles interact with one another and lead historical lives, and shows that these factors affect ideological aspects of reception.

To work out this critique and synthesis, I will examine the same things through the lenses of these different approaches. I will first look through two of the three lenses at general principles of literary history, especially the relation of literary texts to both their local cultures and their later readers. To illustrate and refine these theories, I will scrutinize the concept of genre through all three of their lenses. Then, as a case study to illustrate and clarify these views of literary history and genre, I will look at the pastoral genre and in particular Milton's pastoral elegy "Lycidas." In both genre and poem, I will pay particular attention to certain elements of plot and technique: the plot events of death and resurrection or apotheosis, and, in the representation of those events, the use of the symbolic technique that Hogan calls "alignment." Alignment is the linking of human situations and events with aspects of natural and divine orders, as with the enduring parallel of the course of human life with the cycle of the day, the seasons, and/or the life-story of a god or hero: a human hero's youth may be connected with dawn and spring, their old age with sunset and winter, and they may be as mighty as Thor, as terrible as Shiva, as wise as Athena, as patient as Job, or as beautiful as Helen. I will follow up Hogan's and Frye's suggestions that these plot and technique aspects of the genre are general literary principles and are plausible candidates for literary universals. At the same time, I will also explore in some depth how these candidate universals interact with culturally and historically particular aspects of the production and reception of genres and texts.

The history of pastoral has much to reveal about these routes for exploration. It reveals that certain conventional metaphors the genre uses for alignment are more stable than others, and hence are better candidates for further specific literary universals. Those metaphors, used to symbolize death and resurrection, are the solar metaphor for life that includes death as sunset and rebirth as sunrise, and the vegetable metaphor for life that sees death as plant death in winter and rebirth as new plant life in spring. Other, less stable metaphors are shepherd and flock as leader and people; water as an agent of transformation (potentially bringing both positive and negative change, nourishment and cleansing as well as dissolution and death); and the nuptial metaphors in which romantic love symbolizes the love between the shepherds, and the love of the god for the dead shepherd – and hence wedding symbolizes apotheosis, the reunion of the deceased with the god in heaven.

That genre history also reveals that those more central metaphors, while they are quite general (relating to commonplace experience of sun and plants), interact in certain ways to produce specific emergent meanings and effects, which can serve different conceptual and rhetorical purposes than those of the metaphors taken individually. It reveals that the ways in which alignment is expressed change over time. Not least, it also shows that these factors of stability and specificity affect how the genre can be turned to ideological purposes. We will find that there is stability in the pastoral plot (and in specific variants of the plot), in the techniques used to evoke the themes of those plots, in the metaphors used to manifest those techniques, and even in the ways that pastoral is read, received, and used. Naturally, there can be various reasons for stability, and particular instances of those plots, techniques, metaphors, and receptions also depend very much on cultural context.

General Principles of New Historicism

Stephen Greenblatt's account of new historicism in *Learning to Curse* provides a useful characterization of the school by its main founder and continuing torchbearer. To accomplish this characterization, he contrasts his movement in the first place with the hyper-harmonious marmoreal aesthetic idealism of the New Criticism:

> One of the more irritating qualities of my own literary training had been its relentlessly celebratory character: literary criticism was and largely remains a kind of secular theodicy. Every decision by a great artist could be shown to be a brilliant one ... Behind these exercises was the assumption that great works of art were triumphs of resolution ... the mature expression of a single artistic intention ... Traditional formalism and historicism ... shared a vision of high culture as a harmonizing domain of reconciliation based upon an aesthetic labor that transcends specific economic or political determinants. What is missing is psychic, social, and material resistance, a stubborn, unassimilable otherness, a sense of distance and difference. New historicism has attempted to restore this distance. (168–9)[3]

Unlike some cultural critics, Greenblatt is conscious of the challenges raised by rejecting the above tenets, especially on the issues of pleasure and play. He cites Marx's wonder at art's "apparently transhistorical stability": Marx saw that the difficulty in grasping art's relation to society lay not in seeing how past art works connect with forms of social development, but rather "in understanding why they still afford us aesthetic enjoyment and in certain respects prevail as the standard and model beyond attainment" (qtd. in Greenblatt 9). Greenblatt writes that "this stability poses a problem for any theory that insists in a strong way upon the historical embeddedness of literary texts (or cultural artefacts in general), insists, that is, upon the inseparability of their meaning from the circumstances of their making or reception" (9). Incidentally, other major cultural and new historicist critics have occasionally remarked on the same phenomenon. Raymond Williams, one of Greenblatt's inspirations (or preceptors, to use Frye's word), says:

> Art is one of the primary human activities, and ... it can succeed in articulating not just the imposed or constitutive social or intellectual system, but at once this and an experience of it, its lived consequence, in ways very close to many other kinds of active response ... but of course often more accessibly, just because it is specifically formed and because when it is made it is in its own way complete, even autonomous, and being the kind of work it is can be transmitted and communicated beyond its original situation and circumstances. (*Culture and Materialism* 25)[4]

But Greenblatt rejects the inference from "the supposed continuity of aesthetic response" to "a notion of the inherence in the text itself of the power to produce aesthetic pleasure and ... correspondingly to a notion that this pleasure is outside of history, disinterested and contemplative" (9–10). (A little later: the "monolithic and timeless character of pleasure"; the belief that "aesthetic pleasure is unitary and fixed" (10, 11).) This is the view that new historicism, perhaps by definition, rejects.

I admire Greenblatt's forthright stress on the problem posed for his own approach by the persistence of cultural artefacts, and the various aesthetic pleasures they offer (a later chapter of *Learning to Curse* discusses "resonance" and "wonder"). However, his response to these problems goes to extraordinary lengths to avoid obvious implications – such as that there is important continuity and stability in the creation of, structure of, and response to human meaning (in artworks in particular) over distant times and places, and that we should seek to understand this. Instead, Greenblatt suggests that the transhistorical stability of pleasure is an illusion. Comparing the pleasures of Shakespeare's original Jacobean audience with those of today's audiences, he declares that the "actual nature of that gratification, the objects and sensations and meanings and practices by which it is provoked and to which it is attached, differs significantly" (10). I say "declares" because he gives this opinion with little evidence that pertains to the pleasures enjoyed by either Shakespearean audience, or their kinds and degrees of difference, and thus the belief seems an article of faith rather than a product of reason. Even in a single audience, Greenblatt observes, pleasures may be different for different sectors, occur for different reasons, and respond to different signals. Thus he wants "to historicize pleasure, to explore its shifts and changes, to understand its interests" (10). Important reservations temper this view, however: "There do seem to be long-term continuities in pleasure and in those things that trigger pleasure. Such continuities ... should make us wary of exaggerating the psychological or moral distance that separates us from cultures temporally or geographically distant from our own" (10). And yet all his effort is poured into just such explorations of distance and difference, and scarcely any into continuity. He states the obvious, then ignores it.

Greenblatt goes on to discuss critically a central idea that new historicism inherits from post-structuralism: the challenge to "the distinction between literary and non-literary texts ... the stable difference between the fictive and the actual," given a view of discourse "not as a transparent glass through which we glimpse reality but as the creator of what Barthes called the 'reality-effect'" (13). He insists on the importance of reading "all of the textual traces of the past with the attention traditionally conferred only on literary texts" (14), but also insists that "the post-structuralist confounding of fiction and non-fiction" is inadequate (15). A text's status as fiction or not "fundamentally alters our mode of reading ... and changes our ethical position" toward it. Fabricated non-fiction, for example, is not art but lie. Thus "our belief in language's capacity for reference is part of our contract with the world; the contract may be playfully suspended or broken altogether, but no abrogation is without consequences, and there are circumstances where the abrogation is unacceptable. The existence or absence of a real world, real body, real pain, makes a difference" (15). There is much outside the text, and it matters.[5] (Common sense agrees, and it is possible that most critics agree, too.) Following on this, Greenblatt wants to develop terms to describe how material gets transferred "from social discourse to aesthetic discourse" and vice versa, because aesthetic discourse is "bound up with capitalist venture" and "social discourse is already charged with aesthetic energies" (157). We will presently explore some cases of how this may occur and what the implications are.[6]

Recalling my earlier contrast of the intellectual tendencies to lump and split, I applaud Hogan's argument that despite surface contrasts, a focus on species universals and a focus on cultural and individual differences are not in conflict but rather complementary, indeed "mutually necessary" (*Mind* 10). Opportunities to integrate (another coherence-word, of course) these perspectives are important.[7] There are ways to lump together lumping and splitting. With this in mind, I will now review Frye's kind of historicism – his sense of how literary thought interconnects with literary history.

Frye's Historicism: Concern, Meaning, and Ideology

In Frye's last major work, *Words with Power*, he states clearly, up front, his view of the relation of literature to society and history. He raises precisely the problem for historicism that concerns Greenblatt: criticism that studies "literature as a historical or ideological phenomenon, and its works as documents illustrating something outside literature ... leaves out the central structural principles that literature derives from myth, the principles that give literature its communicating power across the centuries through all ideological changes" (xiii). Not very amazingly, Frye does not turn into the bogeyman who declares aesthetic power, pleasure, and insight inherent in the text and outside history, monolithic, timeless, unitary, and fixed. He recognizes continuity in response, and an element of disinterest (or play) in both creation and response – as Greenblatt does – but he attributes them to the structural principles of myth. Such principles, he argues, "are certainly conditioned by social and historical factors and do not transcend them, but they retain a continuity of form that points to an identity of the literary organism distinct from all its adaptations to its social environment" (xiii). They are neither autonomous nor transcendent, but are continuous and coherent enough to give literature a coherent identity. The evolutionary analogy here, if taken a little further, suggests that there may be stable principles, not only of literary continuity, but also of literary change.[8]

Frye's working out of these ideas in his chapter on "Concern and Myth" has the advantage of a historical sense of the evolution of the social roles of stories, as he compares and contrasts the role of mythologies in early societies with the role of literatures (the descendants of mythologies) in later societies. Early myths have two contexts: literary, due to their structure, and ideological, due to their function; and "when their ideological function disappears, myths ... become purely literary, as Classical mythology did after the rise of Christianity" (31). This contrast develops into a more general view of how the two contexts influence writers and support their communicability in a balanced way. He imagines this relationship as a benign (or at least not very malign) temporal crucifixion: "I think of a poet, in relation to his society, as being at the center of a cross like a plus sign. The horizontal bar forms the social and ideological conditioning that made him intelligible to his contemporaries, and in fact to himself. The vertical bar is the mythological line of descent from previous poets ... which carries on into our own time" (47). That "vertical line of literary descent" enables readers to "understand poets remote from us in time and culture" (47–8). The horizontal bar of ideology is also historical, and a source and condition of (initial, local) intelligibility: it "constitutes the 'historicity' which surrounds the writer as a womb does an embryo, and which many critics think makes up the entire area of criticism" (48). However, Frye says, the ideologies that surround the great writers of the past are "so to speak, a great deal deader" than the writers themselves, and to understand the "communicating power" of the writers, one must study "the place in the history of literature itself" that they inherit and transmit, and "the conventions and genres that [they] found it natural to use" (48). Hence literature, as well as "participating in history as a whole," also "has its own peculiar history, and the center of that history is not biographies of authors or dates of publications, but the modifying of conventions and genres to meet varying social conditions" (48). Crucially, Frye adds that "meeting these conditions, of course, may mean opposing them as well as adapting to them" (48). Additionally, there may be other ways to meet conditions between or beyond opposition and adaptation, including various mixtures of the two.

The distinction between ideology and literature implied in Frye's choice of horizontal and vertical bars as metaphors for them may be overly sharp. After all, horizontal and vertical are literally (simply, geometrically) at cross-purposes to each other, whereas some past ideological contexts affect and communicate with us today in ways analogous to the arts. As I suggested in chapter 3, for example, the contrast, pervasive today, between liberal and conservative, or "left" and "right," began in the nineteenth century, though the two sides seem to have roots in the American and French revolutions of the eighteenth century. As myths of freedom and concern, in Frye's terms, they have a much longer history. Still, Frye's proposal to explain continuity of response to literary texts is more satisfactory than Greenblatt's curious shuffle, which (1) concedes there are continuities in pleasure and its triggers, then forgets about the concession; and then (2) claims that continuity is an illusion because pleasure, even due to the same object, is multiple and historical. The latter point fails to explain why the same object continues to be attended to.

We also need to consider Frye's argument that literature and its conventions and genres focus on primary concern, whereas ideology focuses on secondary concern. Primary concerns are rooted in (and, in part, are themselves) certain aspects of basic human experience, especially bodily experience. They include "food and drink, along with related bodily needs; sex; property (i.e., money, possessions, shelter, clothing, and everything that constitutes property in the sense of what is 'proper' to one's life); liberty of movement" (42). Secondary concerns "arise from the social contract, and include patriotic and other attachments of loyalty, religious beliefs, and class-conditioned attitudes and behavior" (42). Primary concerns are in origin "not individual or social in reference so much as generic, anterior to the conflicting claims of the singular and the plural. But as society develops they become the claims of the individual body as distinct from those of the body politic. A famine is a social problem, but only the individual starves" (42). As regards the relation of concern to belief and expression, "the axioms of primary concern are the simplest and baldest platitudes it is possible to formulate: that life is better than death, happiness better than misery, health better than sickness, freedom better than bondage, for all people without significant exception" (42).[9] Secondary concerns, on the other hand, are closely linked with ideologies, the latter being largely rationalizations of the former (43). While secondary concerns tend to be expressed in ideological prose language, "myths, or story-telling patterns" are the idiom of primary concerns. However, "human life being what it is, it is not so much the satisfaction of these concerns that are featured mythically as the anxiety about not getting them satisfied" (43). A literary work "will reflect the secondary and ideological concerns of its time, but it will relate those concerns to the primary ones of making a living, making love, and struggling to stay free and alive" (43).

Consequently, on the relation of myth to history, Frye's analysis is again orthogonal to historicism in Greenblatt's sense. As a result, it achieves historicism's other major historical goal: to connect the past with the present. It is worth quoting Frye a little extensively on this:

> Myth tends ... to dehistoricize whatever is historical in its structure. ... within literature the shaping of events takes precedence over the history. The mythical structures developed by literature are not anti-historical, but

> counter-historical: they transpose a historical theme into the present tense, and hence modify or alter features that emphasize the pastness of the past. (56)

Myth not only provides historical information, but organizes it under a human perspective. Without this, history has no basis for an ethical position toward that real world with its real bodies. The chapter closes with a strong challenge to the assumptions behind what Frye calls, somewhat askance, the "buzzword" of "historicity":

> It is widely believed, or said, that any dehistoricizing tendency of any kind, whether mythical or not, will corrupt the critical process into some kind of static idealism. To me myth is not simply an effect of a historical process, but a social vision that looks toward a transcending of history, which explains how it is able to hold two periods of history together, the author's and ours, in direct communication. It is very difficult, perhaps impossible, to suggest a social vision of this kind, even within an ideology, without invoking some kind of pastoral myth, past or future ... Such mythical features in social vision do not denigrate history, but help to clarify its function. (60–1)

The ideas of a "transcending of history" as such (and of "direct communication" with the past) may seem anathema to historicists, but Frye's argument is that such visions are great forces in history itself, and are in fact a great part of the reason for having and studying it. Paradoxically, historicism pushed to the extreme, which as Greenblatt says exaggerates the distance between one culture and another, becomes ahistorical. As examples of history combined with pastoral myth – by which he means "a perspective 'above' history" (58) – Frye mentions *The Communist Manifesto*, and then the story of Jesus's crucifixion. He says that it is not that "the myth falsifies history," but rather that history, as "the continuous record of what ascendant ideologies do, falsifies primary concern" (61). As a historical event, the crucifixion becomes assimilated to the events of "all the others who suffered that hideous and obscene death" (61). On the other hand:

> The myth of *the* Crucifixion confronts us with the reminder that we are as much involved in the death of Christ as his contemporaries, the sense of urgency about getting rid of anyone who disturbs our social conditioning being as intense as ever ... Hence it is only the myth in the present tense,

> not the event in the past, that has the power to give all the other poor wretches who have been victims of brutal injustice a place in the center of human vision. (61)

There is reason to believe that new historicists would agree with Frye that primary concern is what makes history meaningful. Think of Greenblatt's celebrated anecdotes that focus on how culture relates to "victims of brutal injustice," and the careful attention of historicists to the experience of groups marginalized for various reasons (race, class, gender, and more). Frye adds to this view that only myth, not history, can frame the original historical context in terms of human concern, and hence make the historical event present and meaningful, and hence challenge us in our own history (our social conditioning, our complicity), and perhaps even guide us through its pitfalls. While there is an ethical principle in seeing culture squarely in its actual historical context without allowing personal perspectives and interests to distort it, there is also an ethical principle in seeing and judging that context from the perspective of the transhistorical factors of the human body, its mind, and their concerns.

I can imagine several responses to Frye's account. First, Greenblatt's anecdotes have something of the effect Frye attributes to myth, yet they are non-literary. He discusses the bland 1586 report by a merchant adventurer of his small fleet landing at Sierra Leone, admiring a town of natives, and on departing burning it to the ground, with its striking "absence of feeling" and "ethical vacancy" (Veeser 5); a 1525 report of the Spanish in Hispaniola using the mythology of the natives of nearby islands to con them into slavery in the gold mines – natives who later committed mass suicide when they discovered the fraud ("Improvisation" 49–50); the equally chilling report from 1603 to 1604 by an agent of the East India Company of his torture and murder of a Chinese goldsmith suspected of theft (*Learning* 13–14). These anecdotes suggest that primary concern is not necessarily mythical (and vice versa). It could be argued, though, that Greenblatt's use of these anecdotes, with his personal response and reflections on their meaning, makes them in some respects literary, and takes them beyond their purely historical contexts via a "higher" perspective. He enacts the very transfer of material across discursive spheres that he studies by stressing the context of primary concern. The anecdotes are horrific because, while they are narratives and therefore prototypically present human-scale events from a human perspective, their narrators appear indifferent to the suffering they describe and both narrators and narratives glibly allow secondary concerns priority over primary.[10]

Second, Greenblatt shows that cultural representations can be callous as well as concerned (or hegemonic as well as resistant/subversive, to use historicist terms). This suggests that "myth" is not necessarily allied to universal primary concern. The clearest example comes from the plastic arts. Albrecht Dürer's plan for a "Monument to Commemorate a Victory over the Rebellious Peasants," referring to the slaughter in the Peasants' War of 1524–5 in Germany, seems ironically to take the side of the rebels because its peasant figure evokes the image of "Christ in Distress" (104). Yet other features and context suggest Dürer accepted the commonly held view that the rebels were, as Luther put it, "agents of the devil" (105) who should be killed mercilessly. Another example, even more telling of literary unconcern or anti-concern, is Shakespeare's quasi-monstrous character Caliban from *The Tempest*, who is despised and punished, though he wins sympathy away from Prospero at certain points: the audience is compelled to acknowledge "the independence and integrity of Caliban's construction of reality," but "the play insists that we judge it and that we prefer another" (31).

Frye also deals with such conflicting impulses in literature. Earlier in *Words with Power*, he contrasts an ideological "overthought," which is often callous, with a less-conscious mythical "underthought," which is concerned. His example comes from Shakespeare's *Henry V*, where a "counterpoint" of different emotions and themes undercuts the patriotic overthought about the heroic English king who invades and conquers France. An image of England's chronicle "rich with praise / As is the ooze and bottom of the sea / With sunken wrack and sumless treasuries" suggests the injustice and horror and futility of the war (57–8). Indeed, this view is analogous to Greenblatt's, epitomized in his title example of Caliban's phrase, which mocks Prospero and Miranda's claims that they have been charitable in educating Caliban – he has only learned, Caliban says, to curse his own misery.[11] As Greenblatt puts it, "Caliban's retort might be taken as self-indictment: even with the gift of language, his nature is so debased that he can only learn to curse. But the lines refuse to mean this; what we experience instead is a sense of their devastating justness. Ugly, rude, savage Caliban nevertheless achieves for an instant an absolute if intolerably bitter moral victory" (25). Yet for Greenblatt, this passing underthought is trumped by the ideological overthought, which the play itself "insists" that the audience prefer (though Greenblatt himself certainly does not prefer it). In both cases the texts present, subliminally, as it were, a concerned and critical view of a situation, while also apparently celebrating a rotten ideology. Frye's remarks do point up the fact that Greenblatt counts on some shared moral sense in his readers that will enable them to see the chilling irony of those anecdotal reports, the contrast of the events described with the emotional and moral vacancy of the narrators. But they leave open questions, which deserve serious investigation, about how to distinguish – both theoretically and in particular cases – the ideological overthought from the mythic underthought, how the texts convey and weight these disjunct visions, and what the consequence is for the various dimensions of reader response. On this last question, one could ask, for starters, how people should, and in fact do, negotiate the conflicts that arise in relation to overthought and underthought among these different dimensions (intellectual, aesthetic, emotional, moral, etc.).

A third potential stumbling block for Frye's account is that the structure of the text is not the only factor that determines meaning. Frye tends to emphasize the potential for concern in the myth or text itself. Thus one might suspect that he is rigging the game by defining myth (and to some extent literature), such that it is necessarily about primary concern. Frye does say "there is no real boundary line between" primary and secondary concern (42), but there is a meaningful distinction. He wants to contrast the properties of myth to the univocality and rationalizing of non-literary ideological discourse, so he claims that the meaning of myth is richly flexible, yet constrained by always being related to primary concern. New historicists, on the other hand, are more interested in how texts are actually read, received, and used by various audiences, in various situations, and for various purposes. These factors are indeed aspects of literary meaning, and we could adapt Frye's ideas to them – for example, by asking how a particular audience's situation and concerns (primary and secondary) affect their sense of overthought and underthought, ideology and myth. Frye at least provides a powerful structure of ideas with which to address the questions that Greenblatt leaves hanging in the air.

A fourth possible objection goes to Frye's initial distinction between primary and secondary concerns rather than to the overthought/underthought analysis he builds on it. In a fascinating essay titled "The Potato in the Materialist Imagination" (in Gallagher and Greenblatt), Catharine Gallagher challenges cultural materialist analyses that "invoke the human body as the ground of all explanation" (135) (e.g., by E.P. Thompson), or that grade phenomena as more to less cultural (e.g., by Raymond Williams) (112), by arguing that the body is cultural all the way down. According to "body history," "mere food" is always already powerfully cultural (112), and what counts as food and what feels like hunger are thoroughly historical (125). In the English food riots of the 1790s, many people going hungry refused to "accept potato substitutes for white bread" (126). They saw potatoes as unfit and inadequate nourishment for humans, so that to subsist on them would be a demeaning and dehumanizing departure from civilized society. Frye does not use the word "culture," but his distinction contrasts bodily and social concerns, whereas Gallagher stresses that the body politic goes deeply into individual bodies.

However, there are no irreconcilable differences between these approaches. While Frye gives the physical body a role in cultural explanation, he does not make it the "ground of all explanation." He sees no sharp line between primary (bodily) and secondary (social) concerns, and his point that famine is social but only individuals starve is compatible with Gallagher's point that hunger is not a straightforwardly physical matter. The body history argument can lead us, then, to elaborate Frye's view. It indicates that primary concerns are to some extent specified differently in different cultures (e.g., what counts as food), and that there are situations in which social concerns become primary. More precisely, as participation in families and communities seems fundamental to human life, sociality may be a point where primary concerns merge into secondary ones. (Community becomes political and ideological by degrees.) Thus just as there can be situations with conflicts among primary concerns, there can also be cases where a social body has as strong a moral claim as a physical body. After all, while the status of the potato has come a long way since the eighteenth century, there are still distinctions between what humans and animals eat, and it would still be as dehumanizing as ever to offer animal food to people in need today. But Gallagher's prioritizing of cultural history over bodily universals leads her to speculate that people may have remained hungry (as some claimed) even when they did eat potatoes (126). A more balanced view would suppose that while there is wide variation in what cultures may reject as *not* human food (what people will find disgusting and sickening), the body demands that *something* must count as food, eating, and hunger, and sets rather strict limits on what *can* be food for a given species (e.g. not rocks, dirt, air, poison). Again, Frye works out a way to encompass two apparently polarized aspects of a crux in human experience, and two clashing perspectives on that crux, each of which is locked into a partial explanation.

Ultimately, Frye is quite consistently "celebratory" about the visionary and liberating power of literature, but he is never naïve or simplistic. He also recognizes the ways in which it is ideologically conditioned, and the ways in which mythical patterns can be dangerously manipulative. His approach offers a valuable counterweight to much literary sociology today, which takes a relentlessly suspicious and accusatory attitude as a first principle. I would suggest that a sociology of production and reception, focused on historicist concerns, but informed by both Frye's literary and social-cultural theory and cognitive research on literary universals, could take criticism beyond both. It could connect meaning derived from specific historical ideological matters with meaning derived from universal body-based cognitive experience and concern (structures of thought and feeling).

The topic of genre is central in new historicism, cognitive poetics, and Frye's theory, and therefore an ideal focus for this conversation. I will now survey the treatment of genre by our three conversants, find their common ground, and imagine how to draft a more complete blueprint for the cultural history of genre by a judicious synthesis.

New Historicism at the Middle Level: Genre and the Poetics of Culture

The concept of genre has been central in the genesis and development of the "cultural poetics" of new historicism. Indeed, Greenblatt invented the term "new historicism" in his introduction to a special issue of the journal *Genre*. He writes:

> The critical practice represented in this volume challenges the assumptions that guarantee a secure distinction between "literary foreground" and "political background" or, more generally, between artistic production and other kinds of social production. Such distinctions do in fact exist, but they are not intrinsic to the texts; rather they are made up and constantly redrawn by artists, audiences, and readers. These collective social constructions on the one hand define the range of aesthetic possibilities within a given representational mode and, on the other, link that mode to a complex network of institutions, practices, and beliefs that constitute the culture as a whole. In this light, the study of genre is an exploration of the poetics of culture. (6)

In an argument (influenced by Greenblatt) for a new historicist sociology of genre, Tony Bennett criticizes traditional approaches to the topic, in which "society always comes first and literature follows on ... as its determined effect ... as essentially epiphenomenal" (108). The result is a "series of equations": "commonality of conditions equals commonality of form which support commonality of function" (80). For example, the realistic and domestic novel arose out of the romantic heroic epic to reflect changing ideas and values as religious feudal monarchies became secular capitalist democracies. Such accounts are vulnerable to deconstructive analyses of meaning construction because they believe genres are defined by the features they possess, rather than by how they contrast with other genres (92–4). As a result, Bennett recommends stressing the entangling and interanimation of literary genres with non-literary ones, and therefore with social relations of power (107–14).

Bennett quotes Leonard Tennenhouse's account of his conversion to this view, in which he mentions Frye as a defender of the idea of the autonomy of the literary or aesthetic realm. Tennenhouse had to jettison the assumptions of conventional genre analysis, embodied in Frye, which sees texts primarily in relation to previous and later texts in a generic tradition. Instead, he had to see texts primarily in relation to the contemporary historical scene – to non-literary forms of discourse and their involvements in the power relations of social institutions and ideologies. Tennenhouse's *Power on Display* aims to avoid imposing modern literary readings on Shakespeare's plays and to reveal the "radical historical otherness" of their political relations by relating them "to royal speeches and proclamations, to ledger reports and parliamentary reports, rather than to earlier or later moments in the evolution of drama" (111):

> To the degree that the Renaissance theatre performed a political function utterly different from the scene of reading, we may assume Shakespeare's plays, unlike the written Shakespeare, were not enclosed within an aesthetic framework. They opened onto a larger arena of events and observed a transgeneric logic. In my account ... stagecraft collaborates with statecraft in producing spectacles of power. The strategies of theatre resembled those of the scaffold, as well as court performance, I am suggesting, in observing a common logic of figuration that both sustained and testified to the monarch's power, a logic which by definition contradicts that inhering in generic study such as Frye's. (qtd. in Bennett 111–12)

That is, Tennenhouse says, arrangement of texts by genre "automatically detaches the work from history and presumes the internal organisation of its meaning," and proposes a "cultural logic intrinsic to a particular form" over "the vicissitudes of political conflict" that actually determine the inter-textual and institutional relations that regulate how literary texts are used (qtd. in Bennett 112).

However, assessing these historicist analyses together, at a distance from their original contexts of intellectual struggle, one senses that they have swung the critical pendulum too far the other way, and thereby lost some of the valuable insights of their predecessors. Tennenhouse's account is distortion through exaggeration – distortion of Frye's thought and of the literary issues themselves. A genre context links a text to a generic history, but also presumes a partly external organization of a text's meaning (in the sense of its complex relations to genre models and members, as well as their conditions of production) and allows for historical and political reference. The monological historicism Bennett proposes closes down the flexibility and multivocality of artworks – it rejects the aesthetic and traditional aspect in favour of the political, rather than acknowledging their interaction. In any case, the genre context cannot simply be jettisoned, because textual allusions often create connections with earlier moments in a genre and suggest connections with later ones, which in turn suggests a pattern of such lineage in literature generally. In fact Hogan proposes "allusion" and "structural assimilation," that is, "the explicit or implicit patterning of one work on the plot of another, often culturally central work," as universals of literary technique ("Literary Universals" 227; *Mind* 21). Thus, we need a more nuanced account of the interaction of universals and particulars in cognition and culture. We can begin tinkering toward such an account by considering an approach that takes Frye's ideas in a direction opposite to that of historicism – the direction of universals of mind and literature.

Universals and Their Uses: Emotional Thought and Genre

For purposes of considering literary universals, the most important cognitive research is that of Patrick Colm Hogan. Several of Hogan's books and articles propose a detailed theory of literary universals, and because the search for universals goes against the grain of contemporary literary study, he takes pains to place his project in intellectual and moral contexts. He dispels the suspicion that research on universals necessarily harbours a nefarious moral and political agenda by distinguishing between normative and empirical universals. Normative universals are local standards of some group that are taken to be universal and used to stigmatize or otherwise impose upon out-groups. Empirical universals, on the other hand, are established by research across distinct traditions. Hogan also relates his project to the predominant literary-critical practice of analysing the connections between cultural texts and their contexts by considering how universals relate to cultural and historical particulars. Pandit and Hogan contrast the tendencies in literary scholarship and in cognitive research:

> Put simply, literary critics and theorists have tended to stress the historical and cultural embedment of literature. In contrast, the focus of most cognitive work has been on universals – not what differentiates us, but what unites us across cultures and across time periods ... Put differently, literary study has tended toward particularity, the particularity of the work or the particularity of its historical and cultural milieu. In contrast, cognitivism has tended toward generality, the generality of the human mind. (2)

However, "cognitivist universalism and literary particularism" may and must be reconciled: "We cannot understand universals without understanding the particulars in which they are instantiated. Conversely, we cannot understand particulars, at least the particulars from another era or culture, without understanding universals. It is universals that provide the common ground against which we define and make sense of differences" (2–3). Echoing Frye's critique of historicism, Pandit and Hogan praise an analysis of literature in terms of cognitive modelling as a perspective that "does not distance us from the work (as thoroughgoing historicism might)," but rather "fuses it with our own horizons": "Too often, staunch New Historicists make historical investigation the end of criticism and theory. In this process, the plays may vanish, and with them their bearing on what we ourselves do outside the classroom or the pages of scholarly journals (4)."[12] New historicists would reply that the reception of literature, that "fusion of horizons" itself, should also be historicized, since the reader's contribution to literary meaning is just as bound to and shaped by historical ideological struggles as the writer's.

The Mind and Its Stories is Hogan's major study of universals of literary narrative based on universals of emotional thought. He remarks that stories in every culture inspire emotion by depicting its causes and effects, and proposes that there are "extensive and detailed narrative universals" that are "the direct result of extensive and detailed universals in ideas about emotions that are themselves closely related to universals of emotion per se" (1–2). He carefully explains and qualifies the concept of universals to dispel mistaken notions about what they are, how they work, and how they are studied. First, he firmly rejects the idea that universals must inhere in every literary text, or even in every literary tradition. Instead, following research on linguistic universals, Hogan proposes that literary universals are "properties and relations found across a range of literary traditions ... with a greater frequency than would be predicted by chance alone" (17, 19). The traditions in question must be "genetically and areally distinct," in other words, "they have distinct origins and have not influenced one another" (with respect to the property in question) (17). The reason is that "if a shared property is the result of a common source ... then that property does not provide evidence of a universal" (17). Absolute universals occur across all traditions, while statistical universals occur in more traditions than chance would predict (19). But even absolute universals can have a statistical element, as they need not occur in all works, as long as they occur with a greater-than-chance frequency (19).

The interrelation of emotion and conceptual prototypes is central to Hogan's theory, and we need to delve into it a little. It is generally accepted that human concepts are represented more in terms of prototypes, or "standard cases," than in terms of definitions that state "necessary and sufficient conditions" for category membership (30). Hogan contrasts prototypes with other representational structures: schemas and exempla (57–62). A schema is "a hierarchy of principles" that defines a concept, organized from the most to the least "central or definitive properties" (57), a folk theory of, for example, "bird." A prototype is "a sort of concretization of the schema with all default values in place" (58), a summary representation of a prototypical bird. An exemplar or exemplum is "any specific instance of a category," such as a remembered bird. All three kinds of representational structure operate in cognition, often for different purposes (61–2), and different people will have differently specified concepts.

Prototypicality is a factor in much if not all categorization, including our understanding of stories. First, emotional interest is a main feature of the stories considered prototypical (unlike e.g., stories of furnace repair) (86–7). Second, emotion concepts themselves involve the feeling of the emotion (typically via personal memories), plus "some account of the kinds of situation that give rise to the emotion and some account of the kinds of expression and action that result from an emotion" (82). Emotion concepts are based on prototype mini-narratives, which include causes and effects (or as Hogan puts it, eliciting conditions and actional/expressive consequences) (82–3). Thus "sad" means roughly "what you feel when someone you love dies and what you express through weeping" (83). Third, narratives are produced, interpreted, and evaluated in relation to prototypes of narrative structure. Genres, for example, have prototypical characters, openings, plots, scenes, etc. (86–7). Fourth, emotion prototypes provide central structural principles of storytelling and guide decisions about tellability, interest, effect, tone, shape, outcome, and more (88–9). Broadly, prototypical stories are "expansions of the micronarratives" that define emotion concepts (88–9).

Before he states his two major hypotheses about prototype narratives, Hogan discusses the relations among types of emotion. He sees a fundamental emotional polarity of happiness and sorrow:

> Happiness and sorrow are, in many ways, general markers for positive and negative feeling, with "positive" here meaning something like "the feeling we wish to achieve and sustain" and "negative" meaning something like, "the feeling we wish to end and avoid." Their phenomenological tone is, roughly, the mental equivalent of what in bodily sensation is termed "pleasure" and "pain." (90)

These "outcome" emotions correspond to enduring conditions and are themselves relatively lasting, whereas others such as anger, disgust, and fear are "punctual," elicited by brief events (90). The latter are evaluated in relation to the former but not vice versa: "Fear is, precisely, fear of what will lead to sorrow or block happiness" (90).

Hogan then proposes, first, that there are two predominant prototypes, a personal one and a social one, for the eliciting conditions of happiness: romantic union and social or political power (including material prosperity). They are the goals protagonists seek in prototypical narratives. The corresponding prototypes for sorrow are the death of the beloved and the complete loss of social or political power, through social and political exclusion in or out of society (94–7). Thus, second, there are two prominent structures of literary narrative cross-culturally, romantic and heroic tragicomedy, which derive respectively from the personal and social prototypes for happiness (with the middles or progressions of the plots typically associated with sorrow) (98–121).[13] Romantic tragicomedy involves

> two lovers who cannot be united due to some conflict between their love and social structure, typically represented by parental disapproval. This conflict commonly involves a rival as well, a suitor preferred by the interfering parents. The lovers are separated, frequently through exile and imprisonment. This separation often involves death or imagery of death. In the end, they are reunited, sometimes following a direct conflict with and defeat of the rival. It may happen that the reunion of the lovers takes place only in the afterlife. (101)

In heroic tragicomedy,

> the rightful leader of a society is displaced from rule or prevented from assuming rule, most often by a close relative. He/she is exiled or imprisoned. This exile or imprisonment is linked with death – imagery of death, the threat of death, and so on. While he/she is in exile or imprisoned, the kingdom is threatened by some outside force, typically a (demonized/bestial) invading army or, less often, a demonic beast. The hero defeats the threat to the kingdom. He/she then battles the usurper, and is restored to his/her proper place as leader of his/her society. (109–10)

I will consider how these universal plots and their imagery relate to pastoral.

Hogan's remarks on how this study of universals relates to the study of cultural particulars are highly instructive, and I will take guidance from them when I explore "Lycidas" as a pastoral that emerges from a particular context and speaks to other particular contexts. Although "most widely admired plots may approximate one or another of these structures," "it hardly follows that most widely admired plots are identical" ("Narrative Universals" 35). There are of course differences between *Romeo and Juliet* and *Sakuntala* or *Titanic*, which result from various kinds of structural transformation:

> The specification of prototypical structures (e.g., the development of the personality traits, appearance, and conditions of the lovers); the rearrangement of prototypical elements in discourse (e.g., altering the order in which the story is told or shifting the focus from the lovers to some apparently ancillary character); the deletion of prototypical events (as in tragedy, where the comic resolution is absent); the addition of further, complicating events, and so on. (35)

Hogan's cognitive account of literature includes not only isolating universals, but also studying "how universality works itself out in particularity" (35). The study of particularization involves two tasks. The first task is "to articulate the general principles by which universal structures are modified and specified" (as in the structural transformations just mentioned) (35). The second task looks at those principles and seeks to "isolate social, typological, or individual patterns" in how they are used. The second task thus considers phenomena such as the following:

> Historical periods, literary traditions, or individual authors may favor one or another way of forming characters, structuring discourse, and so on. Thus we find times and places where tragedy flourishes at the expense of comedy; we find literary traditions developing distinct (though not unrelated) character typologies; we find authors cultivating their own, individual poetic "voice." (35)

Hogan's account of particularizing universals is complex, but goes to the heart of an approach to literature that can blend the cognitive with the cultural. An example of how he applies it will clarify its details.

To examine how an author (Shakespeare, in this case) particularizes universals, Hogan distinguishes among several literary factors. He distinguishes "basic narrative structure" from "various ancillary motifs," that is, "plot elements (usually characters or events) that may be inserted into different story structures in order to provide complication, increase suspense," and so on (36). Examples are the common motif of the protagonist with one main companion, and the related motif of "estrangement and reconciliation between these two figures in the course of the story" (36). There are also "development principles," which are "procedures that may be applied to structures or motifs to intensify the emotion of a section, undermine expectations, prepare the reader for future developments, and so on" (36). Examples are "intensifying conflict through familialization," that is, particularizing conflicts as within a family; and "the alignment of different registers in the plot" (36), that is, as I have noted, establishing parallels between natural conditions and social relations, or character situations (e.g., linking death with winter) (37). I will later delve into the characteristic use of this development principle of alignment in pastoral (and in "Lycidas" especially) as a way of particularizing universals.

Hogan then proposes functions, particularly ideological functions, common to his prototypical narratives. Heroic tragicomedies "cultivate a sense of devotion to and pride in an in-group (roughly, a national in-group), a sense of opposition to an out-group (including anger toward that group), and a sense of respect for hierarchies of authority within the in-group" (37). As for romantic plots, they are more ambivalent in social and ideological function (as might be expected, given that heroic plots are concerned with social emotion, and romantic plots with individual emotion). They typically idealize romantic love and union against all social divisions and restrictions, yet bring lovers together in socially sanctioned ways (i.e., heterosexual marriage) ("Brain in Love" 345):

> On the one hand, romantic tragicomedy is a deeply progressive genre. It opposes hierarchy and social division. It supports individual freedom of choice. But it could hardly have such a prominent place across times and cultures if it were entirely revolutionary, entirely at odds with the operations of society. On the one hand, societies establish and enforce hierarchies, beginning with the family. But, at the same time, they must limit the strength of familial bonds, so that the larger society does not dissolve into familial or tribal units, warring factions like the Montagues and Capulets. Romantic tragicomedy helps to foster the establishment of bonds across such divisions by idealizing the extra-familial union and occluding the loss suffered in the movement away from the family. (353)

However, romance plots can also critique idealization, as in Flaubert's *Madame Bovary*.

One of three development principles central to political functions (of heroic plots, but presumably also romantic ones) is a certain form of alignment: not just "contingent parallels across facts (e.g., death and winter)" but "alignment of norms – moral, spiritual, and social," specifically, alignment of in-group norms with "transcendental moral norms," and with "divine preferences" ("Narrative Universals" 37). For example, a usurper character "violates social law (e.g., fealty), the higher ethical principles (e.g., those of loyalty) that underwrite the social law, and the divine will that underlies both (e.g., "divine right" for English kings ...)" (37). Hogan goes on to describe how the "pattern to the particular motifs, principles, and structural variants" distinctive of Shakespeare's use of the heroic plot modify that plot's ideology by making it "much more ethically ambiguous and emotionally ambivalent" (40).

For all the confusion and bad press that surround the concepts of archetype and anagogy, a fresh look at aspects of "Lycidas" from Frye's perspective can contribute to both tasks of studying "how universality works itself out in particularity": to articulate the principles by which universal structures are modified and specified *by* identifying social, typological, and individual patterns in the ways pastoral, and particular pastorals, adapt general principles of plot and ideology. To get to the point where I can do that, I must first compare Frye's multifaceted approach to the pastoral genre with a new historicist approach.

Frye's Pastoral Genre: Mode and Symbol

Frye's analyses lead to a set of suggestions about the structure of pastoral in relation to broader narrative patterns, and also about the structure of a particular pastoral, Milton's "Lycidas," in the contexts of modal, mythical, and anagogic criticism (as discussed, roughly historical, social, and religious approaches to culture respectively). These suggestions will clarify how these patterns underpin literary continuity and communicability, and also interact with local historical and political factors in contexts of production and reception. I will find that those patterns link the continuous to the local by shaping the use of the technique of alignment.

Frye, too, of course, places great emphasis on tragedy and comedy as basic narrative forms. They are two of the four archetypal narratives of his third *Anatomy* essay, but the first essay in that book, which offers a historical view of fictional modes, also uses a basic contrast between tragic and comic, and gives pastoral a key role in representing the earliest modes. Here he defines modes in terms of the principle of the hero's power of action, which changes over history, and defines tragic and comic modes in terms of the hero's relation to society. Power of action partly concerns the hero's relation to nature, and partly connects with the hero's relation to society. Pastoral (in a broad sense) is important in this scheme because it evokes an identity of the human and natural worlds, so that pastoral heroes are divine or quasi-divine. Thus what changes over history is not just the power and status of the hero, but the quality of the hero's relation to nature and society – from creating and controlling them to being subordinate to them.

The theme of the tragic mode is the exclusion of the hero from society, often through death (35–6). The theme of the comic mode is the integration of society, thus the acceptance and "incorporating of a central character into it" (43). As does Hogan, Frye sees tragic and comic as closely aligned. Since societies can be at two levels, human and divine, exclusion from one can mean inclusion in another. Hence the potential rebirth of the hero into heaven or earth is a pivotal event, which indicates how intimate, and indeed marriageable, tragedy and comedy are, and which can define the genre of a particular story. In tragic modes, stories of dying gods are Dionysiac, whereas comic stories of divine deaths are Apollonian, presenting (Classical) apotheosis or (Christian) salvation (or assumption) (35–6, 43). In both modes, gods are associated with nature, for example, vegetation and sun gods produce imagery of death as autumn and sunset. Moving from myth to romance, the hero becomes half-divine, but similar metaphoric associations of human with natural (especially animal and vegetable) worlds persist. The elegiac mood of "a spirit passing out of nature ... heroism unspoiled by irony" comes from such a hero's death or isolation (36). Pastoral is the "chief vehicle" of the idyllic "mode of romantic comedy corresponding to the elegiac" (43). Like the elegiac, the idyllic also "expresses the theme of escape from society" (by idealizing a simple country life), and as its world is close to nature and easily connected with myth, its imagery often relates to salvation, as in the Bible (43). Thus tragedy and comedy relate to the basic myths of the death and rebirth of the (divine) hero, which in turn are related to metaphors of the hero in terms of recurring cycles of sun and vegetation, and also to later secular stories.

This analysis reappears in the second essay of *Anatomy of Criticism*, informing Frye's arguments for mythical and anagogic symbolism (and their associated forms of criticism), for which a central example is Milton's "Lycidas" as pastoral (99–101, 121–2). To recapitulate, mythical or archetypal criticism concerns the "social aspect" of poetry, as a "mode of communication" and "the focus of a community," in which symbols are archetypes – that is, recurring and communicable units that connect works and help to unify literary experience (99). Thus, Milton's use of clearly conventional pastoral images (and allusions) prompts readers to "assimilate" them to other literary experience (99). The single poem indicates a generic tradition with a significant amount of coherence and suggests a larger order in literature as a whole. This order, while it is in part in the body of literary texts, is also one that readers help to create by reading – somewhat as Milton helped to expand by writing – through that unconscious assimilation and expansion of images and associations across works (100).

Frye imagines the assimilation of "Lycidas" to the pastoral tradition running as follows, across a range of "we thinks." "We think first" of pastoral's descent from Theocritus's elegy adapting the ritual Adonis lament, to Virgil and the "whole pastoral tradition" to Spenser and

Milton. "Then we think" of the pastoral symbolism of the Bible and its churches, and the link of Classical and Christian traditions in Virgil's Messianic Eclogue (99–100). "Then we think" of extensions of pastoral in Sidney's romance (*Arcadia*), Spenser's romantic allegory (*The Faerie Queene*), Shakespeare's forest comedies; "then of the post-Miltonic development" of pastoral elegy in Shelley, Arnold, Whitman, and Dylan Thomas; and perhaps of similar conventions in painting and music (100). Another thing we should think, perhaps, is the thought that Frye's "we think" and the "we think" of you and I may be significantly different. But then, everyone's "thinks" will be different from everyone else's, and a comparative study of "thinks" in relation to literary texts would be revealing and valuable. In any case, the resonance of the text arises from how it evokes these "thinks" and establishes an echo chamber across them.

Beyond specific historical conventions, however, many symbols (such as the sea, the heath, leviathans, and dragons) "cannot remain" in individual works, but get absorbed in the ongoing imaginative experience of them in other texts (100). For pastoral, such symbolism includes herders and herd animals like sheep, the "friendly" nature of pastures, streams, and woods, and nature spirits such as nymphs and satyrs. While few readers may have much direct experience of sheep and shepherding (not to mention musician-poet-shepherds and nature spirits), such symbols also relate to a more general level of socially transmitted and acquired common knowledge and experience. Most people eventually gain some knowledge and experience of forms of human harmony with nature, as in some aspects of agricultural life (with its routines of raising animals; its contrasts of predator versus prey and country versus city; and its dependence on solar, weather, and seasonal cycles), and in recreation that turns to nature as an escape from everyday work. There is also the common knowledge of the love and loss of close companions.

Frye returns again to discuss "Lycidas" in the context of anagogic criticism. He describes the three roles with which Lycidas is identified (god, poet, priest), their main cultural exempla or archetypes, the two key metaphors connected with the first role, and the coherence of the modulations of these metaphors in relation to the other roles. Finally, he discusses how the figure of Christ embodies all of these roles. First, Frye identifies Lycidas with the dying fertility god (Adonis or Tammuz) who is ritually lamented in Mediterranean religion. The god "personifies both the sun that falls into the western ocean at night and the vegetable life that dies in the autumn" and thus partakes of two central metaphors for human life based on solar and vegetal cycles. This dying god myth has been part of pastoral elegy since its beginnings in Theocritus. Second, Frye sees Lycidas as a poet (Orpheus), analogous to the god through his connection with nature's life, and his early death. Third, Frye sees Lycidas as a priest (Peter), analogous to Orpheus through the threat of drowning. Thus, "each aspect of *Lycidas* poses the question of premature death as it relates to the life of man, of poetry, and of the Church." But these three roles and their imagery are integrated in the figure of Christ. He has the roles of the young dying god eternally alive, the word containing all poetry, and the head and body of the church. He embodies the images of the good shepherd of the pastoral world, and the never-setting sun of righteousness – able to raise Lycidas (like Peter) from the waves, as he redeems souls from the "lower world" (as Orpheus failed to do) (121–2).

In Frye's account, the principle of linking and assimilation at the archetypal level is "symbolism" – that is, at this level, literary works are linked by certain images and events that are the basis of the "plot" of a genre (in the case of pastoral, images of sheep, shepherds, and their natural milieu; and stories of the shepherds' loves, singing, and deaths) and that, when applied metaphorically, are the basis of its corresponding theme. Symbols from common human experience are emphasized. The principle of assimilation at the anagogic level seems to be "roles" – that is, at this level, literary works are linked by central activities in human social life that are bound up in complex networks, the actions and images associated with those roles, and the metaphors that link them with natural cycles. Roles are connected with one another, as are their actions and images, but they are also distinguished.[14] The god dying and being reborn is the central figure. A god can naturally enough become priest and poet, whereas those figures cannot readily take on each other's roles, nor of course that of god. This dying god figure also readily connects with the personification metaphors based on natural (solar, vegetal, meteorological, seasonal) cycles at the archetypal level.

Frye's account of "Lycidas" is ultimately more or less the exact opposite of Samuel Johnson's. Milton's practice of mingling of "trifling fictions" in "irreverent combinations" with "the most awful and sacred truths" using a "long train of mythological imagery, such as a College easily supplies," far from polluting, indecent, or impious, is actually the vehicle of the awful and sacred aspects of the educated imagination.

Frye and Hogan Compared: A Digression

There are a number of general similarities between Frye's and Hogan's studies, and a few summarizing words of comparison and contrast may be of use in sharpening the outlines of both.[15] Both focus on story types; and both ground their main story types on a polarization of emotion, related to the pleasure/pain polarity, into what people want and do not want (though they have different ideas about what that is and why). Hogan's discussion of happiness and sorrow as positive and negative emotions related to bodily pleasure and pain is reminiscent of Frye's understanding of positive and negative desire and concern as polarizing factors in literary structure (e.g., WP 42–3, 88). Hogan, echoing Frye, emphasizes imagery types and image-analogies as possible universals related to the story types in which they appear (e.g., imagery of death and rebirth).[16] In addition, Hogan's analysis of aesthetic pleasure as involving "resonance" because the text evokes subconscious associated patterns of situation and event is comparable to Frye's account of literary resonance. However, while Frye's archetypal and anagogic perspectives chiefly evoke structures from cultural traditions, Hogan's "suggestion structure" (following Keith Oatley) also gives a prominent role to memories of personal experiences and emotions (*Mind* chapter 2).[17]

There are, of course, differences. In terms of their aims, Frye makes suggestions about likely universals and their probable bases, while Hogan attempts to establish and specify in detail what is universal and why. In terms of their primary analytic contexts, Hogan puts his analysis of patterns of story and imagery in the context of cognitive research on natural and evolved human emotions, mental structures, narrative, and language. Frye puts his story and image patterns in the context of literary and mythical conventions and traditions. He specifically rejects certain historical (diffusion of myths) or psychological (collective unconscious) explanations of the specific universals he proposes as unnecessary. Instead, he says "there is enough uniformity in the human mind, in the order of nature that that mind works with, and in the physical conditions of the medium itself, to account for all such similarities" ("On Teaching Literature" 435). Frye adapts frameworks of the psychology, anthropology, and aesthetics of his time. His mode of contextualizing patterns in terms of conventions focuses more on the emotions of the audience's relations to characters and events, whereas Hogan focuses more on the emotions of the events themselves. Hence

Frye's contexts can often be highly informative about the structure and implications of specific texts. By contrast, it is not always clear how an understanding of cognitive principles, and of universals, can be informative in this way. Hogan does not aim to enable more interpretations, but he does discuss some implications of his theory for interpretation (*Mind* 71–4). Additionally, Hogan bases his theory on evidence from many cultural traditions (including non-Western literary theory), which as he says better informs research on universals than does Frye's predominant focus on Western literature. However, Frye covers a broader time span, goes more deeply than Hogan does into his literary evidence, and offers more complex dynamics of character types, audience response, rhetoric, and historical development.[18] The two theories are thus effective complements to one another.

As for their treatments of story forms, in general, Frye's approach to narrative structure leans toward the social and thematic aspects, while Hogan's leans toward the individual and event-based aspects. Hogan sees tragicomedy as the most basic narrative form (integrating tragedy into comedy), whereas Frye sees romance as most basic (though romance tends toward either tragedy or comedy, and can integrate tragedy, satire, and comedy). Hogan distinguishes romantic from heroic tragicomedy through their pursuit of different goals with different emotional qualities (individual versus social forms of happiness: love versus power). Frye's distinction between comedy and tragedy first stresses social factors, specifically social integration or exclusion, which are often embodied in love and marriage, or death. Hogan's emotional prototype approach first stresses the ideas of union with, or death of, the individual beloved as the emotional basis of the narrative, and then describes the more detailed plot involving social obstacles.

We may compare Frye's and Hogan's plot types in a little more detail by considering their views of both specific event-types (stories of love, adventure or heroism, and/or death) and individual versus social factors. In Hogan's romantic tragicomedy, the lovers' reunion may occur in the afterlife. This seems to circumvent social integration, but is otherwise reminiscent of Frye's account of comedy, though Frye emphasizes the triumph of the new society that forms around the lovers rather than the conflict with the rival or the possibility of reunion after death. Hogan's heroic tragicomedy, on the other hand, sounds like Frye's account of romance, although for Frye the hero's defeat of the enemy and reclamation of authority is accompanied by wedding his bride. Frye links the plot of the love story with comedy and the plot of adventure and quest with romance, which focuses on "a conflict between the hero and his enemy" (AC 187). However, romance often integrates these two plots. As Frye puts it elsewhere, "the central element of romance is a love story, and the exciting adventures are normally a foreplay leading up to a sexual union" (SeS 24). Frye's quest romance also often integrates individual and social happiness. That is, the hero saves the kingdom by defeating the monster, marries the princess, and ascends the throne (e.g., AC 189, on the "dragon-killing theme" as the "central form of quest-romance"). Tragedy, however, "usually makes love and the social structure irreconcilable and contending forces" (218). As well, Frye sees tragedy as only indirectly death-oriented. Death is rather a main corollary of a more abstract and general principle of structure: tragedy leads up to "an epiphany of law, of that which is and must be" (208). This natural law governs "a world in which existence is itself tragic, not existence modified by an act" and "every new birth provokes the return of an avenging death" (213). This takes the tone or quality of tragedy in a crucially different way: tragedy creates "a vision of death which draws the survivors into a new unity" (215) – and this helps account for the appeal of tragedy, something that is less obvious in Hogan's account.[19] In short, for both genre anatomists, the central factors are stories of love and adventure, and possibly death, outcomes of success or failure, positive and negative emotions, contexts of both individual and social experience, and themes or ideologies. However, as they rank and organize these factors in different ways, they develop different typologies. For Hogan, the distinction between individual versus social goals and emotions distinguishes romantic versus heroic genres, and the focus on individual emotions makes death a more significant genre-defining factor. For Frye, stories of love and heroism both have individual and social dimensions, and a focus on social inclusion/exclusion makes events of love and death less genre-defining and more emotionally complex. The comparison also reveals some of the practical consequences of using different classificatory principles. Frye does not seem to have an obvious place for tragedies that are centrally love stories, and Hogan seems to have no obvious place for irony and satire (or humour generally),[20] or for a heroic plot in which a love story is central (although he discusses how prototypes and plots can be combined). For Frye, Romeo and Juliet and other doomed lovers are outliers in the realm of tragedy, while Hogan demotes the heroism of all those medieval and Renaissance knights questing for their loves (and Don Quixote himself).

This comparison has certain implications for the study of universals and particulars in pastoral, and pastoral elegy especially. Pastoral elegy focuses on lamenting the death of a beloved companion, and/or celebrating his transcendent rebirth. Hogan associates tragedy directly with death and with loss of power (death is the situational aspect of the prototype for sorrow), and comedy with union with the beloved or with winning social power. In his view death must be tragic, although it may later turn comic, on the condition that the lovers are reunited after death. However, pastoral elegy involves only recognition of the companion's ascension into an afterlife, not afterlife reunion. For Frye, death can be simultaneously tragic and comic at different levels, in the case where exclusion from earthly society leads to inclusion in divine society. This "rebirth" event is central in pastoral elegy and in literary plots generally, but the specific afterlife event of reunion with the beloved is not central in Frye's scheme. For Hogan, apotheosis/resurrection can be part of other genres as well, although it is most prominent in romantic tragicomedy. It may be part of the concluding "spiritualization" in heroic tragicomedy (in the not-uncommon "epilogue of suffering," as in the *Iliad*'s turn to the defeated Trojans after Achilles triumphs over Hector), and it is common in *sacrificial* tragicomedy (a genre Hogan adds later in his study as a supplement to his first two, which treats "the genesis and overcoming of famine" [186], as in *Oedipus Rex*) (see e.g., 232–3).[21] But in no case is rebirth definitive of a genre. The celebration-of-rebirth element of pastoral elegy looks more basic to the genre's structure in Frye's account, while the mourning-of-death element looks more basic in Hogan's account.

New Historicism's Pastoral of Power

Despite Frye's implication, historicist analyses often look at genres and conventions, and how they are modified by authors to meet social conditions – though the stress falls on the adaptation to social uses, rather than on the continuity of meaning. Louis Adrian Montrose's rather brilliant essay on the "pastoral of power" was eye-opening for me. It was one of the studies that convinced me that the new historicism was right about the entangling of literary forms in political power, and that Frye's approach tends to downplay this factor in literary reception (though he acknowledges it in literary production). On the other hand, as I have suggested, Frye's expansive view of the social contexts and functions of literature and criticism could put historicist literary sociology in a broader historical and theoretical frame of reference.

Montrose does not have Barthes's genius for melodramatic exaggeration, but he does show how Barthes's view of "mythologizing" as the selection and distortion of historical reality applies to genres. According to Barthes's example, it is the photograph that makes the distortion: a snap out of time and place, stripped of its context in actual life and history. Montrose shows the variety of ideological uses to which a single genre can be put, how these applications make selective use of tradition and are transformed over time, and how the genre frame's roles and relations can distort and cloak certain roles and relations of events in real experience. But, as with Barthes and Greenblatt, Montrose tends to perceive an exclusively political – and an implicitly negative – function for literary forms. There is little complementary sense of how a frame can reveal reality, use its own logic to highlight important aspects of reality, or make an argument, even a true one, even in a good cause.

Montrose analyses uses of pastoral structures and themes in poetry and pageantry to mediate (or again, frame) social relationships. The repertoire of these forms "includes images and metaphors; conventions of person, place, and diction; and distinctive generic features and their combinations" (88). Michael Drayton says pastorals are base in style, subject, and status, but can evoke the highest matters, such as Biblical and classical accounts of the birth of a saviour in Luke's Gospel and Virgil's fourth eclogue (94). The amorous lyric is typical of Elizabethan pastoral poetry, but this natural love can be fused with religious concepts and feelings (94). Christ is paradoxically both the Lamb of God and the Good Shepherd, whose flock is all humanity (95). As for their use, Montrose quotes Puttenham's *Arte of English Poesie* saying that pastoral poetry is not simply intended to represent the "rustical manner of loves and communication: but under the vaile of homely persons, and in rude speeches to insinuate and glaunce at greater matters," including those that would not be safe to discuss in other forms (88).

Montrose is particularly interested in political relationships between Queen Elizabeth, aristocratic elites, and commoners. Pastoral often worked to cast complex "public relationships of power" as "intimate relationships of love ... between the royal shepherdess and her flock, and between the queen of shepherds and the spiritual and temporal pastors who guard her flock" (91). Variations are possible: commoners (actual shepherds) could be pastoral shepherds, and the Queen could be the shepherd's beloved (103–5). In these pastoralized relationships, a veneer of harmony and loyalty conceals the often harsh reality of omnipresent power struggles with their ceaseless competition, conflict, and exploitation.

Montrose provides several examples of pastoral used in various specific media for contrasting political ends. First, the fifteenth century Wakefield Nativity pageants reveal pastoral's grounding in classical and Biblical mysteries (94–7), with their radical social implications of "inversion and levelling" (96). However, the post-Reformation Tudor ideology was anxious about the survival and status of the English nation and was rigidly hierarchical. It created a syncretic "mythology, iconography, and ritual" in which the Queen attracted the symbolism of the Virgin Mary, as well as "the pastoral symbolism of Christ's Nativity and the Church's ministry" (97). It had to suppress radical medieval popular cults, spirituality, and culture, and radical implications "had to be expunged or transformed if pastoral metaphors were to function effectively as benign images" of the stable social hierarchy (95–7). This partly popular, partly official transformation worked to "the emotional benefit of the populace, the political benefit of the government, and the economic benefit of the artists and craftsmen, performers and patrons, who helped to body it forth" (98). Second, Spenser's poem praising Elizabeth "achieves an ideological fusion of classical imperium and Christian reform" and "a poetic fusion of classical and humanist with medieval and native literary traditions" (100). It offers "illusions which sanctify political power" for a reward, and illustrates the "dialectic by which poetic power helps to create and sustain the political power to which it is subservient" (100). Third, and most importantly for Montrose, the "scenarios, speeches, and songs intended for performance" before the Queen at Sudeley during the progress of 1591 have little artistic value, but "exhibit particularly well the social instrumentality of figurative language, the dialectic between power relations and symbolic forms" (102). The royal party encounters people whose livelihoods actually involve sheep, and the discourse between them is fittingly pastoral. Several staged pastoral scenes draw on national, religious, and personal symbolism to flatter the Queen, creating "a complex and hyperbolic role" for her, and at the same time "a simple, collective, and idealized relationship between the Queen and her subjects" (107). This cult of Elizabeth could have complex functions: both psycho-social inspiration in "international politics and religious conflict"; and also socio-political mystification in domestic policy, by procuring "the loyalty, obedience, and service of both the unenfranchised masses and the political nation" (109, 107). It appears that an entertainment could achieve several ends – uniting all groups against an external threat, or the crown with either group against the other as a threat (that is, with commoners against the gentle landed elites, or with elites against the people) (110). Pastorals of power are efficacious instruments for "coupling mildness with majesty" and "intimacy and benignity with authoritarianism," creating the illusion that the Queen had a personal relation with them all (110). Fourth, in 1645 Milton recovers the power of pastoral's radical social roots in a new context: "Lycidas" criticizes the corruption of the church (as Spenser had), and his Nativity poem imagines "a revival and completion of the English Reformation" that is historical and political as well as spiritual (111–12).

Montrose distinguishes the uses of pastoral (clearly, though not overtly) into those he admires (critical of authority) and those he despises (assuaging discontent with authority). Milton's revolutionary poems imply "a recovery of the authentic sources and forms of pastoral power" (112), whereas the pastoral of ruling power is essentially mystification. The central symbolic structure in these social uses is the relation between shepherd and sheep: if the shepherd is responsible (protecting, feeding, guiding) and the sheep are peaceful and obedient, all is well in the world. The radical pastoral stresses ultimate social equality: we are all equally sheep in relation to the only true shepherd, Christ, who heralds a revolution of social justice. It attacks the worldly shepherds as corrupt (bad shepherds, or wolves in sheep's clothing). The royal pastoral, by contrast, stresses harmonious social segmentation: Eliza is Queen of shepherds (and both classically and Christianly divine); the aristocracy, and sometimes the priesthood, are shepherds; and the commoners are sheep. It mystifies complex relations of power as simple personal relations of love.

However, both versions of pastoral can be seen as having positive and negative value, as both are empowering and mystifying. Montrose mentions possible admirable motives and results of the cult of Elizabeth, but stresses the downside. In addition, the royal pastoral might be seen as another kind of mediation because it offers a frame for performances in Goffman's sense (e.g. in *Presentation of Self*). That is, persons and groups standing in various relationships can adopt the fictional roles and relations of a genre in various ways in order to negotiate and enact matters of power in an indirect fashion. These parties do not directly state commands, demands, or complaints, but instead suggest them through masks and play them out in quasi-fictional form, which provides distance and allows parties to make, take up, ignore, or revoke suggestions while saving face. All parties involved could articulate concerns without real confrontation and perhaps achieve consensus. After all, no one really believes that the political relationships are pastoral. (Recall that Frye [e.g., WP 72, cited above] and others [e.g., Talmy, Ricoeur] point out that metaphor often assumes the recognition that it is not literally true, and so there is an ironic quality to its use.) Moreover, the radical pastoral can also be mystifying if it ignores distinctions among individuals within the groups of shepherds and sheep – that is, if it sees all of the sheep as wholly innocent and good, and all of their shepherds as equally abusive and bad. The average priest, for example, would have fit rather awkwardly within the power struggles of the time, and would be ill-represented in the struggles implied in the radical pastoral. Priests, as spiritual shepherds, would be subject to the needs and demands of their flocks and also of their superiors. While any priest might be incompetent or corrupt, he would generally lack the temporal power of the aristocracy: he could not simply be an oppressor. Lower-level "shepherds" in general, spiritual or temporal, would be in like positions.

Montrose's essay articulates an exemplary account of how longstanding literary conventions were turned to specific ideological purposes rooted in highly particular historical situations. Let us now pull together our perspectives on genre to consider how they complement and correct one another: how pastoral conventions and the historical uses into which they are trained and pruned also embody general principles of literary structure rooted in transhistorical properties of the human brain and mind.

Pastoral Reconsidered: History and Particulars of a Universal Technique

This section attempts to *begin* teasing out what is universal from what is not, how these two categories interact, and why. As such, it is necessarily speculative, but also, I think, important. Having lodged my qualifications with the Office of Scholarly Caution, I will now plunge provisionally ahead.

A study of universals will in many ways focus on general rather than specific aspects of phenomena. This can court triviality (e.g., X is verbal art; verbal art is a cultural universal; hence X instantiates a cultural universal, etc.). To get beyond the trivial, I will seek the most specific universal aspects of the most specific qualities of the text. To do so, I will draw on Frye's vision of the interrelations of body-based common human experience, literary structure, literary history, and literary sociology, in order to relate Hogan's ideas about universals more richly to Montrose's new historicist studies of the uses of pastoral for specific ideological purposes. Unlike either Hogan or Montrose, Frye describes how the structures of myth and metaphor in literature underpin its capacity for cross-cultural communication, how they interact in texts, and how they change in patterned ways over history. Thus, by drawing on Frye, I can add to Hogan's principles, and his patterns of use of principles, and can enrich Montrose's sense of how genres are used in historical ideological contexts.

At this point it is also worth recalling how complex the relations between universals and particulars can be. Indeed, these categories are now often seen as matters of degree, and as interacting, rather than as sharply distinguished. Universals are often related to the natural human body, or what is inborn in it, since all humans have human bodies with inborn bodily systems and functions. However, it is often impossible or extremely difficult to distinguish the bodily or natural from the environmental, social, or cultural; and to distinguish the innate from the acquired (through experience or learning). Hogan, citing Antonio Damasio, points out that animal and human emotions are subject to this complex entanglement. Fear, for example, is associated with specific areas and processes in the brain, and also with objects in the environment, and in fact evolution has implanted fear of aspects of objects. That is, Damasio says that humans are born disposed to respond with fear to specific features of stimuli: "Size (as in large animals); large span (as in flying eagles); type of motion (as in reptiles); certain sounds (such as growling)" (qtd. in Hogan, "On Being Moved" 243). However, these innate fear "triggers" do not arise inevitably, but need to be activated by experiences early in life. Hogan goes on to cite another of Damasio's studies that says that a monkey's innate fear of snakes will not develop unless the monkey not merely sees a snake, but sees its mother seeing the snake, and sees her expression of fear of it: "Once is enough for the behavior to kick into gear, but without that 'once' the 'innate' behavior is not engaged" (qtd. in Hogan, "On Being Moved" 243). Indeed this pattern seems quite common: in order for inborn dispositions or capacities to develop, they need to be activated by some specific form of influence from or interaction with the environment, often within a critical period or "window." As with the monkey, its mother, and the snake, this interaction can be a tangled knot of natural, social, and psychological factors. What is hardwired in the brain, and is presumably natural, evolved, and universal, is not inevitable, since its emergence and development depends on the organism's interaction with environmental conditions. Our wiring is wedded to our world. (Compare Richardson, *Neural* 3–10, on how cognitive historicists seek to move beyond the sterile terms of the realism/relativism debate and toward an "interactionist ontology" in which humans are "naturally" cultural.)

The most productive point on which to focus for these purposes is Hogan's literary development principle of alignment, which uses parallels to link narrative elements across registers – social relations and character situations get linked with natural conditions and divine/transcendental elements. Alignment is a very widespread technique, and a fairly abstract one, and it can be embodied in a wide range of particular details (and sub-techniques); it is in addition crucial for ideological applications of literary structures – it is the naturalizing, normalizing, and sanctifying technique *par excellence*. Hogan argues that alignment intensifies emotion and reinforces heroic ideology. Pastoral generally uses alignment to treat a particular kind of human/nature harmony as sanctioned by the divine order, and hence as part of divine harmony. A simple human agricultural order is sanctioned because it accords with the divine-natural harmony of its setting. In pastoral elegy, the events of death and apotheosis are central, and natural and divine orders tend to align with and support the mourning for the companion and the affirmation of his transition to divine existence. Alignment is effective in mourning death: when nature laments with you, it both intensifies and consoles your grief. It has an even greater role in envisioning apotheosis or resurrection. Indeed, given the lack of evidence in the human world for these processes, analogies with natural processes may be the only "evidence" offered as a basis for the vision.[22] As well, the higher perspective glimpsed by the evocation of this natural-divine order may be used to sanction and/or critique human social phenomena. Hogan suggests some social, typological, and individual patterns in the use of development principles like alignment. Frye's analyses point to several additional kinds of patterns: first, there are *historical* patterns in the use of the alignment principle; second, there is a principle of *modification* or *specification* of alignment due to how its conventions intersect with one another; third, both Frye's and Montrose's studies suggest there are patterns in the *reception* of alignment. I will pass all of these patterns under my lenses in turn.

Alignment, Displacement, and Cultural History

Hogan's argument necessarily downplays the historical context of stories in order to establish the extent to which his plots are grounded in universal emotions and emotion-concepts. However, this focus obscures the relations between plots and other literary patterns, including historical ones.

Frye sees degrees of alignment as a factor in the definition of genres and modes. As he also sees literary history as defined by modifications of genres and modes, it is clear that literary history is in part the history of the principle of alignment. For Frye, what Hogan calls alignment is essentially a form of metaphor. As we have seen, metaphor identifies two things with one another, especially human with natural and divine things. Metaphorical alignment of all kinds is common in, and partly definitive of, early mythic and romantic modes, because the conception of the world, characters, and events in those modes involves divinized natural elements.

Frye also emphasizes the deep historical and structural links between those early stories about gods and demi-gods and later literary stories about humans. He points out that the use of alignment steadily declines over the course of literary history, as "realism" (a term he is wary of, but a useful one) gradually increases. When metaphorical alignment does occur, its quality shifts from "identification" of human, divine, and natural realms to much less direct forms of "association," as well as increasing parody. Frye calls this process "displacement":

> The mimetic tendency itself, the tendency to verisimilitude and accuracy of description, is one of two poles of literature. At the other pole is something that seems to be connected both with Aristotle's word *mythos* and with the usual meaning of myth. That is, it is a tendency to tell a story which is in origin a story about characters who can do anything, and only gradually becomes attracted toward a tendency to tell a plausible or credible story. Myths of gods merge into legends of heroes; legends of heroes merge into plots of tragedies and comedies; plots of tragedies and comedies merge into plots of more or less realistic fiction ... We may think of our romantic, high mimetic and low mimetic modes as a series of *displaced* myths, *mythoi* or plot-formulas progressively moving over towards the opposite pole of verisimilitude, and then, with irony, beginning to move back. (AC 51–2)

Later, Frye makes explicit the link of myth with metaphor: "As realism is an art of implicit simile, myth is an art of implicit metaphor" (136). Thus, "the central principle of displacement is that what can be metaphorically identified in a myth can only be linked in romance" – here, romance means humanized but still idealized narrative – "by some form of simile: analogy, significant association, incidental accompanying imagery, and the like. In a myth we can have a sun-god or a tree-god; in a romance we may have a person who is significantly associated with the sun or trees" (137). Thus alignment is a graded factor in literature: texts do not just use or not use alignment, but rather use it to different degrees and may establish it by various narrative and rhetorical techniques. Furthermore, the relative presence of alignment, and the techniques used to establish it, are features that both link and distinguish genres, as displacement links myth to realistic fiction and also distinguishes them. As well, the extent, techniques, and forms of reception of alignment change historically and participate in the process of genre change.

An inference here is that later genres, and later texts within genres, tend to undermine the ideological functions of earlier genres and their texts: idealizing, naturalizing, divinizing certain aspects of society gives way to implicit or explicit critique of those aspects of society. Frye sometimes stresses the continuities between earlier and later narrative, as when he says that "romance is the structural core of all fiction" (SeS 15), though he also recognizes their basic contrast, as when he says that "it would hardly be too much to say that realistic fiction, from Defoe to Henry James, is, when we look at it as a form of narrative technique, essentially parody-romance" (SeS 39). Other critics stress discontinuities, contrast, and critique, but in a way that nonetheless relies on a basic connection between them. For Lukács, the novel is "the epic of a world that has been abandoned by God" (88); for Jameson the novel is "a kind of immanent critique of romance in its restructuration of the form ... something like a dialectical self-consciousness of romance itself" (*Political* 129).

To describe displacement in view of cognitive and historicist approaches, I will need to consider the relation of metaphor to the "literal" storyworld (i.e., what "actually" exists and happens in the storyworld, even though it is fictional) and to reader interpretation of that relation. As an example of displacement, recall Frye's discussion of the history of pastoral narrative and imagery. Alignment is common in pastoral, and is arguably partly definitive of it. The two key metaphors of natural alignment in pastoral that Frye mentions are (in conceptual metaphor theory terminology) PEOPLE ARE PLANTS and A LIFETIME IS A DAY.[23] In the pastoral myth of the Adonis lament, the link between the hero-god's life and sun and vegetation has a literal basis in the storyworld: in the storyworld, it is literally true that there is a direct correspondence between the hero and sun and vegetation.[24] Displacement in later developments of pastoral reveals two major things: the difference between the most central metaphors and the less central ones, and the difference in the metaphors' relations to the literal storyworld. As Frye shows, later developments of pastoral continue to idealize life close to nature even when they do not deal specifically with shepherds. That is, shepherding metaphors, though central to the pastoral genre, are less central and widespread than sun and vegetation metaphors. Moreover, those more central metaphors recur in much later poets' work with no implication of literal truth underlying the metaphoric connections. Whitman's "When Lilacs Last in the Dooryard Bloomed" is a pastoral elegy on the death of Lincoln, and is "in its *form*, as conventional as *Lycidas*, complete with purple flowers thrown on coffins, a great star drooping in the west, imagery of 'ever-returning spring' and all the rest of it" (AC 102). (Of course, the continuities and differences discovered in a genre's history depend greatly on which texts are determined to be in its tradition.)

In "Lycidas," Milton uses natural alignment powerfully – indeed the line about Orpheus, "Whom universal nature did lament" (l. 60), could be an epitome of the technique. However, Milton seems at least equally interested in normative alignment of the divine world with his ethical and social purposes, as when he attacks corrupt clergy through the voice of St Peter, who says he would prefer to have lost many of those existing clergy than Edward King: "How well could I have spared for thee young swain, / Enow of such as for their bellies' sake, / Creep and intrude, and climb into the fold?" (ll. 113–15). It is not obvious how the two natural alignment metaphors of sun and plants are involved in normative alignment. However, as Frye observes, they allude to the story of Christ, and hence indirectly reinforce normative alignment. It seems that in Milton's case, while alignment that relates to Classical imagery and myth is deliberately metaphorical, alignment that relates to Christian imagery and myth is somewhat different. Even here, a close look reveals many complexities. Milton recognizes how shepherd and flock are used metaphorically, but he may well believe in the literal truth of some of the pastoral stories of the Bible, as well as in literal connections between Christ, the sun, and vegetation, at least insofar as the Bible positions God as the creator and ruler of all of those things.

Connecting the principle of alignment with that of displacement highlights both the interaction of several general literary principles (some of them universals) with one another, and also their interaction with various and changing cultural contexts. We begin to trace the tree from roots to branches.

Alignment, Displacement, and Metaphor Interaction

Frye's emphasis on the context of other conventions (in fact, structural principles) operating in conjunction with alignment clarifies alignment in Hogan's sense. I have noted Frye's account of how plot and metaphor are integrated in myth. Also note how in literary narrative multiple metaphors get integrated with one another. The two main metaphors of natural alignment in pastoral are A LIFETIME IS A DAY and PEOPLE ARE PLANTS. I suggested that these metaphors are good candidates for universals. In experience and in cultural texts, universals such as these interact with one another and with other particulars. It might seem that such interaction simply reinforces alignment and makes it more effective, but it can also create unexpected structures, meanings, and effects.

Sun and vegetation metaphors have source domains that are causally connected to each other in the world, and in human experience of the world, because plants need sunlight to grow. The target domains are also causally connected to the sources because humans need both sun and plants to survive and thrive. The target domains themselves, people and human life, are also closely connected and provide another kind of link between the metaphors. The metaphoric mappings are structurally similar because both focus on the complete long-term chronology of individual human lives: the sequence of birth, living, and death. Of course, they have different entailments. A LIFETIME IS A DAY focuses more on absolute beginnings and ends: birth is sunrise and death is sunset. PEOPLE ARE PLANTS focuses more on gains and losses of vitality: birth and youth bud, sprout, and blossom, and decline fades and withers. As well, the sources make different kinds of contribution to human life. The sun provides light and warmth, whereas plants provide food and materials for building and clothing. Thus the two metaphors cohere with each other to some extent, and align with the target of human life in ways that are broadly similar but not identical in detail.

Stories and poems that use both metaphors to establish alignment reflect this partial match and partial clash of structure.

Given this alignment of sun and plant metaphors, it is striking that in Frye's account, a fundamental aspect of the imagery of "Lycidas" – that is, water – is not inherently part of either metaphor, but gets connected with them to elaborate their meanings. Of course, water imagery is suitable to both the particular occasion and the genre. Edward King did die by drowning, and the pastoral setting often includes streams and rivers. But Milton connects these facts with a cluster of mythical and metaphorical details. As Stella Revard writes:

> The underlying image of *Lycidas* is water: the water that drowned Lycidas; the wat'ry tears – melodious and lamenting; the water that causes the sisters of the sacred well to revive their song; the fresh-water stream that bears the head of Orpheus in contrast to the Alpheus's amorous stream that pursues the fountain nymph Arethusa and mingles its waters with hers; the water of triumph on which Christ walked; the water of other streams in the kingdom of the blest. (40–1)

But the meaning of water, she says, "changes as it is linked now with one, now with another figure. It destroys Lycidas and Orpheus; it is the medium of Alpheus's and Arethusa's transformation; it triumphs as Christ rises from the ocean like a resurrected sun; and it is the final benison for the saved Lycidas whose oozy locks are laved with nectar pure – heaven's transformed water" (41). What are the implications of how the water metaphors interact with and modify the other metaphors?

In terms of general conceptual metaphors and their grounding in experience, it seems plausible that water metaphors are universal and primarily positive. Certainly, people have universal experience of water as central to life. However, that experience includes ambivalence, as it is easy to see that water can be both beneficial and destructive. Water is naturally linked with plant life in obvious ways. Its link with solar cycles is less obvious, as sunrise and sunset need not occur over water. But sun and water are connected in common experience through the cycle of evaporation, condensation into clouds, and precipitation that clears the clouds away to reveal the sun again. While the plant cycle depends on the influence of both sun and water, the solar and water cycles oppose one another.

In the total literary cosmology, water has many complex affiliations. It is connected to the solar metaphor via rivers and seas. This connection is established in part by a metonymic extension of both source domains. Frye notes that the sun "falls into the western ocean at night," and rises from the ocean in the morning. This is bad cosmology, of course. The sun does not actually enter the ocean. But it is an effective literary convention. As Revard notes, the water connection is also due to allusion to myths involving water, though Frye's account of the mythology is more comprehensive and coherent than Revard's. Frye stresses that Lycidas, as priest, is compared to Peter and Orpheus because he is threatened with drowning. Christ (but not Orpheus) can raise Lycidas (and Peter) from the waves, as he redeems souls from the lower world. Thus much of the meaning of the poem's imagery, both positive and negative, relies on the mythological idea of water as primal formlessness. To follow Frye's typology, recall that in the opening of the Bible God creates heaven and earth from a watery chaos, to which the world is returned with the Flood. This is connected to all the imagery of triumph over water. Such imagery includes defeating the leviathan; Christ walking on water; Christ and the apostles being "fishers of men"; baptism as rebirth (sometimes thought of as drowning the old man and raising the new); the sea of death and its abolition. These examples stress the negative, demonic side of the image: water as cause of dissolution and death. But many other examples stress the positive side: water as the bringer of life, restorer of health and power, and cleanser of sin and death.[25] Linking early pastoral with the water and fishing imagery of the Bible creates further potential metaphorical parallels: apostles are fishermen as well as shepherds, and people are fish as well as sheep.

Looking at "Lycidas" in the light of this cosmology, there is an evident pattern to the metaphoric affiliations of water. The idea of water as agent of transformation – sometimes positive, sometimes negative – distinguishes the water metaphors from the solar and plant metaphors, which do not share that quality. The sun disappears, but returns again the next day. Plants die, but many only appear to do so according to the season, and (usually) live again in the spring. Thus both sun and vegetation metaphors highlight rebirth rather than destruction and death, and often conceal how and where changes happen. Destructive water, which swallows bodies in storm or flood or even calm, makes the event of death more definite and gives it an active cause and setting. This active cause and setting is something to struggle with and potentially triumph over. In "Lycidas," the figures associated with water are the ones who investigate the causes of Lycidas's death. Neptune questions (personifications of) winds, waves, and rivers. He finds that none of these forces were against Lycidas, and the tragedy was due to a badly built, perhaps cursed, boat ("that fatal and perfidious bark / Built in th'eclipse, and rigged with curses dark"), but still the sea is called "the monstrous world" (ll. 100–1, l. 158). Water imagery can thus turn a story of causeless and inevitable death into a story of active struggle with a kind of enemy or hostile world. The pastoral story of ease and peace, or of mourning over death, becomes a story of conflict and triumph.

The addition of certain imagery can thus result in a change or modulation of genre. When water-as-enemy is added, the pastoral elegy changes, in Hogan's terms, from a romantic tragic story of individual lost love into a heroic comic story of victory over a usurping antagonist. Similarly, a certain passage illustrates Frye's point that (in mythic and romantic modes) tragic exclusion from an earthly society can translate into comic inclusion in a divine one. The translation is due precisely to the use of metaphor to create story events – specifically, by combining the image of death by drowning with the metaphor of LIFE AS A DAY, which entails that sunrise from the sea can be resurrection:

So sinks the day-star in the ocean bed,
And yet anon repairs his drooping head,
And tricks his beams, and with new-spangled ore
Flames in the forehead of the morning sky:
So Lycidas sunk low, but mounted high ... (ll. 168–72)

Again, when the water-antagonist is added to pastoral, there is a change in genre orientation, so to speak. The poem is still pastoral by virtue of the specific types of setting, character, and action it contains, but it has changed from a romantic-tragic kind of pastoral to a heroic-comic/romantic one, by virtue of the more abstract kinds of actions and action-outcomes described (victory over antagonist) and their attendant emotions.

Next, I will consider exactly how the metaphors in "Lycidas" that are based on three main natural-world source domains (sun, plants, and water) work to create alignment with natural and divine orders, by supporting and specifying the central theme of resurrection after premature death.

There are no sharp lines between natural and divine in the world of the poem, but there are some broad associations of certain metaphor domains with certain kinds of alignment. In Frye's account of the conventional metaphors "Lycidas" evokes from cultural mythology, sun and plants are relatively equal in supporting divine alignment: both evoke gods and cycles of rebirth. Looking at the poem in more detail, the solar metaphor is the most significant in specifically expressing resurrection, while the plants in the poem support natural alignment. As it rises again after it sets, the sun is the sign and agent of resurrection, which is associated with Christ. Its earthly, non-metaphorical role in the poem does not seem important. The poem generally gives plant imagery a more earthly function. Flowers are the means and evidence of mourning, and reeds and oats are instruments for songs of both mourning and celebration. As well, fame is seen metaphorically as a plant – though its status as divine or natural is ambiguous, as it is "no plant that grows on mortal soil, / ... But lives and spreads aloft by those pure eyes, / And perfect witness of all-judging Jove" (ll. 78, 81–2). Water imagery is also important for alignment, and its associations are somewhat more complex than those of sun and plants. It is spiritual as a source of poetic inspiration and as an agent of transformation. It is also earthly, an antagonist to humans, and a producer of earthly change. Sun and vegetation images have no such antagonistic role. Near the end of the poem, Lycidas appears among divine groves and streams (l. 175), but this divinizing of plant and water imagery is rare. Hence, while vegetation and water imagery are important divine symbols in the general literary cosmology, in "Lycidas" itself, they tend to align the protagonist and his story with the natural order, while solar imagery aligns the protagonist and his story with the divine order.

Thus natural and divine alignment are not an all-or-nothing affair. Metaphor interaction is another regular principle that complicates the principle of alignment, and particular uses of alignment metaphors can create complex particular effects. Indeed, the cultural metaphors *evoked* by a poem may be *used* by that poem in ways that contradict their typical, expected implications.

Alignment, Ideology, and Reception

Montrose's study suggests social patterns in receptions of universals – that is, in ideological uses of universal plots and of the alignment technique. It indicates how specific historical genre structures get adapted into particular literary texts, and into sub- and extra-literary phenomena, to suit (varying, even contrasting) social and ideological purposes. Frye and Hogan do not address such directly and unambiguously social and ideological uses of literary genres.

Montrose's account of pastoral suggests several possible modifications of Hogan's account of genre ideology. Hogan implies that romantic tragicomedy is generally progressive, that heroic tragicomedy is generally conservative, and that the latter but not the former prefers the technique of normative alignment of social and ethical orders with divine ones. Montrose shows how in cases where Elizabeth was projected into the pastoral plot, the romantic story of lovers uniting served the kind of authoritarian ideology Hogan associates with the heroic story – and that the romantic story used natural and divine alignment to reinforce its vision. Also contrary to Hogan's expectations, Montrose's account of the ideology of Milton's "Lycidas" shows how the heroic story of a divine ruler who returns to drive out usurpers, similarly using natural and divine alignment, can also be progressive.

Montrose's two types of political pastoral, royal and radical, map onto Hogan's plot types in definite but curious ways. In such political pastoral, the predominant story prototypes operate in combination with the genre's conventional equation of individuals with social groups and its more specific metaphorical equation of shepherds and sheep with, respectively, representatives of social/political power and the subjects of that power. The royal pastoral celebrates social harmony in terms of the harmony of personal love – love of the shepherd for the lady (Queen), love among shepherds, love of the sheep for the (royal) shepherd, and love of the shepherds for the sheep. It celebrates the political power of the metaphoric shepherds, which includes their protection of their subjects, the obedience of the latter, and the prosperity of the nation. (This harmony is spiritualized for the Virgin Queen, and operates in connection with her religious cult.) From Hogan's perspective, this pastoral plot is a romantic comedy, but the projection of that plot to social groups gives it a dimension of heroic comedy (i.e., it deals with social emotion, though it frames it in terms of individual emotion). The radical pastoral laments the death of the beloved shepherd, and also the loss of social power of the "sheep" through corruption of other shepherds, who deny them food and protection. The radical pastoral also looks forward to the return of the Good Shepherd to set things to rights. It is therefore heroic, and tragic insofar as it laments loss of life and power, but comic insofar as it celebrates the anticipated victory of the right shepherds and sheep. "Lycidas" is an example of how this radical pastoral pattern can be informed by the structures of romantic and heroic tragicomedy. More specifically, in terms of its cultural-historical context, both Edward King and Milton were excluded from the social power of the church (an important sub-group within society) by the new laws against Puritans. This exclusion spurred Milton to throw himself into politics, and the poem represents and enacts his shift in attitude (see Evans, especially 52–3). This situation presents a complex interaction of universals and particulars in the interaction of universal plot structures with a particular historical genre, particular political uses of variants of that genre, individual and social emotions (real and fictional), and Milton's even more particular personal and political situation.

Because a genre is so flexible in its social uses, one can imagine a use of "Lycidas" in the context of mourning for AIDS victims, as the final epigraph of this chapter indicates. Here, the implied wedding of Lycidas in heaven would come to the fore, and the divine "nuptial" associations would become linked with the earthly relationship between the two shepherds. The implied role of spouse for Lycidas (and perhaps for his mourner) would be at once divinized and naturalized (see Boehrer on this aspect of the poem's symbolism). In fact, highlighting this nuptial context would add a dimension Frye did not focus on to the symbolism reviewed above. Wedding symbolism in the Bible and throughout Western culture would enrich the associations of sun, vegetation, and water metaphors, and the roles of god, poet, and priest that Frye outlines. Emphasis would be on union and the success and transcendence it symbolizes. Thus, wedding imagery would foreground the flowering and fruit (spring and summer) cycles of vegetation imagery and the sunrise and zenith aspects of solar imagery. Further, the wedding schema would draw attention to the relations of Lycidas's roles to other roles that can be figured as wedding-like: god to worshippers, poet to muse and to audience, and priest to god and to congregation.[26]

Surveying the pastoral landscape I have roamed over with the aid of my three guides, I can pick out some significant points about universals and particulars and their applications. First, both of these cases suggest that a genre will not convey a certain ideology consistently in multifarious contexts. Rather, a genre's function is to present a more abstract theme (similar to Frye's "underthought" of imagery), which authors and audiences can sharpen into ideological uses in particular texts and receptions (the discursive "overthought"). Whether such ideologies are conservative or progressive depends on the particular text, how it defines in-groups and out-groups, and what the values and relative power relations of those groups are. When it comes to ideological uses of genres, it is helpful to make Todorov's distinction between historical and theoretical genres – that is, between "the classes of texts that have been historically perceived as" genres (*Genres* 17), such as pastoral elegy, and much broader categories developed for theoretical purposes, such as tragedy and comedy as Frye and Hogan use them. With ideological uses of historical genres, one must give cultural specificity its due. Only in certain cultures, at certain points in history, are the appeal of historical genres and their instances broad enough to be effective in political rhetoric. Beyond those restrictions of time and place, historical genres can be effective for later readers mainly in literature, because in literary art readers have an expectation of, and interest in, confronting traditions of ideas and conventions that may be alien to them. Certainly the use of traditional pastoral in political rhetoric, as Montrose describes it, is highly particular to its time. Politicians can and do still use allusions to the Bible and other major texts, and they still appeal to their audiences by using well-known metaphors (such as the body politic and national family). But pastoral and its shepherd and sheep metaphors is, for politics, a thing of the past. It comes across to modern minds as antiquated – and more importantly as undemocratic, as Frye points out:

> The conventional honors accorded the sheep in the animal world provide us with the central archetype of pastoral imagery, as well as with such metaphors as "pastor" and "flock" in religion. The metaphor of the king as the shepherd of his people goes back to ancient Egypt. Perhaps the use of this particular convention is due to the fact that, being stupid, affectionate, gregarious, and easily stampeded, the societies formed by sheep are most like human ones. (AC 143)[27]

Immediately afterward, he indicates how pastoral in the broader sense may be relevant to other cultures, and even remain useable today: "But of course any other animal would do as well if the poet's audience were prepared for it." That is, this structure does not depend on specific concepts (sheep and shepherds) but rather on higher-level concepts, such as "the animal world" or more specifically herding activity. As long as there are groups with leaders and followers, whether family, clan, tribe, community, city, country, or any other such association, such herds and herders will have some purchase. Not only that, we continue to hear hopes of entering or re-entering a Golden Age, and the related idea of regaining harmony with nature in some way. The association of politicians and political movements with sun and vegetation cycles also persists, as in talk of a new "dawn," "day," "season," or "spring," and of "growth," "budding," "blooming," "blossoming," "flourishing," and so on. However, contemporary audiences seem to prefer different specific story types and popular genres. These may well partake of those broader genre structures that Todorov calls theoretical – such as Hogan's universal plots. Fairy tale structures are still common in political rhetoric, as Lakoff shows, and action films sometimes influence the marketing of politicians (as Greenblatt points out). Yet archaic genres may also be effective in other contexts of reception involving an imaginative response closer to the literary. Mourning is an example of a context in which people expect and want to be connected to cultural tradition and to encounter and accept some transpersonal authority. Like literature, mourning involves personal contemplation of existential matters, organizing vision and feeling in relation to a wider worldview. Politics, by contrast, typically involves direct persuasion to belief and/or action, so appeals to authoritative tradition may well seem evasive or deceitful, especially since (democratic) politicians are supposed to be the equals or even servants of their constituencies. The broader point is that the continuing viability of the universals and particulars of a literary genre depends on the rhetorical, discursive, and social situations in which the genre is used. These contexts can change the ways a universal structure may be used, and hence the way it appears. The study of universals should also consider these factors of reception or "uptake" – matters of where, when, why, and how a structure such as a genre is found, taken up, and recreated.

Conclusions

Ultimately, this analysis leads back to those questions of which elements of literary structure and response exhibit continuity and contribute to trans-contextual communication, and how and why they do so. Clarifying continuity helps to delineate what changes over time and to explain why it does so. That in turn clarifies the nature of the pleasures and uses of literature. The resources of Frye's analyses have enabled me to connect several foci into a more synoptic vision. A focus on universals merges with a focus on historical particulars. Frye's studies of general literary principles and plausible universals of plot and imagery support Hogan's arguments about the existence and importance of literary universals. Both of these approaches – which together forge a stronger alloy – work against the new historicist suggestion that there is no significant continuity or stability in literary structure and response, and consequently in the concept of literature itself. On the other hand, the new historicists are highly persuasive in selling the idea that literary structures, techniques, and response do carry over into fields of non-literary thought and discourse, and similarly that the production and reception of literary discourse is deeply implicated in ideological and political genres and purposes. Frye makes a strong case that these general principles are also tied in to bodily experience, and so to literature's transcultural communicating power, as opposed to its local ideological dimension. Yet some of the ideological uses of literary genre I have examined suggest that Frye's contrast between the mythical and the historical/ideological as "underthought" and "overthought" may be too sharp.

This chapter has sought an integrated assessment of continuity and change in a genre by offering further proposals about general patterns in the use of the principle of alignment. First, there is a historical pattern here: alignment is gradually displaced in terms of its extent and its techniques. As well, earlier uses of alignment are always available for allusion and recreation, and are an important part of literary education, in that they supply a major aspect of the meaning of later uses. Second, the metaphors that establish alignment interact with each other, and with narrative events, in a variety of ways to create further structures and effects, some of which are culturally specific, and some of which are more general. Literary works may differ in the way they use metaphors to establish natural or normative alignment. Third, there are patterns in the ideological uses of alignment in pastoral. There is a contrast between royal and radical pastoral, yet these political subcategories can use either comic (idyllic) or tragic (elegiac) versions of the plot and may focus on either or both romantic or heroic aspects of it.

In short, while pastoral, like many genres and texts, is from some points of view highly particular, idiosyncratic, and even peculiar, it can still have powerful effects in many contexts because its structure relies on general cognitive and cultural structures and principles shared across those contexts. Yet both general and particular are part of any text and any response, not just later responses to earlier texts. Literary structures and principles are "conditioned by social and historical factors and do not transcend them" yet "retain a continuity of form" (Frye) and a power of communication due to cultural mythological traditions with roots in cognitive universals, even as they put readers in touch with "stubborn, unassimilable otherness, a sense of distance and difference" (Greenblatt).

Conclusion Minds Transfigured Together: Metaphor, Myth, and Culture in Mind

HIPPOLYTA
'Tis strange, my Theseus, that these lovers speak of.

THESEUS
More strange than true. I never may believe
These antique fables, nor these fairy toys.
Lovers and madmen have such seething brains,
Such shaping fantasies, that apprehends
More than cool reason ever comprehends.
The lunatic, the lover, and the poet
Are of imagination all compact.
One sees more devils than vast hell can hold:
That is the madman. The lover, all as frantic,
Sees Helen's beauty in a brow of Egypt.
The poet's eye, in a fine frenzy rolling,
Doth glance from heaven to earth, from earth to heaven,
And as imagination bodies forth
The forms of things unknown, the poet's pen
Turns them to shapes, and gives to airy nothing
A local habitation and a name ...

HIPPOLYTA
But all the story of the night told over,
And all their minds transfigured together,
More witnesseth than fancy's images,
And grows to something of great constancy;
But howsoever, strange and admirable.

Shakespeare, *A Midsummer Night's Dream*, 5.1.1–27

Both Frye and the cognitive critics discuss the relation of metaphor to mind by joining in the imaginary conversations devised by Shakespeare in *A Midsummer Night's Dream*. Where Frye picks up Theseus's remarks on imagination, Lakoff and Turner take the side of Theseus's interlocutor, Hippolyta, to make another point. Theseus, they say, speaks for the (mistaken) literal meaning theory. He says that figurative language is all illusion; it is about things that are not there. Hippolyta, on the other hand, sees that his dichotomy between fancy and truth is mistaken: poets are imaginative *and* truthful, and can see something that "grows to ... great constancy," since to explore conceptual metaphor is "to discover that one has a worldview, that one's imagination is constrained, and that metaphor plays an enormous role in shaping one's everyday understanding of everyday events" (*More* 214). Hippolyta says that if we are to understand our worldviews, we must understand the metaphorical processes of imagination. Moreover, "poets can appeal to the ordinary metaphors we live by in order to take us beyond them" (214–15). Therefore metaphor and poetry have many powers. Among them is that "*power of revelation*" explored above, that is, "the power that metaphor has to reveal comprehensive hidden meanings to us, to allow us to find meanings beyond the surface, to interpret texts as wholes, and to make sense of patterns of events" (159).

Frye, too, confounds Theseus by taking his point to its extreme. He introduces Theseus's formula about the lunatic, the lover, and the poet being "of imagination all compact" into a discussion of the varieties of "personally involving metaphor" (WP 78). A metaphor is an assertion of a kind of identity that contrasts with "identity *as*" (categorization). Metaphors that say "A is B" express an "identity *with*" that is not ordinarily found in experience. There are exceptions to this limitation of experience, which include our sense of identity with all the personalities we have been or had, our sense that all our body parts are parts of the same thing, and our sense that what enters the continuum of our experience is all part of our life. Here, identity means unity with variety (WP 78). (This kind of metaphor is what *Anatomy* called "anagogic" [124–5].) Frye relates the erotic experience of two bodies becoming one flesh to other kinds of identification – "with the natural environment, with society or a social group, or with a predecessor in the literary tradition" (WP 81). In this context, Frye says, lunatics, lovers, and poets are groups of people who take identity-with seriously. Taken a little further, this reaches into "existential" (or following Heidegger, "ecstatic") metaphor, an extension of the use of metaphor that "not merely identifies one thing with another in words, but something of ourselves with both" (WP 75–6).

The conceptual party sees conventional metaphor as part of everyday experience, and Frye sees unconventional, personally involving metaphor as foreign to normal experience. Lakoff and Turner discuss the cognitive aspect of "projection" and "mapping" in metaphor where Frye treats "identification" psychically. Although they take on different roles in this play, their interpretations of those roles are complementary: this is what Gibbs Jr. calls the paradox of metaphor. Each also recognizes the emphasis of the other. They would agree that metaphor can effectively connect mind and world rather than being merely ornamental or delusive, can structure and create the world in some ways, is systematic rather than random, and relies on schematic thought. While these passages are about metaphor, much the same applies to myth, which can embody and unfold metaphors in local habitations and names. These are strong claims for the power of myth and metaphor, and connecting these arguments can only support, clarify, refine, and extend them.

This book has reconsidered some of the central tenets of Frye's theories of thought, language, literature, society, and culture. In scholarly terms, the reconsideration is motivated by a significant convergence between Frye's ideas and those of cognitive linguistics and poetics on the one hand, and some of the major concerns of current schools of cultural studies and new historicism on the other. While I give due weight to the elementary observation that both Frygean and cognitive poetics partly conflict with, and criticize, the post-structuralist ideas that strongly inform those current schools, my interest is in using the encounters worked out to develop all of the theories involved. As a result, this enterprise has issued in proposed partial syntheses of Frygean and cognitive poetics and cultural theory. To return to our metaphors for scholarship, the conversations prompted explorations, which led to sketching and building new configurations. Frye's schematologies supplied the maps and ground patterns throughout. The results are gratifying, particularly the discovery of points where further exploration and building could begin – directions to move in, obstacles to overcome, gaps to fill in, and structures to extend or make anew. In general, I have sought to point to paths just beginning to open and to make some progress along them. This means leaving behind some ideas in favour of others, yet also raising new questions more than giving final answers.

Mythologies and Cosmologies: Ways Forward

My syntheses suggest a number of questions for the future about literary mythologies and cosmologies. I offer a sketch of those that seem most important to me, in the spirit of a last round for the *cena*, in the hopes of whetting others' appetites.

Structure and Variation

- What are the fundamental elements and relations of the world's mythologies and cosmologies? How must/can they be organized? For example, do these worlds always have an *axis mundi*? An ultimate boundary? Can we use inventories of basic image schemas and metaphors, and principles of their grouping and combination, to approach these questions?
- What exactly is included in the generic literary cosmos? Is there more to it than what Frye specifies? How exactly does this generic world-picture relate to all of a culture's past mythologies, and its literary mythologies in all their diversity?
- In what way is Frye's generic cosmos unified? Does it make more sense to speak of multiple cosmologies? What is gained and lost by suppositions of unity and of plurality? Can the coherence of the generic cosmos be understood in terms of principles of conceptual coherence for image schemas and metaphors, as I suggest? Are some such structures interconnected in an overall model of the everyday human world in the cognitive unconscious?
- How do we square the idea that a cosmology is a coherent map of the literary universe with the experience of variant meanings for its elements? Does a cosmology tend to assign a standard meaning to an image or story, with non-standard alternatives, or are elements polysemous? How do people deal with variant meanings when they conflict? What constitutes a conflict? Do we somehow integrate the conflicting elements, or drop the problematic one, or shift between them, or somehow hold them apart or ignore the conflict? Frye remarks on different meanings of a single archetype in Dantean and Yeatsian roses (AC 125). The conceptual party points out that "it's all downhill" can metaphorically mean either that something is easy or that something is getting worse; but Dante integrates these and makes evil an easy downward path and good a difficult upward one.

- How important is the Bible for this cosmos? Frye recognizes body-based structures in the cosmos, and pre- and extra-Biblical analogues, but argues that the Bible is its most important epitome and the source of its continuing cultural influence in the West. The conceptual party, on the other hand, suggests that conceptual structures come primarily from embodied experience.
- How does the cosmos change over time? Frye examines a systematic inversion and introversion of the cosmos around the eighteenth century, such that the locus of value, meaning, and causation in the world was relocated from up there outside to down here within. Are there other systematic changes? How exactly are these brought about?
- How does the cosmology relate to cognitive models in other areas of thought, feeling, and action? To the plurality of deep frames in psychology, politics, history, and so on? (Both Frye and Lakoff and Turner discuss how the Great Chain of Being was applied to theology, science, and society.) To models for people, as in stereotypes; for how the world works, as in folk theories of natural and technological things and processes? If these are not part of it, how do we delimit the mythological/cosmological model from other models?
- How do cosmological models relate to non-cosmological literary texts focused on small-scale realities, as in many short stories? To texts with cosmological ambitions, but that are highly "realistic," such as Joyce's *Ulysses*? Or scientific, such as Pynchon's novels? How do traditional and "high culture" mythology and cosmology relate to those of pop culture and subcultures?

Learning and Use

- How are mythologies and cosmologies built up in individual minds over time – on the basis of analogies across stories that lead us to build up conventional categories of elements (images, characters, etc.)? How do they develop over lifetimes?
- How is mythology acquired and developed from things other than "Great Books" – nature, social structure, institutions, customs and practices, language and discourse, history, material things, technologies, and personal life? How is it carried forward in time and space beyond the individual lifetime?

- How and to what extent do mythologies and cosmologies differ between individuals in a culture? How do people who inherit one mythology live with or in another? What conflicts, congruencies, and negotiations arise?
- How do people use mythologies and cosmologies in various aspects of everyday life (ethical, aesthetic, political, practical, etc.)?
- Frye does not draw the line clearly between his generic cosmos and what belongs to individual authors. How do the mythologies and cosmologies of individuals draw on and modify and challenge inherited ones? How does the production, structure, and reception of individual texts relate to the whole cosmos and its parts? If a mythology is as all-encompassing as Frye implies, how are originality and innovation achieved?

Principles of Imagination

- Both Frye and Turner and Fauconnier see thought as primarily integrative, constructive, and organizing. Frye sees meaning as broadly metaphorical, in that centripetal attention must link what is merely juxtaposed and construct patterns at many scales (words to sentences to texts to mythologies). Turner and Fauconnier chart the intricate details of mapping and blending at smaller scales (words, grammar, brief texts, images, scenes, and models). We should be able to use each to expand the other's topics and framework: how do conceptual integration processes operate in the larger contexts of narrative, mythology, identity, and culture? What role does imaginative identification (with self, nature, other people, myths, and gods) play in conceptual integration?
- How do the elementary structures of literary thought that I have reviewed relate to one another, and to mythologies and cosmologies? Primary, basic, and plausibly universal concerns, emotions, genres, symbols, folk models of everyday physics, metaphors, and image-schemas must form and accumulate in the cognitive unconscious during comparable windows of development. How do they interact with one another in experience and thought? Do they become interwoven into one or more coherent schematologies? There is something of how such integration could work in Dante's cosmos; and something akin to that integrated model is needed to understand many other literary works.

The Body, Primary Concern, and Underthought and Overthought

- Frye's account of primary concerns developing metaphorical spiritual aspects is analogous to Lakoff and Johnson's account of basic well-being developing into moral systems via metaphor. How might these clarify each other? For Lakoff and Johnson, well-being grounds metaphoric source domains of health, purity, strength, control, freedom, wealth, protection, care, light, uprightness, and balance (*Philosophy* 291). Frye's body-based primary concerns of property, sex, eating, and movement develop into concerns to make and create, to love, "to sustain oneself and assimilate the environment," and "to escape from slavery and restraint" (WP 139). Non-metaphoric experiential morality and concern can only be expressed as platitudes: "Health is good," "It is better to be cared for than uncared for," "Everyone ought to be protected from physical harm," "It is good to be loved" (*Philosophy* 325), "life is better than death, happiness better than misery, health better than sickness, freedom better than bondage" (WP 42). Are the metaphors projected in mythologies and cosmologies? Are the concerns and their myths and metaphors found in moral systems?
- How can Frye's overthought/underthought analysis be supported and developed? Does the distinction inherit the fuzziness of the primary/secondary concern distinction? Can and should it be clarified? Is there some clear way to distinguish these dimensions in a text, or a reading? How important is it to read in these terms? What factors determine how they play out in a text or a reading? If, as research suggests, personal values, feelings, and identity play an important role in literary response and interpretation, how does this affect how primary and secondary concerns are perceived?
- Is it possible to enrich and fine-tune a sense of what belongs to the universal and the particular in literature and culture, and how they interact, by contrasting the proposals for universals from embodied cognitive science, conceptual metaphor theory, and Hogan's and Frye's linking of body, mind, and literary structures with the challenges that regard body as well as mind as deeply shaped by culture and history?

To move out from the scholarly details, this study is motivated by the conviction that the topics dealt with here go to the heart of literature and culture, and that the best prospects for making progress in understanding them lie with the recovery of Frye's remarkable thinking in the light of the remarkable contemporary discoveries about the mind. Frye's brilliant schematologies can and should participate in the ongoing rediscovery in cognitive science (and its new humanistic subfields) of those two fundamental processes and structures of the mind, metaphor and myth. These are the structures we create, play with, build with, and struggle with. We can get to know them, savour them, transform and blend them, create new ones, recreate old ones, and use them in new ways. They can give us joy and terror, they can blind us and make us see, they can trap us and liberate us. Yet while we create them, they also create us, and our worlds. We inherit them, and they outlast us. They are intricately connected with one another, and part of the fabric of culture that surrounds us. We live by metaphors and myths, but they also live by us, and what we do with them we may pass on. The better we understand them, the better we understand ourselves, as individuals, groups, and humans, and the better we can use them to experience, know, and act on our selves, our cultures, and our worlds.

Notes

Introduction

1 Denham's *Annotated Bibliography* (1987), *Northrop Frye Newsletter, Northrop Frye Handbook,* and posts on *The Educated Imagination* website (ed. Adamson) provide indispensable documentation of work by and about Frye. See Denham, "Auguries," "Frye's International Presence," and "Pity" on Frye's influence.

2 These thinkers make much of their own notions of similarity and coherence. Foucault's early analyses turn on his arguments for the likenesses and samenesses that he finds in unusual places. He proposes that at the end of the eighteenth century there was "an event that is of the same type" in the spheres of general grammar, natural history, and the analysis of wealth (*Order* 257). In short, the event is a shift in how the objects of these spheres are conceived: from grids of elements and divisions based on visible structure to analysis in terms of internal structure, relations, and laws. Gallagher and Greenblatt discuss the consequences of the new historicist fascination with the possibility of treating whole cultures as single texts, of "treating all of the written and visual traces of a particular culture as a mutually intelligible network of signs" (*Practicing* 7). Jameson also develops his own Marx-inspired total theory of literature in *The Political Unconscious.*

3 Among the most prominent of "spillover" developments are those of Robert Nozick in philosophy, Hayden White in history, and Roy Schafer in psychology. Others include Robin West in legal theory and even Rebecca Hagey in nursing studies (Denham, "Auguries" 82–3). Denham does not mention Clifford Geertz (perhaps because Geertz leans more on Kenneth Burke and

Suzanne Langer than on Frye). In "Deep Play," where he famously treats the Balinese cockfight as an art form to articulate his "symbolic" or "interpretive" view of social science, Geertz builds on Frye's remarks about how literary works like *Macbeth* and *King Lear* coordinate and focus impressions of life in Aristotelian "typical" or "universal" events (446–51). But Geertz's tendency has been toward cultural particularity, and away from generalizations and unifications; he has been a strong influence on new historicist critics, most notably Stephen Greenblatt, whom I discuss in relation to Frye in chapter 4. Gallagher and Greenblatt discuss the influence of Geertz on their school (*Practicing*, chapter 1).

4 Frye was, however, somewhat sceptical about Bakhtin's "buzzword," "dialogism," and again preferred his favoured term "interpenetration." See Denham's essay on "Interpenetration" in Frye, especially 148–9 and 160 (footnotes 16 and 19), and in a later version his *Religious Visionary*, 49–50 and 296.

5 Here and throughout I present image schema names in small caps, to follow the convention that has developed in the literature.

6 For details of the disputes, see *The Journal of Consciousness Studies*. There are also such disputes in more popular media, and there is even a blog, *The Neurocritic*, devoted to "deconstructing the most sensationalistic recent findings in Human Brain Imaging, Cognitive Neuroscience, and Psychopharmacology."

7 More recently but similarly, Slingerland's framework for a cognitive approach to culture uses philosophy of science to argue for a comparable "vertical integration" of disciplines, in which lower-level findings limit the kinds of hypotheses that are viable at higher levels, and knowledge and hypotheses at those higher levels in turn guide and contextualize what is known about lower levels. A more general challenge informed by philosophy of science, Paisley Livingston's *Literary Knowledge* skewers "framework relativist" views of science, and also sets out an original program for "oriented readings" to "challenge and to refine, to complexify and perfect hypotheses within the other anthropological disciplines" (260). The new *Journal of Literary Theory* has a number of important discussions of the possible relations between the humanities and the sciences (especially cognitive and brain sciences).

8 In a later paper, Hogan maps out in more detail the levels around which mind meets matter, and separates various strata of psychology as it touches biology. He distinguishes among four levels of "cognitive architecture": intentionalism, representationalism, connectionism, and neurobiology ("On Being Moved," 239). Again, patterns at each level can be studied on their

own, though it is also important to relate each level to the others, eventually. Hogan himself is often concerned to discern patterns at the representational/conceptual level, but at times he moves across levels, explaining higher-level patterns by lower-level principles. Thus he explains standard poetic line length in terms of the nature of rehearsal memory ("Literary Universals"), explains some audience emotional responses in terms of experiential triggers based in neurobiological architecture ("On Being Moved"), and explains mirth patterns in terms of certain child-like practices and evolutionarily-guided attitudes toward children ("Laughing Brains"). Writing a few years earlier, in the appendix to *Philosophy in the Flesh*, Lakoff and Johnson discuss the relation between brains and minds and concepts in the context of the "Neural Theory of Language Paradigm." They seek to bridge the "enormous gap between physical brain structures and the level of human concepts and language," in "a small set of precise steps" (570). The "common paradigm" in cognitive science specifies descriptions of "high-level cognition" (above), "the relevant neurobiology" (below), and the level of "neural computation relating these" in the middle. Lakoff and Johnson instead set out five levels of analysis, and split neural computation into three levels to make the task of linking cognition to neurobiology "more manageable" (570). The details of this penta-plex are not important here.

1. "Systems That Won't Quite Do"

1 Frye's influences are many, but few are shared with the conceptual party, and as they do not refer to him, so he shows no direct familiarity with Lakoff, Johnson, and Turner. Regarding metaphor, he acknowledges theoretical debts to Paul Ricoeur's *The Rule of Metaphor*, Max Black's *Models and Metaphors*, Philip Wheelwright's *Metaphor and Reality*, and Christine Brooke-Rose's *A Grammar of Metaphor* (GC 238n). Of these, Black seems to have been the strongest influence on the conceptual theory of metaphor, although Turner's *Death is the Mother of Beauty* (1987) also cites Brooke-Rose, Ricoeur, and Wheelwright. Both Frye and Turner also refer to Fenollosa's study of the Chinese written character as a medium for poetry, as both are interested in how to "translate the diagram" of one concept to another: Frye through Pound's reference (GC 56); Turner in an epigraph to the final chapter of *The Literary Mind*, on language (140). In *Cognitive Dimensions of Social Science* (2001) Turner discusses Geertz's "Deep Play" extensively (8–59) (see note 3 to Introduction, above). Critics have considered Frye's thought in relation to semiotics – see e.g., the special issue of *RS/SI* 13.3 (1993) edited by Adamson – but rarely in relation to linguistics. Gill briefly discusses Lakoff

and Johnson in connection with Frye's relation to phenomenology and postmodern mythography ("Flesh," *Phenomenology* 188–9, 191–3).

2 Cognitive linguistics is said to be "all-inclusive or all-embracing" (Dirven et al. 3), and "heading for its own built-in final destination, that of cognitive semiotics" (2). New subfields include cognitive versions of discourse analysis, sociolinguistics, poetics, narratology, stylistics, rhetoric, anthropology, and religious studies. It is also very concerned with "worldview, that is, with everyday conceptualization, reasoning, and ... language," and common sense (Lakoff, *Moral* 3–4). Cognitive approaches to literature and other arts have mushroomed since the mid-1980s. Even in 1989 Bordwell noted the difficulty of keeping up with such research. Richardson's "Studies in Literature and Cognition: A Field Map" (2004) provides an excellent overview of the field, and his introduction to *The Neural Sublime* (2010) is an important update. Valuable introductions are Stockwell, *Cognitive Poetics* (2002); Semino and Culpeper, eds., *Cognitive Stylistics* (2002); Gavins and Steen, eds., *Cognitive Poetics in Practice* (2003); Hogan, *Cognitive Science, Literature, and the Arts* (2003); and Zunshine, ed., *Introduction to Cognitive Cultural Studies* (2010). Herman, ed., *Narrative Theory and the Cognitive Sciences* (2003) provides an overview of cognitive narratology. See also the annotated bibliography on Richardson's *Literature, Cognition, and the Brain* website, and the bibliography on Claiborne Rice's *Cognitive Approaches to Literature* website. *Poetics Today* has hosted important discussions in essays and special issues. See especially Shen, ed., "Aspects of Metaphor Comprehension" (1992) and "Metaphor 2" (1993), Fludernik, Freeman, and Freeman, eds., "Metaphor and Beyond" (1999), Richardson and Steen, eds., "Literature and the Cognitive Revolution" (2002), and discussion of the latter in Adler and Gross (2002) and in issue 24.2 (Summer 2003: "The Cognitive Turn?: A Debate on Interdisciplinarity"), Sternberg, "Universals of Narrative" (I) and (II) (2003), and the issue on "Cognitive Themes" (30.3, 2009). There is a special issue of *Style* on "Cognitive Approaches to Figurative Language" (36.3, Fall 2002). *Language and Literature* and *Metaphor and Symbol* frequently publish papers using cognitive linguistics, and the *Journal of Literary Theory* also has important discussions of cognitive literary and cultural studies. Cognitive approaches to the other arts are also flourishing (e.g., *The Artful Mind*, Turner, ed. 2006).

3 For some representative early responses to Frye, see Krieger, ed., *Northrop Frye in Modern Criticism* (1966). Krieger's "Northrop Frye & Contemporary Criticism" (1966) replies to common criticisms, as does Frye's "Reflections in a Mirror," in the same volume. Denham responds to critiques of Frye's modal literary history (*Critical Method* 18–27). Even serious Frye criticism

often struggles with the difficulty of making all the necessary dimensions of theoretical evaluation converge: contextualization, application, and critical development. For the comparable complaints against the conceptual party, see Jackendoff and Aaron's review of Lakoff and Turner's *More Than Cool Reason* (1991), Miall's discussion of Johnson's *The Body in the Mind*, "The Body in Literature" (1997), Gross, "Cognitive Readings" (1997), Tsur, "Lakoff's" (2000) and "'EVENT STRUCTURE'" (2001), Adler and Gross, "Adjusting the Frame" (2002), Swan, "Life without Parole" (2002), Jackson, "'Literary Interpretation'" (2003), Van Oort, "Cognitive Science" (2003), and various chapters in Fludernik, ed., *Beyond Cognitive Metaphor Theory* (2011). For responses to Adler and Gross, see Hernadi, "On Cognition" (2003), Spolsky, "Cognitive Literary Historicism" (2003), and Richardson and Steen, "Reframing the Adjustment" (2003). One major difference in the impact and growth of the two approaches has to do with the relation of their development to that of other approaches. I see cognitive poetics as entering a phase of self-criticism and careful development and consolidation, after an initial phase of exploration and ground-laying, a following phase of enthusiastic application, and a consequent phase of broad attack and defence and counter-attack. Cognitive poetics is strengthened by its awareness of the post-structuralist critique of language and meaning, and by its symbiotic relationships with linguistics, psychology, and empirical research. Frye's theories, however, while they reached the phase of enthusiastic application and general attack and defence, were rather taken by surprise and thrown aside when post-structuralist theory stormed over North America in the late 1960s and afterwards. I would like to see Frye studies go further in the phase of critical development – as studies of Bakhtin have, for example.

4 See Hamilton's *Anatomy* for fuller discussion of the critical context. Scholarship on the relation of cosmological models to literary meaning includes Arthur O. Lovejoy's *The Great Chain of Being*, E.M.W. Tillyard's *The Elizabethan World Picture*, and C.S. Lewis's *The Discarded Model*. *Fearful Symmetry*, Frye's study of Blake's mythological universe, led toward his overarching literary theory, and he studied the mythologies of many other writers along the way (*Fables of Identity*, in particular, is conceived as a "practical" companion piece to the *Anatomy*). Frye identified Vico as "the first modern thinker to understand that all major verbal structures have descended historically from poetic and mythological ones" (WP xii), and also admired Spengler, who like Vico presented a complete analogical model of cultural history in terms of organic cycles. Frye notes that "from Frazer on, there have been many remarkable essays on what Graves in *The White Goddess* calls a historical grammar of the language of poetic myth. These would include the

works of Mircea Eliade, Joseph Campbell, and several Freudian, Jungian and other psychological studies. But as a rule these still show only a perfunctory interest in literature" (WP xiii). Frye acknowledges archetypal theorists Maud Bodkin, Kenneth Burke, Gaston Bachelard, Francis Fergusson, and Philip Wheelwright (AC 358). These are related to studies of unifying myths by Joseph Campbell, Lord Raglan, Jane Harrison, and Carl Jung, and to studies of the birth of the hero by Otto Rank, Jung, and Kerényi (361). Jessie L. Weston's *From Ritual to Romance* and F.M. Cornford's *The Origin of Attic Comedy* were influential in arguing the evolution of literary genres from ritual. Russell's *Northrop Frye on Myth* (1998) examines Frye's relation to theorists of myth, and emphasizes Frazer, Spengler, Cassirer, and Jung. Gill's *Northrop Frye and the Phenomenology of Myth* (2006) compares Frye favourably with myth theorists Eliade, Jung, and Campbell. Willard's "Archetypes" (1994) examines Frye's relation to Jungian archetypes, and Willard's "Alchemy" (1983), Alter's "Northrop Frye" (2002), and Burgess's "From Archetype" (2002) discuss Frye's connecting archetypal criticism with Biblical typology.

5 Frye sees myth and metaphor as "informing principles" in the human sciences, as mathematics is for the natural sciences. Literary critics and mathematicians study these elements in their essentially hypothetical form. Denham critiques Frye's science analogies (*Critical Method* 192–204). Chamberlin discusses Frye's ideas about mathematics.

6 Frye's arguments are prominent in Culler's key theoretical chapters in Part I, "Structuralism and Linguistic Models," and Part II, "Poetics." More precisely, Frye wrote that structuralism "interests me because it seems to me a movement heading in the direction of what I call interpenetration, the interrelating of different subjects in a way that preserves their own autonomy, instead of subordinating them to some grandiose program of mental imperialism" (SM x). Interestingly, Turner objects to structuralism precisely because he sees it as imperialistic, uniting various subjects under one theory. Instead of an "organizing hypothesis," he proposes a "grounding activity" for criticism: an "integrated approach to language and literature" as acts of the everyday human mind (*Reading* 6–7), which he calls "cognitive rhetoric." Steen and Gavins connect cognitive poetics (favourably) with structuralism. (It cannot be said that cognitivist thinkers have always been careful to avoid imperialistic directions: see Simon's "Literary Criticism" for an avowedly imperialist strategy of absorbing literary studies into cognitive science.) Other cognitive critics have identified Saussurean linguistics as a source of post-structuralism's theoretical weaknesses – see Turner (*Death, Reading*), Holland (*The Critical I*), McConachie and Hart. Jackson's *Poverty*

also surveys literary theory's inheritance of errors of structuralism. Pinker, Norris, and others have also critiqued the linguistics of Derrida and Lacan. See chapter 3 for some key details. Denham comments on the "analogy of Frye's alphabet of forms to Chomsky's syntactic rules ... Both rely on a finite set of principles to create an infinite number of sentences (in Chomsky's case) and literary works (in Frye's)" (*Religious* 342 n48).

7 Lakoff and Johnson acknowledge Kant (Johnson, *Body* xxv–xxix, xxxvii), Merleau-Ponty, and John Dewey (Lakoff and Johnson, *Philosophy* xi). Johnson's *Meaning* cites John Dewey and William James extensively, and declares his debt to phenomenology and American pragmatism. Frye draws considerably on Kant (see Forst), and his phenomenology is indebted to Hegel and Merleau-Ponty (on the relevance of the latter for Frye, see Gill, *Phenomenology*). Frye cites Vico as a major influence (see Cotrupi for discussion). Adler and Gross see Vico's mark on the conceptual party (206), but Richardson and Steen note Lakoff and Johnson's distinctness from Vico and other Romantic precursors ("Reframing" 154–5). Geeraerts's study of the philosophical ancestry of cognitive semantics lays stress on continental rather than analytic philosophy, and indicates links with the phenomenological tradition initiated by Husserl, especially that of Merleau-Ponty, but contrasts it with Derrida. Jäkel goes over other neglected precursors to conceptual metaphor theory, including Locke, Vico, Herder, Franz Wüllner, and especially Kant (and neo-Kantian Cassirer), Hans Blumenberg, and Harald Weinrich. I would add that Ricoeur is a good representative of the more traditional approach to humanities scholarship, which reviews all major metaphor theories in a historical survey. However, such an approach can lack a strong theoretical view, and skimp on developing theories and analyses in detail, as Ricoeur's does.

8 Frye is one of only two critics whose work appears in both volumes of the Adams and Searle anthologies, *Critical Theory Since Plato* and *Critical Theory since 1965* (the other is Murray Krieger). In fact, Searle's "Afterword" is ambivalent about Frye. It contrasts the 1965 English Institute's tribute to Frye (extraordinarily devoted to a living critic) with the 1966 conference on structuralism at Johns Hopkins University, where deconstruction began its conquest of North America. Most of the essay is devoted to deconstruction. Since the late 1960s, the explosion of criticism obviously reversed Frye's perspective that criticism needed its own "conceptual universe," and now we need to "know something about linguistics and language theory, historiography, anthropology, psychoanalysis, hermeneutics, and semiotics," which may make it "unmanageable, if not unthinkably difficult," and lead to a "loss of focus" (859). On Frye and post-structuralism,

see work by Adamson, Hamilton, and White, the special issue of *RS/SI* 13.3 (1993) (ed. Adamson), and many of the essays in *The Legacy of Northrop Frye* (ed. Lee and Denham). In the latter collection, Hutcheon (1994) and Kristeva (1994) find much to admire in Frye.

9 Although "schemata" may be the more formal plural for "schema," I will use the word "schemas," which has become conventional within cognitive linguistics and poetics.

10 Turner also argues for a view of "cultural literacy" as a capacity to use a dynamic, rich, complex conceptual system for understanding, invention, and thought, as against E.D. Hirsch's "Dictionary" of arbitrary, inert, and isolated pieces of information (*Reading* 216–38).

11 The postulation of co-existing "discrepant representations" seems more typical of literary than linguistic study. For example, Pettersson quotes Ricoeur as saying: "'Seeing X as Y' encompasses 'X is not Y'; seeing time as a beggar is, precisely, to know also that time is not a beggar. The borders of meaning are transgressed but not abolished" (qtd. in Pettersson, "Literary," 108). This is somewhat different from the view that metaphor involves recognizing a linguistic "deviation" then finding a meaning that renders it comprehensible.

12 For cognitive linguistic approaches to cultural models and ideologies, see Holland and Quinn, eds., *Cultural Models*, Dirven et al., eds., *Cognitive Models*, and Lakoff's *Moral Politics, Don't Think of an Elephant, Thinking Points, Whose Freedom?*, and *The Political Mind*. In chapter 4 I will consider how Patrick Hogan's research on literary universals relates to Frye's studies. Sweetser draws on Lakoff and Turner to show how the same conceptual metaphors are present in very distant structures of Indo-European culture: the world of Greek mythology and everyday English language ("Metaphor"). Comparable to Frye's studies of authorial mythologies, Margaret Freeman discusses the "conceptual universe" of Emily Dickinson in conceptual metaphor terms ("Metaphor"), and Elena Semino uses conceptual metaphor theory to define "mind style" in narrative – that is, "language reflects the particular conceptual structures and cognitive habits that characterize an individual's world view" ("Cognitive" 95). Mind style is not synonymous with, but is complementary to, "ideology," which is more sociocultural in character (97). Schauber and Spolsky take Frye's model of romance as a central example in their approach to genre, which is cognitive-linguistic but draws on Jackendoff's notion of "preference rules" rather than the Lakoff-Langacker school (*Bounds*). Cognitive critics as a whole have been somewhat slow to take up the cultural-studies themes of ideology and worldview, but see Zunshine's collection *Introduction to*

Cognitive Cultural Studies, which includes Bruce McConachie's proposal for a cognitive approach to Gramsci's idea of cultural hegemony. The other essays occasionally reflect on ideology and "culture" in some sense, but it would be fair to say that rather than dealing with the typical topics and foci of the school known as cultural studies, they aim to connect cognitive science with a wide range of contemporary literary and cultural theory.

13 Beyond literary study as such, MacCormac (*Cognitive* 40–1, 194–9), while working out a cognitive theory of metaphor in contrast to Lakoff and Johnson (see chapter 3), makes Frye the representative of a "diaphoric" view of metaphor as special and literary, which stresses the suggestiveness of the discrepancies between vehicle and tenor. (The polar opposite is Monroe Beardsley, whose "epiphoric" view sees metaphor as everyday and paraphrasable, and stresses similarities across domains.) Carveth ("Analyst's") draws on Frye's ideas of analogy and metaphor in his discussion of the relation of conceptual metaphor theory to psychoanalysis, but tends to a deconstructive view.

14 Hogan (*Cognitive* 44–7) discusses schemas, prototypes, and exempla as increasingly specific cognitive semantic structural complexes.

15 For studies of the nature of image schemas, and the constraints on the amount and kind of image-schematic structure projected in metaphorical mapping, see Johnson's *Body in the Mind* and the studies of the "Invariance Hypothesis": Lakoff, "Invariance," Turner, "Aspects," and Brugman, "What is." On image schema transformations as the basis for metaphoric polysemy, see Johnson on "balance" (*Body* 74–96), Brugman and Lakoff on "over" (Lakoff, *Women*, 416–61), Sweetser (*Etymology*), and Ekberg on "up," "out," "above," and "behind" ("Mental"). See Mandler on image schemas in conceptual development ("How"), and Gibbs and Colston for evidence bearing on their "psychological reality" ("Cognitive"). Cienki provides an effective overview and synthesis of principles of image schemas ("Some Properties"). The collection edited by Hampe, *From Perception to Meaning*, represents the current state of image schema research and debate by leading scholars. Johnson's *The Meaning of the Body* presents his most recent thinking about the role of image schemas in human experience and thought.

16 The study of "spatial form" in literature relates to the centripetal/centrifugal distinction, as Frye notes (GC 63), but it is defined somewhat differently. Denham notes the similarities of Frye's moving/stationary contrast with Lévi-Strauss's syntagmatic-diachronic chain/paradigmatic-synchronic pattern (*Critical Method* 86–7). For Salusinszky, the "topo-analysis" offered in Bachelard's 1958 *Poetics of Space* is "the most obvious

structuralist analogue to Frye" ("Art of Memory" 53 n3). Cotrupi's *Poetics of Process* corrects the notion that Frye neglects "process" in favour of "product": they are complementary parts of the complete experience of literature.

17 Hamilton finds this argument "outrageously circular" (*Anatomy* 109), but it is so only if archetype is defined as any perceived association at all. Frye stresses that this coherence exists in literature but that reader cognition can reflect it. He does not say that readers never miss associations, never make mistaken ones, or always see real ones. Any such categorization processes face ordinary (non-vicious) hermeneutic circularity: for cats, cars, or character types, you need to experience the exemplars to form the category, but you need the category to grasp the exemplars. Of course, Frye was an exceptionally cultivated reader, but the principle that assimilation and expansion occur naturally for everyone – and is assumed by writers – seems quite sound. One can observe it in one's own responses and in students at every level. A bigger problem is that it is far from obvious how we can tell when an analogy or association is off-base. Another is that Frye excludes (or does not take very seriously) the possibility that archetypes exist – in the sense of widespread schematic types based on valid associations – but do not resolve into a total system.

18 Frye's formulations allow ambiguity on this point. Here the centre is in the "order of words"; earlier he argues criticism should "locate" this centre, from which literature is "spread out in conceptual space" (AC 17).

19 Frye's interest in anagogic monads persists, under the rubric of "interpenetration" – meaning that this microcosmic relation of whole-in-part pertains to all parts. It is an abstract term that is applicable in various contexts. Denham shows how Frye found versions of the idea in Spengler (history, society, and culture), Whitehead (philosophy and science), and Suzuki (Oriental religion) ("Interpenetration" 142–4). He stresses Frye's preference for "experiential and intuitive" versions, and their importance for his grasp of "spiritual vision" (152–3), yet as a concept Frye expresses it as a "thematic or spatial idea" (153). According to Hamilton the metaphor was suggested by Keats (*Anatomy* 19). Frye also discusses the "literary" resonance of elements of the Bible (GC 216–24), and the significance of *kerygma*, meaning "proclamation," cf. "apocalyptic" or "prophetic" (WP 100), which might be called "applied resonance." Regarded as the vehicle of revelation, *kerygma* is a figurative verbal aspect of the Bible that is not quite rhetoric or poetry. It is "on the *other side* of the poetic" (101) because its literary basis of free mythical and metaphorical hypothesis is harnessed to existential concern, on the principle

that "you are what you identify with" (116–17; cf. GC 29–30). The distinctly kerygmatic theme, "life more abundant," produces a distinctive construct, the "myth to live by," a "model for continuous action" that "even the most penetrating literature, even Dante or Shakespeare, does not attempt" (116–17). See also Denham's *Religious Visionary* for his most recent account of Frye's thinking about these concepts as revealed in his notebooks.

20 "Analogy and identity produce, not only the two commonest figures of poetic speech [simile and metaphor], but the two major patterns of poetic imagery. One of these is the cyclical pattern, based on the assimilation of the death and rebirth of life in the human world to the natural cycles of sun, moon, water and the seasons. The other we may call the dialectical rhythm, the movement towards a separation of happiness from misery, the hero from the villain, heaven from hell" (SM 247).

21 Hamilton notes Frye's changing attitudes toward the relation of the traditional to the Romantic cosmos (*Anatomy* 196, 271–2 n6).

22 Denham reports that as early as 1949 Frye wrote in a diary that he wanted to write a book "on the geometry of vision, which will analyse the diagrammatic patterns present in thought which emerge unconsciously in the metaphors of speech, particularly prepositions (up, down, beside & the like)" (qtd. in Denham, *Religious* 314).

23 Denham explores Frye's analyses of journey metaphors and relates them to Frye's own critical development, including his use of the metaphor of the critic as architect (*Religious* 251–6).

24 Compare Donald Freeman on the coherence of the image-schematic metaphors used to depict character psychology in Shakespeare's *Antony and Cleopatra* (and how they inform language, imagery, plot, and on- and off-stage business) ("'The rack dislimns'").

25 To preserve their gestalt structure, Johnson resists analysing his image schemas into components (*Body* 44), but this sine wave can be symbolized as comprising a PATH projected onto a field defined by two linked axes, the horizontal corresponding to time, and the vertical corresponding to the experienced value of events in time.

26 Frye notes that "its ancient forms have been studied by Gertrude Rachel Levy in *The Gate of Horn* and *The Sword from the Rock*" (SM 163). Gibbs also argues that myths "reflect patterns of imaginative thinking rooted in metaphor" (*Poetics* 192), citing Joseph Campbell on the "monomyth" of the hero's journey, and Mircea Eliade on journeys to heights and depths, as well as Frye's discussions of literary patterns of journey and spiral ascent in *Myth and Metaphor* (187–92).

27 Mandala-like images include cosmological diagrams, meditative diagrams as in the I Ching and kabbalah, and the tarot sequence of pictorial visions (Ayre "Geometry" 828). More mainstream examples are the wheel of fortune in Emile Mâle's *Gothic Image*, S. Foster Damon's diagrams of Blake's zoas, Austin Farrer's diagrams of the geometry of the Last Judgment in *A Rebirth of Images*, and Joseph Campbell's heroic quest wheel in *The Hero with a Thousand Faces* (830–2). Ayre also discusses diagrams by Levi-Strauss ("Chart" 169–70), and G. Wilson Knight (174–6), and the cosmological patterns Frye found in Paul Gallico's popular novel *The Poseidon Adventure*, and Hesse's *Glass Bead Game* (179–83).

Frye published only the most temperate diagrams and downplayed their importance. But he inspired many other efforts – Denham's *Critical Method* diagrams many *Anatomy* schemas. And as Salusinszky points out, Frye's notebooks reveal that he "drew hundreds of *real* diagrams, much more 'ingenious' than those suggested by anyone, even Denham" ("Art" 47). However, it is not clear how consistent the diagrams of Frye's myths and genres are or could be: for one thing, their principles of similarity and contrast often have more than two dimensions. For discussion, see Ayre's "Geometry" and "Chart," Dolzani's "Introduction," and Denham's *Religious Visionary*, which presents more of Denham's ingenious diagrams as well as some of Frye's.

28 Elaborations on this structure use more specific types of imagery and story: descents may enter the belly of a beast or involve fighting monsters (Frye, SeS 112). They may also mix the logics of action and metaphor: for example, unlike "earth-mother" myths of creation by natural birth, "sky-father" myths of creation by artificial design require metaphoric "fall" myths to explain mortality (GC 109–10). Frye describes the association of the former with the sense of nature as a "force of growth or energy" (*natura naturans*), the latter with the sense of nature as a "structure or system" (*natura naturata*), and notes the analogy of these conceptions with his contrasting movement/structuring processes (68, 69, 71).

29 Note that the coherence of complex constructs may be partly conventional and unconscious rather than the product of a specific construction in context, as in conventional metaphoric models (e.g., ANGER as HEATED FLUID IN A CONTAINER). Somewhat as sentences are structured by grammar, and literary texts may be structured tacitly on the cultural models of genres, or of story types like "the Fall," such cognitive models may function as tacit input spaces to a blend, even though no part of them is explicitly referred to. In blending theory, the "Invariance Hypothesis" about the image-schematic constraints on metaphor must be replaced with

a "Topology Principle" about how image-schematic projection should be maximized – subject to the imperatives of the five other optimality principles. See Fauconnier and Turner, "Conceptual Integration" 33–49, and *The Way We Think* chapters 6, 7, and 16, on competition and cooperation among optimality principles. Their "Rethinking Metaphor" is a good example of how their recent thinking contrasts with Lakoff's. They propose that metaphors are not simply source-target mappings of concepts – rather, a network of related models of targets (of time, in their example) enters into particular metaphors in discourse in various ways. In short, they advocate rethinking metaphor theory from the perspective of blending theory. Lakoff has recently advocated the opposite ("Afterword, 2003").

2. Spatial and Spiritual Orders

1 Dante's narrative can be treated as a conceptual blend. While the capacity of metaphors to integrate into a consistent narrative world is a strong indicator of at least partial coherence (as partial cross-space mapping is necessary for blending), blends may modify the metaphors they project from inputs to blend space, and so coherence across inputs may not carry over directly into the blend. The other side of this classification is that integration networks do not automatically inherit the limitations on coherence among conceptual metaphors: they may use only one or some of the specific mappings for, say, time (they do not need to integrate the structures of all source domains), and grounding scenarios are not definitive for characterizing mappings and coherence.

2 Cognitive analyses of narrative should support the enterprise of investigating how metaphor is projected in narrative. Yet Sternberg notes that (outside of Turner's *Literary Mind*) "the two primary thrusts of cognitivist discourse analysis, the figurative and the narrative, seldom meet" ("Universals (I)" 321 n16). Pettersson makes a similar observation, and advocates further interaction ("Afterword" 310–16, "Literary"). For some interesting exceptions, see Kimmel's "From Metaphor" and Steen's "Love stories." More recent cognitive literary analyses have lighted on this issue (see Fludernik, ed., *Beyond*).

3 Other geometrical shapes could be used as containers, but the series of spheres dominated, presumably due in part to the idea of the sphere's perfection according to considerations of symmetry, balance, and harmony.

4 I ignore for the moment the complex relations possible among locations, orientations, and movements (one can face forward while moving backward, etc.). Suffice it to say that characterizing location requires conceptualizing

one or more oriented grounds (e.g., a setting or object with a recognized front, top, etc.), relative to which it is possible to identify the position of one or more figures (e.g., the spot is in the middle of the top of the desk on the house's bottom floor). Characterizing orientation and movement require the same kind of context, relative to which something can be pointed or directed, or move in a direction. All three spatial qualities can cohere: you can answer "up" to all three questions Where is X? Which way is X facing? and Which way is X moving?

5 At least arguably. Dante tends to speak of his location relative to east and west, and to the sun and stars (*Purgatory* 2, 17ff., 31–2). But as Dante's shadow is on his left (49), he must be facing perpendicular to the mountain face on his left. So, viewing the mountain from the side, the upward path goes from left to right, and after approaching it from the side, one turns right to ascend. Cf. Krzeszowski on the RIGHT-LEFT axiology ("Axiological" 323–5). I would add that one traditionally turns left to enter a labyrinth.

6 The question of whether or not this shift is a figure-ground reversal is too complex to answer easily. The shift in context involves reframing not which parts of the scene are moving and which stationary, but rather a whole set of related conceptualizations of the moving part's orientation, direction, etc. In fact, the shift from geocentric to heliocentric cosmologies is a better candidate for "duality."

7 Of course, the conceptual party's view is the opposite of Dante's in the sense that his cosmos is primarily conscious and intelligent: matter descends from mind. They would say that Dante built up this vision by connecting metaphors grounded in bodily experience: mind ascends from matter.

8 A number of other scholars in different areas have offered further evidence for the (perhaps universal) human capacity to map across sensory modes, and have discussed its implications for metaphor and related symbolic capacities. As noted earlier, Ramachandran and Hubbard link metaphor and even the origin of language with evidence for "natural constraints on the ways in which sounds are mapped on to objects" plus a "sensory-to-motor synaesthesia" (e.g. matching music to movement, as in dance) ("Synaesthesia" 19). Shen studies synaesthetic metaphor in language and literature. Citing this and other research, Slingerland suggests that conceptual metaphor is "voluntary, partial, and communicable synaesthesia" (160–2). In his essay on metaphor and art, Kennedy considers the significant agreement across people asked to match certain kinds of forms with certain kinds of symbolic functions (e.g., circle with soft, good, weak, and summer, versus square

with hard, evil, strong, and winter) by reference to abstract cross-modal feature matching (453–4). Cacciari reviews and discusses a range of research on how synaesthesia relates to metaphorical language. Examining the "grounding of meaning in bodily experience and feeling" that helps create the sense of a "core self" (*Meaning* 41), Johnson reviews evidence that "neonates have an inborn ability to recognize a single identical pattern present in two or more different perceptual modalities" (42; see also 136–45).

9 There are a number of *catascopias* in Dante: for example, his view of "this puny threshing-ground of ours" (*Paradise* 27, 1.85). Hammil discusses many uses of this convention; cf. Lewis, *Discarded* 26.

10 Although our understanding of the cosmological order has changed radically, gravity continues to be a powerful source domain for a range of metaphors, probably because it is a continual powerful aspect of experience and still a (somewhat mysterious) part of our cosmology. On the other hand, the metaphor of love as the force governing the universe has faded, because we no longer project the emotional forces of everyday experience as cosmological forces.

11 This critique prompts Herder's innovative recognition of multiple cultures, the "specific and variable cultures of different nations and periods," and "social and economic groups within a nation" (Williams, *Keywords* 79). Both insights are central to cultural studies and new historicism.

12 Frye and the conceptual party do not stress some of these correspondences, perhaps because they are contingently rather than necessarily associated with orientational schemas – e.g., heat and cold.

13 Dante uses all of the primary metaphors that Lakoff and Johnson mention in *Philosophy in the Flesh* (48ff.), though whether they are coherent overall is another question.

3. Family, City, and Body Politic

1 Ideology "saturates everyday discourse in the form of common sense" so it "cannot be bracketed off from everyday life as a self-contained set of 'political opinions' or 'biased views'" (Hebdige 363). Other statements on the unconscious and common-sense quality of ideology could be offered. Compare, for example, Stuart Hall's remark that common sense becomes "at one and the same time, 'spontaneous', ideological and *unconscious*" (qtd. in Hebdige 362).

2 Barthes's *Mythologies* and Hall's "Encoding, Decoding" are central for the use of structuralism and semiology in cultural analysis. For discussion of "the theoretical advances which were made by the encounters with

structuralist, semiotic, and post-structuralist work," see Hall, "Cultural Studies" (283–4).

3 I focus on Barthes for several reasons. *Mythologies* came out in the same year as Frye's *Anatomy* (1957), was a major influence on cultural studies, and continues to be extracted and discussed. Frye refers to Barthes in his published works, and privately associates him with the post-structuralist "Holy Family" with its "sacred cow" of "the omnipresence of ideology, & the impossibility of ever getting past it" (qtd. in Adamson, "Treason," 76–7). Also, Barthes's view of ideology in culture is more representative than Althusser's more famous and extreme view, which has met with some critique. Michael Bérubé's blog (www.michaelberube.com), though now retired, was valuable in alerting me to the complexity of cultural studies, including its internal divisions, and in critiquing some of its major theoretical figures (e.g., Althusser, Jameson, and Fish). For Bérubé's valuable critical assessment of Althusser, see his blog entry for 9 August 2005 (www.michaelberube.com/index.php/weblog/theory_tuesday_iv). Bérubé's engaging style and sense of humour offer a refreshing change from cultural studies in the lugubrious Althusserian mode.

4 In CP chapter 1, Frye returns to the "two mental operations" of all media experience: pre-critically following a linear narrative, then studying its structure as a "simultaneous unity" (25–7); he uses "centrifugal" and "centripetal" only as the names of fallacies (32–3). Cf. the discussions of centrifugal and centripetal attention elsewhere (AC 73–4ff., GC 56–63, WP 3ff.).

5 I might also note Moretti's support (reminiscent of Frye) for a scientific criticism, and his disapproval of deconstructive word-play: "Criticism ... has always taken its own empirical foundations lightly, and, instead of struggling to set up a scientific community with common aims and clear rules, has tacitly preferred to legitimate a state of affairs where everyone is free to do as they like. The lexico-grammatical euphoria of the last few years is only the latest episode in a long and illustrious tradition of intellectual irresponsibility ... If criticism can give itself a reasonably testable foundation, then rhetorical analysis will necessarily acquire a different status within the 'stronger' social sciences" (*Signs* 24). Zunshine reveals Raymond Williams's surprising (and overlooked) interest in how the then-new sciences of the human mind inform the meaning of culture and cultural study ("Introduction").

6 See for example Williams's revisions of base and superstructure (*Culture* 31–49) and his concept of "structures of feeling" (22–7); Stuart Hall's "articulation" and "preferred/negotiated/oppositional" kinds of readings (see Nelson et al. 8; Storey, "Introduction" ix); Althusser's "relative autonomy"

of Ideological State Apparatuses; Gramsci's "hegemony" as the dominance of provisional social alliances by popular consent (Gramsci; see also Hebdige 357–67; Williams, *Culture* 37–40, and "Hegemony" in *Keywords*). Also significant are Volosinov/Bakhtin's view of ideological struggle within language by reaccentuating signs. Useful overviews of this post-Marxism: Hebdige; Hall, "Cultural Studies"; and McRobbie. The original formulations of Marx and Engels are briefly extracted in Storey (196–201).

7 Similarly, Larry Grossberg writes: "A theory of articulation denies an essential human subject without giving up the active individual who is never entirely and simply 'stitched' into its place in social organizations of power ... There are always a multiplicity of positions, not only available but occupied, and a multiplicity of ways in which different meanings, experiences, powers, interests and identities can be articulated together" (qtd. in Giroux, "Resisting," 202).

8 On the topic of genre, for example, see Radway's sociology of romance and Williams's materialist account of drama (*Culture* 125–47). I will discuss Montrose's analysis of political uses of pastoral in the next chapter.

9 For cognitive studies of ideology and culture, see note 12 to chapter 1, above.

10 In 2000, Lakoff and colleagues established the Rockridge Institute to counter the decades-long think-tanking of the right (it closed in April 2008). His work soon came into the political spotlight. Prominent democrats (including the Clintons) heard, read, and recommended his work, and consulted with him. *Don't Think of an Elephant!* was praised by progressive luminaries, became a *New York Times* bestseller, and got Lakoff publishing, appearing, and talked about in major opinion journals, and on radio and television. The story of Lakoff's rise is told in Matt Bai's *New York Times Magazine* cover story, "The Framing Wars." Goldstein's "Who Framed George Lakoff?" in the *Chronicle of Higher Education* offers a valuable later overview.

11 Pinker's scathing review prompted an angry exchange of letters (noted in my citations). His full account of liberal and conservative visions is in *The Blank Slate*, chapter 16.

12 This account from *Spiritus Mundi* appears in a slightly different form in *The Critical Path*, chapter 7. Note that Frye speaks of "radical" rather than liberal views. He later develops his view of the relation of culture and ideology, especially in *Words with Power*.

13 Goffman is a strong intellectual link between cognitive linguistics and cultural studies. He is cited or discussed by Foucault ("Space" 164), Bourdieu ("How" 343, 348), de Certeau ("Practice" 478, 484 n9), Jameson ("On

Goffman's") and Radway ("Reading" 286), as well as Lakoff (*Thinking* 25–28, *Political Mind* 22, 248–49) and Pinker (264). Given Stephen Greenblatt's analysis of cultural life as the performance (e.g., by authors and others) of diverse and sometimes conflicting roles, often modeled on literary roles and narratively structured, it is remarkable that he does not (so far as I know) cite Goffman. Frye, too, occasionally sounds as though he is referencing Goffman. In "On Teaching Literature," he writes that "we are continually playing roles in society" and even "dramatize ourselves to ourselves, and the mask never really comes off ... There is never anything under a persona except another persona. It follows that we spend our entire lives playing roles, and are never in a situation which is not to some degree a structured and dramatic situation" (457).

14 For discussions of narrative structures (especially "fairy tale") in political discourse, see Lakoff, "Metaphor and War"; *Don't* 71–2; *Whose* 151–4; and *Political Mind*, especially chapter 1. "Metaphor and War" analyses the rationale for the US war against Saddam Hussein in Kuwait as a hero rescuing a victim from a villain. Lakoff looks back on this paper in *Don't*, noting how "self-defense" and "rescue" variants of classical fairy tales are used to frame "just wars" (71–2). He also treats the conservative "economic liberty myth" as a fairy tale and the related "ownership society myth" as a "radical conservative utopia" (*Whose* 151–3, 154). *The Political Mind* goes more deeply into narrative elements and types and how they are experienced and used, and proposes some cognitive and neural underpinnings of narrative structure. Rockridge's Glenn Smith critiqued the over-reliance on such nuance-less "melodrama" structures in American thought and discourse generally.

15 Lakoff's emphasis on family concepts may be due in part to the American political context, where some powerful radical conservatives are fixated on "traditional family values," including forceful discipline. Conservatives in Canada and elsewhere seem more concerned with the kinds of values Frye and Pinker describe. See Lakoff's discussion of James Dobson's Focus on the Family group as evidence for his Strict Father model (*Don't* 6, *Moral* 182–3, 339–48). However, it has been observed that Stephen Harper too "takes his counsel from the likes of Darrel Reid, the PMO deputy chief of staff and former president of the anti-choice Focus on the Family, as well as the ultra-conservative former Christian educator Paul Wilson, the PMO's director of policy" (Zerbisias). Perhaps in Canada Harper cannot be very open about such affiliations.

16 *Leviathan* also links family metaphors with body politic metaphors in an incidental way, as when colonies are seen as children of the

commonwealth-mother (Part II, chapter 24). There are also links between political and religious family metaphors, as when the right to determine and enforce religious laws, and to interpret the word of God, is assigned to the male sovereign because in the Bible God is the father and speaks only to the fathers of families (especially Abraham and his descendants) (Part III, chapter 40). Someone is exempt from the obligation to obey the sovereign in matters of religion only if they have spoken with God directly. Part III, chapter 42, mentions that monarchy, aristocracy, and democracy mark out three sorts of sovereigns as masters of families, but the only point here is to contrast that paternal role with the role of pastors, who are like schoolmasters for children (577).

17 In Book III, chapter VI, Rousseau pointedly rejects the conjoining of monarchy with the family metaphor. He condemns a sophism used by royalist political theorists, which "consists not only in comparing civil government to household government and the king to the head of a family, an error that has already been refuted, but also in generously attributing to the king all the virtues he should have, and in always assuming that he is what he ought to be" (64).

4. Pastorals with Power

1 New historicism is unusual in being so much identified with the work of one person, Stephen Greenblatt, and his works are the best way to get a sense of the school (see e.g., *Renaissance Self-Fashioning*, *Shakespearean Negotiations*, and *Learning to Curse*, especially the introductions). It is not easy to define the school in terms of a set of principles, since its prime mover is sceptical and suspicious of general principles and theories. Greenblatt discusses his sense of what new historicism is, and how it relates to the major neighbouring theories of post-structuralism and Marxism, in "Towards a Poetics of Culture" (in Veeser, ed., *The New Historicism*, reprinted as chapter 8 in *Learning to Curse*) (see notes 5 and 6, below). Gallagher's collaboration with Greenblatt, *Practicing New Historicism*, provides a valuable account of the origins and later directions of the school (especially the introduction and chapters one and two). Veeser's introductions to his two edited collections on new historicism are useful overviews of the movement. Further, the essays in his *New Historicism* are often refreshingly critical of the titular school (and its various assumptions, post-structuralist, Marxist, Foucauldian, and anthropological). The collection *Cultural Mobility* offers an update and "manifesto" about how to approach cultural study, according to recent developments of the new historicist ideal.

2 An important segment of cognitive critics consider themselves to be undertaking the kind of merger of new historicism and the human sciences of mind that I attempt here (though in different ways). The main proponents of "cognitive historicism" (or "neural historicism," in Richardson's playful coinage) include Mary Crane, Ellen Spolsky, F. Elizabeth Hart, Lisa Zunshine, and Richardson himself. No doubt there are others following in their footsteps. These critics aim to combine some of the insights of post-structuralism with cognitive views of language, thought, behaviour, and culture, and with "contextualist" views manifesting the "hard-won recognition of the historical imperative" (Spolsky, qtd. in Richardson, *Neural* 3), especially new historicist accounts of the deep interweaving of literary texts with non-literary discourses, and with local social and cultural backgrounds shaped by power relations. They trace patterns in cultural history in terms of conceptual structures supplied by cognitive theory. They use these cognitive vocabularies to supplement rather than displace new historicist recourse to vocabularies of power, discursive regimes, ideology, subject formation, performance, etc. These investigations show some promise to address the problems Greenblatt finds so intractable within his own set of assumptions and methods.

3 Although Greenblatt does not mention Frye in this passage, it is easy to see how Frye could be tarred with this brush – he often has been. Another principle Greenblatt rejects, that of avoiding value judgments, was strongly associated with Frye, while other critics at the time rejected (and often misunderstood) it. Greenblatt says the American 1960s and 1970s, especially the opposition to the Vietnam War, decisively shaped his critical practices, and "writing that was not engaged, that withheld judgments, that failed to connect the present with the past seemed worthless" (*Learning* 167). Frye's position is rather that aesthetic value judgments are a side-effect of criticism, and should not be its aim. He does not withhold moral judgments: he sees criticism as a "social and moral struggle" of the genuine mythology of literature against the debased social mythology of cliché and stereotype ("Reflections" 143–4). See Frye's "The University and Personal Life" for his critical remarks on the New Left and the university ferment of the 1960s and 1970s, and his opposition to the Vietnam war (in SM 27–48).

4 Similarly, Cornel West writes:

> I call demystificatory criticism "prophetic criticism" – the approach appropriate for the new cultural politics of difference – because while it begins with social structural analyses it also makes explicit

its moral and political aims ... Yet the aim of this evaluation is neither to pit art-objects against one another like race-horses nor to create eternal canons that dull, discourage, or even dwarf contemporary achievements. We listen to [these artists] not in order to undergird bureaucratic assents or enliven cocktail party conversations, but rather to be summoned by the styles they deploy for their profound insights, pleasures, and challenges. Yet, all evaluation – including a delight in Eliot's poetry despite his reactionary politics, or a love of Zora Neale Hurston's novels despite her Republican party affiliations – is inseparable, though not identical or reducible to social structural analyses, moral and political judgements, and the workings of a curious critical consciousness. The deadly traps of demystification – and any form of prophetic criticism – are those of reductionism, be it of sociological, psychological, or historical sort. (213–14)

5 The way Greenblatt distinguishes his approach on the issue of "the real" from post-structuralism here is reminiscent of some cognitive criticism (e.g., F. Elizabeth Hart, Spolsky, McConachie): the fiction/non-fiction divide is a cognitive factor (mode of reading) with ethical implications rooted in human embodiment. This similarity will help to develop some "cognitive historicist" synthesis, although Greenblatt's understanding of the relation of language to body and world remains highly conventionalist (it is a "contract"). The interest in pleasure and play seems to be another point that distinguishes new historicism from cultural studies and could link it to cognitive criticism dealing with emotion and aesthetic pleasure (e.g., in Hogan). Greenblatt writes, "I am frequently baffled by the tendency especially in those explicitly concerned with historical or ideological functions of art to ignore the analysis of pleasure or, for that matter, of play ... Literature may do important work in the world, but each sentence is not hard labor, and the effectiveness of this work depends upon the ability to delight" (*Learning* 9).

6 Greenblatt also contrasts his approach with Marxism (in Jameson) and post-structuralism (in Lyotard) on the issue of capitalism and culture. He urges a less monolithic view, and rejects Jameson's claim that capitalism demarcates the aesthetic sphere and aligns it with the private, "the psychological, the poetic, and the individual, as distinct from the public, the social, and the political" (*Learning* 148), and Lyotard's claim that capitalism wants to obliterate boundaries between discursive domains. Neither Marxism nor post-structuralism can "come to terms with the apparently contradictory historical effects of capitalism" (151).

7 Hogan effectively critiques the view that research on universals means a hegemonic imposition of one culture's norms on another, and he remarks on the "intellectual and political value of studying universals" (*Mind* 15–16). Indeed, genuine empirical research on universals opposes such naturalizing of false or pseudo-universals offered in bad faith (8–10).

8 Of course, it is tricky to know how far it is possible to take an analogy. Frye does not seem to want to push this one too far. By adaptation to the environment, he seems to mean the literary author's (or the text's) deliberate appeal to the knowledge and attitudes of contemporary readers. But adaptation by natural selection has more to do with things dying out unless and until a random mutation confers an advantage of survival or reproduction on a species. That is, organisms do not adapt during individual lifetimes, and they do not adapt by choice. Nature selects, not organisms. Franco Moretti, however, applies just this kind of extended and detailed evolutionary analogy to literature. He compares surviving genre lineages with extinct ones (e.g., subgenres of the mystery novel), and seeks the reasons for survival in the "genes" of features that survive because they offer some appeal to readers that exceeds that of their competitors (*Graphs* 67–92, on "Trees"; see also Alberto Piazza's afterword on the evolutionary analogy, 95–113).

9 Frye distinguishes four primary concerns, but the exact number may not be that important. It seems that Frye finds four because four is Frye's favourite number. Here, health seems also to be a primary concern, and elsewhere he also speaks of breathing as "the most primary of all primary concerns" (WP 126). One can imagine others. Johnson speaks of intersubjective communication, for example, as primary and essential to human life – not just language but coordination (e.g., between parent and child) of faces, voices, body movements, and more (*Meaning* 36–41).

10 Turner stresses the human scale of narrative and blending (*Literary*), Fludernik sees "experientiality" as characteristic of literary narrative (*Towards*), and Hogan and others stress the emotional aspect of narratives that people consider "prototypical," i.e., "tellable." Herman argues that narrative theory has close affinities with five key concepts from recent discourse psychology: the mind's positioning relative to others, its embodiment, its social distribution, its models of emotion, and its qualia or consciousness ("Narrative Theory").

11 As for Frye's other example, there is no shortage of evidence that the Crucifixion has been invoked and interpreted to support all manner of horrors. Elsewhere he points to how far in another direction its reception might swing: "One sometimes gets the impression that the audience of Plautus

and Terence would have guffawed uproariously all through the Passion" (AC 178).

12 The passage is worth quoting in full. The cognitive approach

> does not distance us from the work (as thoroughgoing historicism might), but ... fuses it with our own horizons (as Gadamer might put it ...). On the other hand, this use of modeling is also historically situated and need not depart from the useful practices of New Historicism. Rather, it shows ways to incorporate history while moving beyond the overburdened historicization that sometimes absorbs all of a critic's attention, leaving little time or energy for the literary work itself or its relevance to contemporary readers and modern life. Too often, staunch New Historicists make historical investigation the end of criticism and theory. In this process, the plays may vanish, and with them their bearing on what we ourselves do outside the classroom or the pages of scholarly journals. Literary criticism and theory cannot forever benefit from losing sight of the aesthetic, linguistic, existential, and political archive that a play itself presents, especially a Shakespearean play. (Pandit and Hogan 4)

13 Hogan's account of how his two plots are variants of a single more basic one is evocative of Frye's ideas about how comedy and tragedy are in a sense parts of a larger total form:

> I use "tragicomedy" to refer to plots that pass through or closely approach an apparently tragic conclusion before resolving happily ... I shall argue that tragicomedy, in this sense, is the fullest and most widespread literary form cross-culturally ... [T]ragedy is not a component of tragicomedy, but a derivative of tragicomedy – in effect, a shortening of tragicomedy. Indeed ... tragedy is only possibly as a failed comedy, for the nature of narrative development is necessarily oriented toward comedy. (24n3)

But he insists he is not proposing a "key to all stories," a "monomyth," or a "duomyth" (101).

14 However, recall that the anagogic level seems to be a perspective that the reader may bring to an individual text. It does not apply directly to particular genres, although it is true that some genres and texts invite this perspective more than others – those that deal with cosmic, religious, or epic themes.

15 There is a personal connection: Hogan was Frye's student in 1977, and worked with him later (Frye contributed an essay to a collection Hogan edited, *Criticism and Lacan*). Hogan acknowledges his debt to Frye, but

observes that it is not as obvious as it may seem. Where their accounts of romantic tragicomedy overlap, neither is greatly original, and their explanatory frameworks are different. Frye influenced him broadly, in "adopting an inductive approach aimed at isolating recurrent literary structures through empirical study of actual literary works" (13n7), but also in sensitizing him to some of their specific structures. He also mentions as influences Frye's commentators, Hayden White, Hernadi, and Todorov.

16 These raise similar questions, which might apply to any effort to discuss "types of structures": what are the limits of "variation"? How far can the structure be pushed and still retain its identity? What is the significance of borderline cases? These questions may be less pressing for Hogan, as he does say stories can be about anything, need not be (very) emotional, and are frequently not of these forms. He also cites cognitive scientific research on how thought is organized in terms of exemplars, prototypes, and schemas – for which issues of strict definition are beside the point.

17 In more detail, Hogan says many formal literary techniques "function to maximize relevance or patterning across encoded properties or relations *with a normative limit at the point where such maximization would surpass the threshold of forced attentional focus*" ("Literary Universals" 240). Suggestion structure is in large part a matter of "the clouds of nondenumerable, nonsubstitutable, nonpropositional suggestions that surround these texts" (*Mind* 51). The production and reception of literature are inseparable from "the patterned, cumulative priming of personal memories" that are "representationally congruent with the literary situations developed in the course of the work," the emotional components of which "serve as the primary source for our empathic emotional response to literary situations" (*Mind* 74–5).

18 Elsewhere, Hogan mistakenly attributes a Jungian view of archetypes to Frye, a common misconception: "I explain these universals by reference to a well-defined, neuro-cognitive account of emotion, not by reference to the semi-mystical, Jungian idea of archetypes" ("Narrative Universals" 61n5).

19 Interestingly, apropos of the tragic figure of the "suppliant," Frye remarks that pathos is "even more terrifying" a mood than tragedy because its "basis is the exclusion of an individual from a group, hence it attacks the deepest fear in ourselves that we possess – a fear much deeper than the relatively cosy and sociable bogey of hell" (AC 217). Perhaps for Frye social exclusion would be the situational prototype for the central negative emotion, and hence the basis of tragic myth, even more than death. However, Frye associates this situation with fear rather than sorrow.

20 However, see Hogan's "Laughing Brains" for a cognitive analysis of humour in literature.

21 In sacrificial narratives, a violation of divine prescriptions leads to a divine/human conflict. Humans overstep proper bounds through arrogance and/or greed, which leads to famine and death (and death imagery). To reconnect human and divine worlds, the community must make a sacrifice, which often involves the institution of a food-related ritual. The sacrifice is often of a human, and it leads to the restoration of plenty by a now benevolent deity (*Mind* 188–9).

22 It is hard to see how the idea of death leading to participation in an afterlife community could be derived directly from body-based universals of experience or emotion, as it is not part of bodily experience. One can certainly see the indirect connections of the idea with those universals, in that primary concerns are largely associated with basic survival, and the idea is motivated by the deep human fear of death and desire for life (as literature is motivated by anxieties around primary concern). The afterlife idea helps people to support and maintain positive emotions and avoid negative emotions. Presumably, the idea of human rebirth after death is to some extent also based on analogy with the emotional experience of renewal in natural cycles (days, seasons, etc.), which makes the corresponding metaphors central in formulating the idea.

23 How deep do these general metaphoric connections go? They are certainly widespread in Western literature, and may well be universals that hold across other traditions. It does not seem extravagant to say that humans universally have experience of the solar cycle and of vegetable life, however widely the particulars of that experience may vary, so it seems natural, and perhaps universal, that these cycles are used to understand human life metaphorically. These metaphors are more appropriate for stories of death than stories of love, as they highlight the passage of time, particularly beginnings and endings, but do not highlight union of two things. Hogan suggests that the connection of bird imagery with his love plot may be a universal, based on the metaphoric association of positive emotions with the direction *up* (*Mind* 26). In any case, the question of what features are universal is an empirical one, but such features likely depend on factors other than the cultural and historical.

24 From the perspective of the reader who does not accept the possibility of such direct correspondence in the real world, those links exist only in the world of the story, and they exist there because the author is using them to convey a meaning that is, for the reader, metaphorical. One

could say, then, that such links are, in such a reader's world, fictional and metaphorical, rather than literal in the sense of representing the reader's reality.

25 On imagery of water of life and death in the Bible, see GC 144–7, and 189–92 on the related imagery of sea creatures (leviathan, fish, and fishing): "Metaphorically, a monster in the sea *is* the sea; hence the landing of the leviathan is much the same thing as the abolition of the sea of death" (190).

26 One should not neglect to condemn the idea of purging "Lycidas" (or any other text) from syllabi or the canon on the suspicion that it might corrupt young minds. In fact, the suggestion is itself a curious kind of textual reception or use that should be investigated and indicted by cultural studies.

27 Rousseau's *Social Contract* similarly criticizes metaphors of rulers as herders. He mentions Grotius, who suggests that

> the human race is divided into herds of cattle, each with a ruler who watches over it in order to devour it.
>
> Since a herder is of a nature superior to that of his herd, the herders of men, their rulers, are of a nature superior to that of their peoples. Such was the reasoning of the Emperor Caligula, as reported by Philo. He concluded from this analogy that either kings were gods or peoples were animals.
>
> Caligula's reasoning is equivalent to that of Hobbes and Grotius. Before any of them, Aristotle had also said that men were not naturally equal, but that some were born to be slaves and others to be masters. (10)

Works Cited

Abrams, M.H. *A Glossary of Literary Terms*. 4th ed. New York: Holt, Rinehart, and Winston, 1981.

Adamson, Joseph. "Northrop Frye, Semiotics, and the Mythological Structure of Imagery." *Recherches sémiotiques/Semiotic Inquiry* 13.3 (1993): 85–100.

---. "The Treason of the Clerks: Frye, Ideology, and the Authority of Imaginative Culture." *Rereading Frye: The Published and Unpublished Works*. Ed. David Boyd and Imre Salusinszky. Toronto: U of Toronto P, 1999. 72–102.

---, ed. *The Educated Imagination*. Website <http://fryeblog.blog.lib.mcmaster.ca/>

---, ed. "Northrop Frye and Contemporary Literary Theory." Special issue, *Recherches sémiotiques/Semiotic Inquiry* 13.3 (1993): 7–116.

Adler, Hans, and Sabine Gross. "Adjusting the Frame: Comments on Cognitivism and Literature." *Poetics Today* 23.2 (2002): 195–220. <http://dx.doi.org/10.1215/03335372-23-2-195>.

Alter, Robert. "Northrop Frye between Archetype and Typology." *Semeia* 89 (2002): 9–21.

Althusser, Louis. "Ideology and Ideological State Apparatuses." *Cultural Theory and Popular Culture: A Reader*. Ed. John Storey. New York: Harvester Wheatsheaf, 1994. 151–62.

Ayre, John. "Frye's Geometry of Thought: Building the Great Wheel." *University of Toronto Quarterly* 70.4 (2001): 825–38. <http://dx.doi.org/10.3138/utq.70.4.825>.

---. "Northrop Frye and the Chart of Symbolism." *Northrop Frye: New Directions from Old*. Ed. David Rampton. U of Ottawa P, 2009. 169–85.

Bai, Matt. "The Framing Wars." *New York Times Magazine* 17 July 2005. 38–45, 68–71.

Barkan, Leonard. *Nature's Work of Art: The Human Body as Image of the World*. New Haven: Yale UP, 1975.

Barthes, Roland. *Mythologies*. 1957. Trans. Annette Lavers. Frogmore: Paladin, 1973.

Bennett, Tony. *Outside Literature*. London: Routledge, 1990.

Berlin, Isaiah. *The Hedgehog and the Fox: An Essay on Tolstoy's View of History*. Chicago: Elephant, 1993.

Bérubé, Michael. *American Airspace*. Weblog. 15 Oct. 2010. <www.michaelberube.com>.

Black, Max. *Models and Metaphors*. Ithaca: Cornell UP, 1962.

Boehrer, Bruce. "'Lycidas': The Pastoral Elegy as Same-Sex Epithalamium." *PMLA* 117.2 (March 2002): 222–36. <http://dx.doi.org/10.1632/003081202X61377>.

Bordwell, David. "A Case for Cognitivism." *Iris* 9 (1989): 11–40.

---. "Contemporary Film Studies and the Vicissitudes of Grand Theory." *Post-Theory: Reconstructing Film Studies*. Ed. David Bordwell and Noël Carroll. Madison: U of Wisconsin P, 1996. 3–36.

---. "Convention, Construction, and Cinematic Vision." *Post-Theory: Reconstructing Film Studies*. Ed. David Bordwell and Noël Carroll. Madison: U of Wisconsin P, 1996. 87–107.

Bordwell, David, and Noël Carroll, eds. *Post-Theory: Reconstructing Film Studies*. Madison: U of Wisconsin P, 1996.

Bourdieu, Pierre. "How Can One Be a Sports Fan?" *The Cultural Studies Reader*. Ed. Simon During. London: Routledge, 1995. 339–56.

Boyd, David, and Imre Salusinszky, eds. *Rereading Frye: The Published and Unpublished Works*. Toronto: U of Toronto P, 1999.

Brooke-Rose, Christine. *A Grammar of Metaphor*. London: Secker & Warburg, 1958.

Brugman, Claudia. "What Is the Invariance Hypothesis?" *Cognitive Linguistics* 1.2 (1990): 257–68. <http://dx.doi.org/10.1515/cogl.1990.1.2.257>.

Burgess, Margaret. "From Archetype to Antitype: A Look at Frygian Archetypology." *Semeia* 89 (2002): 103–24.

Cacciari, Cristina. "Crossing the Senses in Metaphorical Language." *The Cambridge Handbook of Metaphor and Thought*. Ed. Raymond W. Gibbs, Jr. Cambridge: Cambridge UP, 2008. 425–43.

Carroll, Noël. "Prospects for Film Theory: A Personal Assessment." *Post-Theory: Reconstructing Film Studies*. Ed. David Bordwell and Noël Carroll. Madison: U of Wisconsin P, 1996. 37–68.

Carveth, Donald. "The Analyst's Metaphors: A Deconstructionist Perspective." *PsyArt: A Hyperlink Journal for the Psychological Study of the Arts*. 1984.

19 September 2001. 21 June 2004 <http://www.psyartjournal.com/article/show/l_carveth-metaphor_and_psychoanalysis_the_analysts>.

Chamberlin, J. Edward. "Mathematics and Modernism." *The Legacy of Northrop Frye*. Ed. Alvin A. Lee and Robert Denham. Toronto: U of Toronto P, 1994. 230–40.

Cienki, Alan. "Some Properties and Groupings of Image Schemas." *Lexical and Syntactic Constructions and the Construction of Meaning*. Ed. Marjolijn Verspoor, Kee Dong Lee, and Eve Sweetser. Amsterdam: John Benjamins, 1997. 3–15.

Clancey, William J. "Folk Theory of the Social Mind: Policies, Principles, and Foundational Metaphors." *Proceedings of the 27th Annual Meeting of the Cognitive Science Society*, July 2005. Ed. Bruno G. Bara, Lawrence Barsalou, and Monica Bucciarelli. Mahwah: Lawrence Erlbaum. 465–70. Accessed January 2008 <http://bill.clancey.name/>.

Cook, Eleanor, Chaviva Hošek, Jay Macpherson, et al., eds. *Centre and Labyrinth: Essays in Honour of Northrop Frye*. Toronto: U of Toronto P, 1983.

Cornford, Francis M. *The Origin of Attic Comedy*. 1914. Cambridge: Cambridge UP, 1934.

Cotrupi, Caterina Nella. *Northrop Frye and the Poetics of Process*. Toronto: U of Toronto P, 2000.

Culler, Jonathan. *Structuralist Poetics: Structuralism, Linguistics, and the Study of Literature*. London: Routledge & Kegan Paul, 1975. <http://dx.doi.org/10.4324/9780203449769>.

Curtius, Ernst Robert. *European Literature and the Latin Middle Ages*. Trans. Willard R. Trask. New York: Harper Torchbooks–Harper & Row, 1963.

Dante. (Dante Alighieri). *The Divine Comedy: Inferno, Purgatory, Paradise* (3 vols.). 1314–21. Trans. Mark Musa. New York: Penguin, 1984.

De Certeau, Michel. "The Practice of Everyday Life." *Cultural Theory and Popular Culture: A Reader*. Ed. John Storey. New York: Harvester Wheatsheaf, 1994. 474–85.

Denham, Robert. "Auguries of Influence." *Visionary Poetics: Essays on Northrop Frye's Criticism*. Ed. Robert Denham and Thomas Willard. New York: Peter Lang, 1991. 77–99.

---. "Frye's International Presence." *The Legacy of Northrop Frye*. Ed. Alvin Lee and Robert Denham. Toronto: U of Toronto P, 1994. xxvii–xxxii.

---. "Interpenetration as a Key Concept in Frye's Critical Vision." *Rereading Frye: The Published and Unpublished Works*. Ed. David Boyd and Imre Salusinszky. Toronto: U of Toronto P, 1999. 140–63.

---. *Northrop Frye: An Annotated Bibliography of Primary and Secondary Sources*. Toronto: U of Toronto P, 1987.

---. *Northrop Frye: Religious Visionary and Architect of the Spiritual World*. Charlottesville: U of Virginia P, 2004.

---. *Northrop Frye and Critical Method*. University Park: Pennsylvania State UP, 1978.

---. *The Northrop Frye Handbook: A Biographical and Bibliographical Guide*. E-book. Jefferson, NC: McFarland, 2011.

---. "'Pity the Northrop Frye Scholar'? *Anatomy of Criticism* Fifty Years After." *Northrop Frye: New Directions from Old*. Ed. David Rampton. U of Ottawa P, 2009. 15–34.

---, ed. *Northrop Frye Newsletter*. Salem: English Department, Roanoke College.

Denham, Robert, and Thomas Willard, eds. *Visionary Poetics: Essays on Northrop Frye's Criticism*. New York: Peter Lang, 1991.

Dirven, René, Roslyn Frank, and Martin Pütz, eds. *Cognitive Models in Language and Thought: Ideology, Metaphors and Meanings*. Berlin: Mouton de Gruyter, 2003.

Dolzani, Michael. "The Book of the Dead: A Skeleton Key to Northrop Frye's Notebooks." *Rereading Frye: The Published and Unpublished Works*. Ed. David Boyd and Imre Salusinszky. Toronto: U of Toronto P, 1999. 19–38.

---. "The Infernal Method: Northrop Frye and Contemporary Criticism." *Centre and Labyrinth: Essays in Honour of Northrop Frye*. Ed. Eleanor Cook, Chaviva Hošek, Jay Macpherson, et al. Toronto: U of Toronto P, 1983. 59–68.

---. "Introduction." *The "Third Book" Notebooks of Northrop Frye, 1964–1972: The Critical Comedy*. Ed. Michael Dolzani. Toronto: U of Toronto P, 2002. xix–lvi.

---. "Wrestling with Powers: The Social Thought of Frye." *The Legacy of Northrop Frye*. Ed. Alvin Lee and Robert Denham. Toronto: U of Toronto P, 1994. 97–102.

During, Simon, ed. *The Cultural Studies Reader*. London: Routledge, 1995.

Ekberg, Lena. "The Mental Manipulation of the Vertical Axis: How to Go from 'Up' to 'Out', or from 'Above' to 'Behind'." *Lexical and Syntactic Constructions and the Construction of Meaning*. Ed. Marjolijn Verspoor, Kee Dong Lee, and Eve Sweetser. Amsterdam: John Benjamins, 1997. 69–88.

Eliade, Mircea. *The Myth of the Eternal Return or, Cosmos and History*. Trans. Willard R. Trask. Princeton: Princeton UP, 1954.

Evans, J. Martin. "*Lycidas*." *The Cambridge Companion to Milton*. Ed. Dennis Danielson. Cambridge: Cambridge UP, 1999. 39–53. <http://dx.doi.org/10.1017/CCOL052165226X.003>.

Fauconnier, Gilles. *Mappings in Thought and Language*. Cambridge: Cambridge UP, 1997.

Fauconnier, Gilles, and Mark Turner. "Conceptual Integration Networks." *Cognitive Science* 22.2 (April–June 1998): 133–87.

---. "Conceptual Projection and Middle Spaces." San Diego: University of California, Department of Cognitive Science Technical Report 9401, 1994. 27 Oct. 2008 <http://ssrn.com/abstract=1290862>.

---. "Rethinking Metaphor." *The Cambridge Handbook of Metaphor and Thought*. Ed. Raymond Gibbs, Jr. New York: Cambridge UP, 2008. 53–66.

---. *The Way We Think: Conceptual Blending and the Mind's Hidden Complexities*. New York: Basic Books, 2003.

Fletcher, Angus. *Allegory: The Theory of a Symbolic Mode*. Ithaca: Cornell UP, 1964.

Fludernik, Monika. "Narratology in the Twenty-First Century: The Cognitive Approach to Narrative." *PMLA* 125.4 (October 2010): 924–30. <http://dx.doi.org/10.1632/pmla.2010.125.4.924>.

---. *Towards a 'Natural' Narratology*. London: Routledge, 1996. <http://dx.doi.org/10.4324/9780203432501>.

---, ed. *Beyond Cognitive Metaphor Theory: Perspectives on Literary Metaphor*. New York: Routledge, 2011.

Fludernik, Monika, Donald C. Freeman, and Margaret H. Freeman, eds. "Metaphor and Beyond: New Cognitive Developments." Special issue, *Poetics Today* 20.3 (1999).

Forst, Graham Nicol. "Kant and Frye on the Critical Path." *Northrop Frye: Eastern and Western Perspectives*. Ed. Jean O'Grady and Wang Ning. Toronto: U of Toronto P, 2003. 19–28.

Foucault, Michel. *The Archaeology of Knowledge and the Discourse on Language*. Trans. A.M. Sheridan Smith. New York: Pantheon, 1972.

---. *The Order of Things: An Archaeology of the Human Sciences*. 1966. London: Routledge, 2008.

---. "Space, Power and Knowledge." *The Cultural Studies Reader*. Ed. Simon During. London: Routledge, 1995. 161–9.

Freeman, Donald. "'The rack dislimns': Schema and Metaphorical Pattern in *Antony and Cleopatra*." *Poetics Today* 20.3 (1999): 443–60.

Freeman, Margaret. "Metaphor Making Meaning: Dickinson's Conceptual Universe." *Journal of Pragmatics* 24.6 (1995): 643–66. <http://dx.doi.org/10.1016/0378-2166(95)00006-E>.

Frow, John. *Genre*. New Critical Idiom Series. Ed. John Drakakis. London: Routledge, 2006.

Frye, Northrop. *Anatomy of Criticism: Four Essays*. 1957. Princeton: Princeton UP, 1971.

---. *Creation and Recreation*. Toronto: U of Toronto P, 1980.

---. *The Critical Path: An Essay on the Social Context of Literary Criticism*. Bloomington: Indiana UP, 1971.

---. *The Double Vision: Language and Meaning in Religion*. Toronto: U of Toronto P, 1991.

---. *Fables of Identity: Studies in Poetic Mythology*. New York: Harcourt, Brace & World, 1963.

---. *Fearful Symmetry: A Study of William Blake*. Princeton: Princeton UP, 1947.

---. *The Great Code: The Bible and Literature*. Orlando: Harcourt Brace Jovanovich, 1981.

---. *Myth and Metaphor: Selected Essays, 1974–1988*. Ed. Robert D. Denham. Charlottesville: UP of Virginia, 1990.

---. "On Teaching Literature." *Northrop Frye's Writings on Education*. Ed. Jean O'Grady and Goldwin French. Toronto: U of Toronto P, 2000. 432–61.

---. "Reflections in a Mirror." *Northrop Frye in Modern Criticism: Selected Papers from the English Institute*. Ed. Murray Krieger. New York: Columbia UP, 1966. 133–46.

---. *The Return of Eden: Five Essays on Milton's Epics*. Toronto: U of Toronto P, 1965.

---. *The Secular Scripture: A Study of the Structure of Romance*. Cambridge: Harvard UP, 1976.

---. *Spiritus Mundi: Essays on Literature, Myth and Society*. 1976. Richmond Hill: Fitzhenry & Whiteside, 1991.

---. *The Stubborn Structure: Essays on Criticism and Society*. Ithaca: Cornell UP, 1970.

---. *T.S. Eliot*. New York: Grove Press, 1963.

---. *Words with Power: Being a Second Study of "The Bible and Literature."* Orlando: Harcourt Brace Jovanovich, 1990.

Gallagher, Catherine, and Stephen Greenblatt. *Practicing New Historicism*. Chicago: U of Chicago P, 2000.

Gallese, Vittorio. "Mirror Neurons." *The Oxford Companion to Consciousness*. Ed. Tim Bayne, Axel Cleeremans, and Patrick Wilken. Oxford: Oxford UP, 2009. 445–6.

Gavins, Joanna, and Gerard Steen, eds. *Cognitive Poetics in Practice*. London: Routledge, 2003. <http://dx.doi.org/10.4324/9780203417737>.

Geeraerts, Dirk. "Cognitive Semantics and the History of Philosophical Epistemology." *Conceptualizations and Mental Processing in Language*. Ed. R. Geiger and B. Rudzka-Ostyn. Berlin & New York: Mouton de Gruyter, 1993. 53–79.

Geertz, Clifford. "Deep Play: Notes on the Balinese Cockfight." *The Interpretation of Cultures: Selected Essays*. New York: Basic Books, 1973. 412–53.

Geiger, R., and B. Rudzka-Ostyn, eds. *Conceptualizations and Mental Processing in Language*. Berlin & New York: Mouton de Gruyter, 1993.

Gibbs, Raymond W., Jr. "Metaphor and Thought: The State of the Art." *The Cambridge Handbook of Metaphor and Thought*. Ed. Raymond W. Gibbs, Jr. Cambridge: Cambridge UP, 2008. 3–13.

---. *The Poetics of Mind: Figurative Thought, Language, and Understanding*. Cambridge: Cambridge UP, 1994.

---, ed. *The Cambridge Handbook of Metaphor and Thought*. Cambridge: Cambridge UP, 2008.

Gibbs, Raymond W., Jr., and Herbert Colston. "The Cognitive Psychological Reality of Image Schemas and Their Transformations." *Cognitive Linguistics* 6.4 (1995): 347–78. <http://dx.doi.org/10.1515/cogl.1995.6.4.347>.

Gibbs, Raymond, Jr., and Gerard Steen, eds. *Metaphor in Cognitive Linguistics. Selected Papers from the Fifth International Cognitive Linguistics Conference, Amsterdam, July 1997*. Amsterdam: John Benjamins, 1999.

Gill, Glen. "The Flesh Made Word: Body and Spirit in the New Archetypology of Northrop Frye." *Frye and the Word: Religious Contexts in the Writings of Northrop Frye*. Ed. Jeffery Donaldson and Alan Mendelson. Toronto: U of Toronto P, 2004. 123–36.

---. *Northrop Frye and the Phenomenology of Myth*. Toronto: U of Toronto P, 2006.

Giroux, Henry. "Resisting Difference: Cultural Studies and the Discourse of Critical Pedagogy." *Cultural Studies*. Ed. Lawrence Grossberg, Cary Nelson, and Paula A. Treichler. New York: Routledge, 1992. 199–212.

Goffman, Erving. *The Presentation of Self in Everyday Life*. New York: Doubleday, 1959.

Goldstein, Evan R. "Who Framed George Lakoff?" *The Chronicle of Higher Education*. 15 August 2008. <http://chronicle.com/article/Who-Framed-George-Lakoff-/24778/>.

Grady, Joe, Sarah Taub, and Pamela Morgan. "Primitive and Compound Metaphors." *Conceptual Structure, Discourse, and Language*. Ed. Adele E. Goldberg. Stanford: CSLI, 1996. 177–88.

Gramsci, Antonio. "Hegemony, Intellectuals and the State." *Cultural Theory and Popular Culture: A Reader*. Ed. John Storey. New York: Harvester Wheatsheaf, 1994. 215–21.

Graves, Robert. *The White Goddess: A Historical Grammar of Poetic Myth*. London: Faber and Faber, 1952.

Greenblatt, Stephen. "Cultural Mobility: An Introduction." *Cultural Mobility: A Manifesto*. Stephen Greenblatt, with Ines G. Županov, Reinhard Meyer-Kalkus, Heike Paul, Pál Nyíri, and Friederike Pannewick. Cambridge: Cambridge UP, 2010. 1–23.

---. "The Improvisation of Power." *The New Historicism Reader*. Ed. H. Aram Veeser. New York: Routledge, 1994. 46–87.

---. "Introduction." *Genre*: Special Topics 7 (1982): 3–6.

---. *Learning to Curse: Essays in Early Modern Culture*. New York: Routledge, 1990.

---. *Renaissance Self-Fashioning: From More to Shakespeare*. Chicago: U of Chicago P, 1980.

---. *Shakespearian Negotiations: The Circulation of Social Energy in Renaissance England*. Oxford: Clarendon Press, 1988.

---. "Theatrical Mobility." *Cultural Mobility: A Manifesto*. Stephen Greenblatt, with Ines G. Županov, Reinhard Meyer-Kalkus, Heike Paul, Pál Nyíri, and Friederike Pannewick. Cambridge: Cambridge UP, 2010. 75–95.

Greenblatt, Stephen, with Ines G. Županov, Reinhard Meyer-Kalkus, Heike Paul, Pál Nyíri, and Friederike Pannewick. *Cultural Mobility: A Manifesto*. Cambridge: Cambridge UP, 2010.

Gross, Sabine. "Cognitive Readings; or, The Disappearance of Literature in the Mind." Rev. of *Reading Minds: The Study of English in the Age of Cognitive Science*, by Mark Turner (1994). *Poetics Today* 18.2 (1997): 271–97. <http://dx.doi.org/10.2307/1773435>.

Grossberg, Lawrence, Cary Nelson, and Paula A. Treichler, eds. *Cultural Studies*. New York: Routledge, 1992.

Grush, Rick, and Nili Mandelblit. "Blending in Language, Conceptual Structure, and the Cerebral Cortex." *International Journal of Linguistics Acta Linguistica Hafniensia* 29 (1998): 221–37. <http://mind.ucsd.edu/>.

Hall, Stuart. "Cultural Studies and Its Theoretical Legacies." *Cultural Studies*. Ed. Lawrence Grossberg, Cary Nelson, and Paula A. Treichler. New York: Routledge, 1992. 277–94.

---. "Encoding, Decoding." *The Cultural Studies Reader*. Ed. Simon During. London: Routledge, 1995. 90–103.

---. "Notes on Deconstructing 'the Popular'." *Cultural Theory and Popular Culture: A Reader*. Ed. John Storey. New York: Harvester Wheatsheaf, 1994. 455–66.

---. "The Toad in the Garden: Thatcherism among the Theorists." *Marxism and the Interpretation of Culture*. Ed. Cary Nelson and Lawrence Grossberg. Urbana: U of Illinois P, 1988. 35–57.

Hamilton, A.C. "The Legacy of Frye's Criticism in Culture, Religion, and Society." *The Legacy of Northrop Frye*. Ed. Alvin Lee and Robert Denham. Toronto: U of Toronto P, 1994. 3–14.

---. *Northrop Frye: Anatomy of His Criticism*. Toronto: U of Toronto P, 1990.

---. "Northrop Frye and the Literary Canon." *English Studies in Canada* 19.2 (June 1993): 179–93.

---. "Northrop Frye and the New Historicism." Special issue, *Recherches sémiotiques/ Semiotic Inquiry* 13.3 (1993): 73–83.

---. "Northrop Frye as a Cultural Theorist." *Rereading Frye: The Published and Unpublished Works*. Ed. David Boyd and Imre Salusinszky. Toronto: U of Toronto P, 1999. 103–21.

Hammil, Carrie Esther. *The Celestial Journey and the Harmony of the Spheres in English Literature 1300–1700*. Fort Worth: Texas Christian UP, 1980.

Hampe, Beate, ed. (with Joseph Grady). *From Perception to Meaning: Image Schemas in Cognitive Linguistics*. Berlin: Mouton de Gruyter, 2005.

Hart, F. Elizabeth. "Embodied Literature: A Cognitive-Poststructuralist Approach to Genre." *The Work of Fiction: Cognition, Culture, and Complexity*. Ed. Alan Richardson and Ellen Spolsky. Burlington: Ashgate, 2004. 85–106.

Hart, Jonathan. *Northrop Frye: The Theoretical Imagination*. London: Routledge, 1994.

Hebdige, Dick. "From Culture to Hegemony." *The Cultural Studies Reader*. Ed. Simon During. London: Routledge, 1995. 357–67.

Herman, David. "Narrative Theory after the Second Cognitive Revolution." *Introduction to Cognitive Cultural Studies*. Ed. Lisa Zunshine. Baltimore: Johns Hopkins UP, 2010. 155–75.

---, *Story Logic: Problems and Possibilities of Narrative*. Lincoln: U of Nebraska P, 2002.

---, ed. *Narrative Theory and the Cognitive Sciences*. Stanford: CSLI, 2003.

Hernadi, Paul. *Beyond Genre: New Directions in Literary Classification*. Ithaca: Cornell UP, 1972.

---. "Entertaining Commitments: A Reception Theory of Literary Genres." *Poetics* 10.2–3 (June 1981): 195–211. <http://dx.doi.org/10.1016/0304-422X(81)90034-6>.

---. "On Cognition, Interpretation, and the Survival of Literature: A Response to Hans Adler and Sabine Gross." *Poetics Today* 24.2 (2003): 185–90. <http://dx.doi.org/10.1215/03335372-24-2-185>.

Hobbes, Thomas. *Leviathan*. 1651. Ed. C.B. Macpherson. Harmondsworth: Penguin Books, 1968.

Hogan, Patrick Colm."The Brain in Love: A Case Study in Cognitive Neuroscience and Literary Theory." *Journal of Literary Theory* 1.2 (2007): 339–55. <http://dx.doi.org/10.1515/JLT.2007.021>.

---. *Cognitive Science, Literature, and the Arts: A Guide for Humanists*. New York: Routledge, 2003.

---. "Laughing Brains: On the Cognitive Mechanisms and Reproductive Functions of Mirth." *Semiotica* 2007.165 (2007): 391–408. <http://dx.doi.org/10.1515/SEM.2007.049>.

---. "Literary Universals." *Poetics Today* 18.2 (1997): 223–49. <http://dx.doi.org/10.2307/1773433>.

---. *The Mind and Its Stories: Narrative Universals and Human Emotion.* Cambridge: Cambridge UP, 2003. <http://dx.doi.org/10.1017/CBO9780511499951>.

---. "Narrative Universals, Heroic Tragi-Comedy, and Shakespeare's Political Ambivalence." *College Literature* 33.1 (2006): 34–66. <http://dx.doi.org/10.1353/lit.2006.0007>.

---. "On Being Moved: Cognition and Emotion in Literature and Film." *Introduction to Cognitive Cultural Studies.* Ed. Lisa Zunshine. Baltimore: Johns Hopkins UP, 2010. 237–56.

Holland, Dorothy, and Naomi Quinn, eds. *Cultural Models in Language and Thought.* Cambridge: Cambridge UP, 1986.

Holland, Norman. "Books, Brains, and Bodies." Presented at the State University of New York at New Paltz, 15 April 1998, and Bogaziçi University (Istanbul) on 28 May 1998. <http://www.clas.ufl.edu/users/nholland/bksbrns.htm>.

---. *The Critical I.* New York: Columbia UP, 1992. <http://www.clas.ufl.edu/users/nholland/criti.htm>.

---. "The Trouble(s) with Lacan." *Literature and Psychology: Proceedings of the Seventh International Conference on Literature and Psychology, Urbino, July 6–9, 1990.* Lisbon: Instituto Superior de Psicologia Aplicada, 1991. 3–10. <http://www.clas.ufl.edu/users/nholland/lacan.htm>.

Hutcheon, Linda. "Frye Recoded: Postmodernity and the Conclusions." *The Legacy of Northrop Frye.* Ed. Alvin Lee and Robert Denham. Toronto: U of Toronto P, 1994. 105–21.

Jackendoff, Ray, and David Aaron. Review article of *More Than Cool Reason: A Field Guide to Poetic Metaphor* by George Lukoff and Mark Turner. *Language* 67.2 (1991): 320–38. <http://dx.doi.org/10.2307/415109>.

Jackson, Leonard. *The Poverty of Structuralism: Literature and Structuralist Theory.* New York: Longman, 1991.

Jackson, Tony. "'Literary Interpretation' and Cognitive Literary Studies." *Poetics Today* 24.2 (2003): 191–205. <http://dx.doi.org/10.1215/03335372-24-2-191>.

Jäkel, Olaf. "Kant, Blumenberg, Weinrich: Some Forgotten Contributions to the Cognitive Theory of Metaphor." *Metaphor in Cognitive Linguistics.* Ed. Raymond Gibbs, Jr., and Gerard Steen. Amsterdam: John Benjamins, 1999. 9–27.

Jameson, Fredric. "On Goffman's *Frame Analysis.*" *Theory and Society* 3.1 (1976): 119–33. <http://dx.doi.org/10.1007/BF00158482>.

---. *The Political Unconscious: Narrative as a Socially Symbolic Act*. Ithaca: Cornell UP, 1981.

Johnson, Mark. *The Body in the Mind: The Bodily Basis of Meaning, Imagination, and Reason*. Chicago: U of Chicago P, 1987.

---. *The Meaning of the Body: Aesthetics of Human Understanding*. Chicago: U of Chicago P, 2007.

Johnson, Samuel. "From *Milton*." *Rasselas, Poems, and Selected Prose*. Ed. Bertrand H. Bronson. New York: Holt, Rinehart and Winston, 1965. 446–69.

Kennedy, John M. "Metaphor and Art." *The Cambridge Handbook of Metaphor and Thought*. Ed. Raymond W. Gibbs, Jr. Cambridge: Cambridge UP, 2008. 447–61.

Kimmel, Michael. "From Metaphor to the 'Mental Sketchpad': Literary Macrostructure and Compound Image Schemas in *Heart of Darkness*." *Metaphor and Symbol* 20.3 (2005): 199–238. <http://dx.doi.org/10.1207/s15327868ms2003_3>.

Kövecses, Zoltán. *Metaphor and Emotion: Language, Culture, and Body in Human Feeling*. Cambridge: Cambridge UP, 2000.

Krieger, Murray. "Northrop Frye and Contemporary Criticism: Ariel and the Spirit of Gravity." *Northrop Frye in Modern Criticism: Selected Papers from the English Institute*. Ed. Murray Krieger. New York: Columbia UP, 1966. 1–26.

---, ed. *Northrop Frye in Modern Criticism: Selected Papers from the English Institute*. New York: Columbia UP, 1966.

Kristeva, Julia. "The Importance of Frye." Trans. Joseph Adamson. *The Legacy of Northrop Frye*. Ed. Alvin Lee and Robert Denham. Toronto: U of Toronto P, 1994. 335–37.

Krzeszowski, Tomasz P. "The Axiological Parameter in Preconceptual Image Schemata." *Conceptualizations and Mental Processing in Language*. Ed. R. Geiger and B. Rudzka-Ostyn. Berlin & New York: Mouton de Gruyter, 1993. 307–30. <http://dx.doi.org/10.1515/9783110857108.307>.

Kuhn, Thomas S. *The Structure of Scientific Revolutions*. 2nd ed. Chicago: U of Chicago P, 1970.

Lakoff, George. "Beyond Beauty and Wonder: Understanding the Mind Is Necessary to Understanding Politics." The Rockridge Institute. 30 October 2006. <http://georgelakoff.com/writings/rockridge>.

---. "The Contemporary Theory of Metaphor." *Metaphor and Thought*. Ed. Andrew Ortony. 2nd ed. Cambridge: Cambridge UP, 1993. 202–51.

---. "Defending Freedom. A Response to Steven Pinker." *The New Republic* 16 Oct. 2006. <http://www.tnr.com>.

---. *Don't Think of an Elephant!: Know Your Values and Frame the Debate*. White River Junction: Chelsea Green, 2004.

---. "How Unconscious Metaphorical Thought Shapes Dreams." *PsyArt: A Hyperlink Journal for the Psychological Study of the Arts*, 18 December 2001. 21 June 2004 <http://www.psyartjournal.com/article/show/lakoff-metaphor_and_psychoanalysis_how_metaphor>.

---. "The Invariance Hypothesis: Is Abstract Reason Based on Image-Schemas?" *Cognitive Linguistics* 1.1 (1990): 39–74. <http://dx.doi.org/10.1515/cogl.1990.1.1.39>.

---. "Metaphor and War: The Metaphor System Used to Justify War in the Gulf." 1991. E-mail. <http://georgelakoff.com/writings/allwritings/>.

---. *Moral Politics: How Liberals and Conservatives Think*. 2nd ed. Chicago: U of Chicago P, 2002.

---. "The Neural Theory of Metaphor." *The Cambridge Handbook of Metaphor and Thought*. Ed. Raymond W. Gibbs, Jr. Cambridge: Cambridge UP, 2008. 17–38.

---. *The Political Mind: Why You Can't Understand 21st-Century American Politics with an 18th-Century Brain*. New York: Viking, 2008.

---. *Whose Freedom? The Battle over America's Most Important Idea*. New York: Farrar, Strauss and Giroux, 2006.

---. *Women, Fire and Dangerous Things: What Categories Reveal about the Mind*. Chicago: U of Chicago P, 1987.

Lakoff, George, and Mark Johnson. "Afterword, 2003." *Metaphors We Live By*. 2nd ed. Chicago: U of Chicago P, 2003. 243–76.

---. *Metaphors We Live By*. 2nd ed. Chicago: U of Chicago P, 2003.

---. *Philosophy in the Flesh: The Embodied Mind and Its Challenge to Western Thought*. New York: Basic Books, 1999.

Lakoff, George, and Mark Turner. *More Than Cool Reason: A Field Guide to Poetic Metaphor*. Chicago: U of Chicago P, 1989.

Lakoff, George, and Rafael Núñez. *Where Mathematics Comes From: How the Embodied Mind Brings Mathematics into Being*. New York: Basic Books, 2000.

Lakoff, George, and the Rockridge Institute. *Thinking Points: Communicating Our American Values and Vision*. New York: Farrar, Straus and Giroux, 2006.

Langacker, Ronald W. *Concept, Image, and Symbol: The Cognitive Basis of Grammar*. Berlin: Mouton de Gruyter, 1990.

Lee, Alvin, and Robert Denham, eds. *The Legacy of Northrop Frye*. Toronto: U of Toronto P, 1994.

Lewis, C.S. *The Discarded Image: An Introduction to Medieval and Renaissance Literature*. London: Cambridge UP, 1964.

Livingston, Paisley. *Literary Knowledge: Humanistic Inquiry and the Philosophy of Science*. Ithaca: Cornell UP, 1988.

Lodge, David. *Consciousness and the Novel: Connected Essays.* Cambridge: Harvard UP, 2002.

Lovejoy, Arthur O. *The Great Chain of Being: A Study of the History of an Idea.* The William James Lectures delivered at Harvard University, 1933. Cambridge: Harvard UP, 1957.

Lukács, George. *The Theory of the Novel: A Historico-philosophical Essay on the Forms of Great Epic Literature.* 1920. Cambridge: The MIT Press, 1989.

MacCormac, Earl R. *A Cognitive Theory of Metaphor.* Cambridge: The MIT Press, 1985.

Mandler, Jean. "How to Build a Baby: II. Conceptual Primitives." *Psychological Review* 99.4 (Oct. 1992): 587–604. <http://dx.doi.org/10.1037/0033-295X.99.4.587. Medline:1454900>.

McConachie, Bruce. "Toward a Cognitive Cultural Hegemony." *Introduction to Cognitive Cultural Studies.* Ed. Lisa Zunshine. Baltimore: Johns Hopkins UP, 2010. 134–50.

McConachie, Bruce, and F. Elizabeth Hart, eds. *Performance and Cognition: Theatre Studies and the Cognitive Turn.* London: Routledge, 2006.

McRobbie, Angela. "Post-Marxism and Cultural Studies: A Post-script." *Cultural Studies.* Ed. Lawrence Grossberg, Cary Nelson, and Paula A. Treichler. New York: Routledge, 1992. 719–30.

Miall, David. "The Body in Literature: Mark Johnson, Metaphor, and Feeling." *Journal of Literary Semantics* 26.3 (1997): 191–210. <http://dx.doi.org/10.1515/jlse.1997.26.3.191>.

Milton, John. "Lycidas." *John Milton: A Critical Edition of the Major Works.* Ed. Stephen Orgel and Jonathan Goldberg. Oxford: Oxford UP, 1991. 39–44.

Montrose, Louis Adrian. "'Eliza, Queen of Shepheardes,' and the Pastoral of Power." *The New Historicism Reader.* Ed. H. Aram Veeser. New York: Routledge, 1994. 88–115.

Moore, Kevin. "Deixis and the FRONT/BACK Opposition in Temporal Metaphors." *Conceptual and Discourse Factors in Linguistic Structure.* Ed. Alan Cienki, Barbara J. Luka, and Michael Smith. Stanford: CSLI Publications, 2001. 153–67.

Moretti, Franco. *Graphs, Maps, Trees: Abstract Models for a Literary History.* London: Verso, 2005.

---. *Signs Taken for Wonders: On the Sociology of Literary Forms.* 1983. London: Verso, 2005.

Morris, Meaghan. "Things to Do with Shopping Centres." *The Cultural Studies Reader.* Ed. Simon During. London: Routledge, 1995. 295–319.

Musa, Mark. "An Introduction to Dante and His Works." *The Divine Comedy, vol. I: Inferno.* Dante Alighieri. Trans. Mark Musa. New York: Penguin, 1984. 15–55.

---. "Introduction to the *Paradise.*" *The Divine Comedy, vol. III: Paradise.* Dante Alighieri. Trans. Mark Musa. New York: Penguin, 1986. ix–xxix.

---. "Introduction to the *Purgatory*." *The Divine Comedy, vol. II: Purgatory*. Dante Alighieri. Trans. Mark Musa. New York: Penguin, 1985. ix–xxiv.

Nelson, Cary, Paula A. Treichler, and Lawrence Grossberg. "Cultural Studies: An Introduction." *Cultural Studies*. Ed. Lawrence Grossberg, Cary Nelson, and Paula A. Treichler. New York: Routledge, 1992. 1–22.

Ning, Wang. "Northrop Frye and Cultural Studies." *Northrop Frye: Eastern and Western Perspectives*. Ed. Jean O'Grady and Wang Ning. Toronto: U of Toronto P, 2003. 82–91.

Norris, Christopher. "On Noam Chomsky: Language, Truth and Politics." *Theoria* 91 (1998): 45–52.

Ortony, Andrew, ed. *Metaphor and Thought*. 2nd ed. Cambridge: Cambridge UP, 1993.

Pandit, Lalita, and Patrick Colm Hogan. "Introduction: Morsels and Modules: On Embodying Cognition in Shakespeare's Plays." *College Literature* 33.1 (2006): 1–13. <http://dx.doi.org/10.1353/lit.2006.0004>.

Pettersson, Bo. "Afterword: Cognitive Literary Studies: Where to Go from Here." *Cognition and Literary Interpretation in Practice*. Ed. Harri Veivo, Bo Pettersson, and Merja Polvinen. Helsinki: Helsinki UP, 2005. 307–22.

---. "Literary Criticism Writes Back to Metaphor Theory: Exploring the Relation between Extended Metaphor and Narrative in Literature." *Beyond Cognitive Metaphor Theory: Perspectives on Literary Metaphor*. Ed. Monika Fludernik. New York: Routledge, 2011.

Pinker, Steven. "Angels and Demons: A Response to George Lakoff." *The New Republic* 19 Oct. 2006. <http://www.tnr.com/>.

---. *The Blank Slate: The Modern Denial of Human Nature*. New York: Viking Penguin, 2002.

---. "Block That Metaphor! A Review." Rev. of *Whose Freedom?: The Battle over America's Most Important Idea*, by George Lakoff. *The New Republic* 2 Oct. 2006. <http://www.tnr.com/>.

---. "Metaphorical Limits: George Lakoff's Tendentious Theory of Everything." *The New Republic* 3 Nov. 2006. <http://www.tnr.com/>.

Pound, Ezra. *Jefferson and/or Mussolini: L'idea Statale: Fascism as I Have Seen It*. New York: Liveright, 1970.

Quintero, Ruben, ed. *A Companion to Satire*. Malden: Blackwell, 2007.

Radway, Janice. "The Institutional Matrix of Romance." *The Cultural Studies Reader*. Ed. Simon During. London: Routledge, 1995. 438–54.

---. "Reading *Reading the Romance*." *Cultural Theory and Popular Culture: A Reader*. Ed. John Storey. New York: Harvester Wheatsheaf, 1994. 284–301.

Ramachandran, V.S., and E.M. Hubbard. "Synaesthesia – A Window into Perception, Thought and Language." *Journal of Consciousness Studies* 8.12 (2001): 3–34.

Reddy, Michael J. "The Conduit Metaphor – A Case of Frame Conflict in Our Language about Language." *Metaphor and Thought*. Ed. Andrew Ortony. 2nd ed. Cambridge: Cambridge UP, 1981. 164–201.

Revard, Stella P. "Alpheus, Arethusa, and the Pindaric Pursuit in *Lycidas*." *Of Poetry and Politics: New Essays on Milton and His World*. Ed. P.G. Stanwood. Binghamton: Medieval & Renaissance Texts and Studies, 1995. 35–45.

Rice, Claiborne, ed. *Cognitive Approaches to Literature*. Website. <http://www.ucs.louisiana.edu/~cxr1086/coglit/index.html>.

Richardson, Alan. *The Neural Sublime: Cognitive Theories and Romantic Texts*. Baltimore: Johns Hopkins UP, 2010.

---. "Studies in Literature and Cognition: A Field Map." *The Work of Fiction: Cognition, Culture, and Complexity*. Ed. Alan Richardson and Ellen Spolsky. Burlington: Ashgate, 2004. 1–29.

---, ed. *Literature, Cognition & the Brain*. Website. <https://www2.bc.edu/~richarad/lcb/home.html>.

Richardson, Alan, and Francis F. Steen. "Reframing the Adjustment: A Response to Adler and Gross." *Poetics Today* 24.2 (2003): 151–9. <http://dx.doi.org/10.1215/03335372-24-2-151>.

---, eds. "Literature and the Cognitive Revolution." Special issue, *Poetics Today* 23.1 (2002).

Ricoeur, Paul. *The Rule of Metaphor: Multi-disciplinary Studies of the Creation of Meaning in Language*. Trans. Robert Czerny with Kathleen McLaughlin and John Costello, SJ. Toronto: U of Toronto P, 1977.

Rousseau, Jean-Jacques. *The Social Contract*. 1762. *The Essential Rousseau*. Ed. and trans. Lowell Bair. New York: Penguin Books, 1975. 1–124.

Russell, Ford. *Northrop Frye on Myth: An Introduction*. New York: Garland, 1998.

Salusinszky, Imre. "Frye and the Art of Memory." *Rereading Frye: The Published and Unpublished Works*. Ed. David Boyd and Imre Salusinszky. Toronto: U of Toronto P, 1999. 39–54.

---. "Frye and Ideology." *The Legacy of Northrop Frye*. Ed. Alvin Lee and Robert Denham. Toronto: U of Toronto P, 1994. 76–83.

---. "Towards the *Anatomy*." *English Studies in Canada* 19.2 (June 1993): 229–40.

Schaeffer, John D. "The Use and Misuse of Giambattista Vico: Rhetoric, Orality, and Theories of Discourse." *The New Historicism*. Ed. H. Aram Veeser. New York: Routledge, 1989. 89–101.

Schauber, Ellen, and Ellen Spolsky. *The Bounds of Interpretation: Linguistic Theory and Literary Text*. Stanford: Stanford UP, 1986.

Searle, Leroy. "Afterword: Criticism and the Claims of Reason." *Critical Theory since 1965*. Ed. Hazard Adams and Leroy Searle. Tallahassee: Florida State UP, 1986.

Semino, Elena. "A Cognitive Stylistic Approach to Mind Style in Narrative Fiction." *Cognitive Stylistics: Language and Cognition in Text Analysis*. Ed.

Elena Semino and Jonathan Culpeper. Amsterdam: John Benjamins, 2002. 95–122.

Semino, Elena, and Gerard Steen. "Metaphor in Literature." *The Cambridge Handbook of Metaphor and Thought*. Ed. Raymond W. Gibbs, Jr. Cambridge: Cambridge UP, 2008. 232–46.

Semino, Elena, and Jonathan Culpeper, eds. *Cognitive Stylistics: Language and Cognition in Text Analysis.* Amsterdam: John Benjamins, 2002.

Shakespeare, William. *A Midsummer Night's Dream. The Oxford Shakespeare: The Complete Works.* Ed. Stanley Wells and Gary Taylor. Oxford: Clarendon Press, 1998. 311–33.

Shen, Yeshayahu. "Cognitive Constraints on Verbal Creativity: The Use of Figurative Language in Poetic Discourse." *Cognitive Stylistics: Language and Cognition in Text Analysis.* Ed. Elena Semino and Jonathan Culpeper. Amsterdam: John Benjamins, 2002. 211–30.

---. "Metaphor and Poetic Figures." *The Cambridge Handbook of Metaphor and Thought*. Ed. Raymond W. Gibbs, Jr. Cambridge: Cambridge UP, 2008. 295–307.

---, ed. "Aspects of Metaphor Comprehension." Special issue, *Poetics Today* 13.4 (1992).

---, ed. "Metaphor 2." Special issue, *Poetics Today* 14.1 (1993).

Simon, Herbert. "Literary Criticism: A Cognitive Approach." Special issue, *Stanford Humanities Review* 4.1 (1994). <http://www.stanford.edu/group/SHR/4-1/text/toc.html>.

Simpson, Paul. *On the Discourse of Satire: Towards a Stylistic Model of Satirical Humour*. Amsterdam: John Benjamins, 2003.

Slingerland, Edward. *What Science Offers the Humanities: Integrating Body and Culture.* Cambridge: Cambridge UP, 2008.

Smith, Glenn W. "Snidely, Saddam and Melodramocracy." Web page. The Rockridge Institute. 18 June 2007. <http://www.rockridgeinstitute.org/research/rockridge/snidely-saddam-melodramocracy/>.

Spolsky, Ellen. "Cognitive Literary Historicism: A Response to Adler and Gross." *Poetics Today* 24.2 (2003): 161–83. <http://dx.doi.org/10.1215/03335372-24-2-161>.

---. "Darwin and Derrida: Cognitive Literary Theory as a Species of Post-Structuralism." *Poetics Today* 23.1 (2002): 43–62. <http://dx.doi.org/10.1215/03335372-23-1-43>.

---. *Gaps in Nature: Literary Interpretation and the Modular Mind*. Albany: State University of New York Press, 1993.

---. *Satisfying Skepticism: Embodied Knowledge in the Early Modern World*. Aldershot: Ashgate, 2001.

Steen, Gerard. "The Contemporary Theory of Metaphor – Now New and Improved!" *Review of Cognitive Linguistics* 9.1 (2011): 26–64. <http://dx.doi.org/10.1075/rcl.9.1.03ste>.

---. "'Love Stories': Cognitive Scenarios in Love Poetry." *Cognitive Poetics in Practice*. Ed. Joanna Gavins and Gerard Steen. London: Routledge, 2003. 67–82.

Steen, Gerard, and Joanna Gavins. "Contextualising Cognitive Poetics." *Cognitive Poetics in Practice*. Ed. Joanna Gavins and Gerard Steen. London: Routledge, 2003. 1–12.

Sternberg, Meir. "Universals of Narrative and their Cognitivist Fortunes (I)." *Poetics Today* 24.2 (2003): 297–395. <http://dx.doi.org/10.1215/03335372-24-2-297>.

---. "Universals of Narrative and Their Cognitivist Fortunes (II)." *Poetics Today* 24.3 (2003): 517–638. <http://dx.doi.org/10.1215/03335372-24-3-517>.

Stockwell, Peter. *Cognitive Poetics: An Introduction*. London: Routledge, 2002.

Storey, John. "Introduction: The Study of Popular Culture within Cultural Studies." *Cultural Theory and Popular Culture: A Reader*. Ed. John Storey. New York: Harvester Wheatsheaf, 1994. vii–xii.

---, ed. *Cultural Theory and Popular Culture: A Reader*. New York: Harvester Wheatsheaf, 1994.

Swan, Jim. "'Life without Parole': Metaphor and Discursive Commitment." *Style* 36.3 (2002): 446–65.

Sweetser, Eve. *From Etymology to Pragmatics: Metaphorical and Cultural Aspects of Semantic Structure*. Cambridge: Cambridge UP, 1990.

---. "Metaphor, Mythology, and Everyday Language." *Journal of Pragmatics* 24.6 (1995): 585–93. <http://dx.doi.org/10.1016/0378-2166(95)00005-D>.

Talmy, Leonard. "Fictive Motion in Language and 'Ception'." *Language and Space*. Ed. Paul Bloom, Mary A. Peterson, Lynn Nadel, and Merrill F. Garrett. Cambridge: The MIT Press, 1996. 211–76.

Tillyard, E.M.W. *The Elizabethan World Picture*. 1943. Harmondsworth: Penguin Books, 1979.

Todorov, Tzvetan. *The Fantastic: A Structural Approach to a Literary Genre*. Trans. Richard Howard. Cleveland: Case Western Reserve UP, 1973.

---. *Genres in Discourse*. Trans. Catherine Porter. Cambridge: Cambridge UP, 1990.

Tsur, Reuven. "Aspects of Cognitive Poetics." *Cognitive Stylistics: Language and Cognition in Text Analysis*. Ed. Elena Semino and Jonathan Culpeper. Amsterdam: John Benjamins, 2002. 279–318.

---. "'EVENT STRUCTURE' Metaphor and Reductionism (an exercise in functional criticism)." 17 Aug. 2001. <http://www.tau.ac.il/%7Etsurxx/Emily_Dickinson.html>.

---. "Lakoff's Roads Not Taken." *Pragmatics and Cognition* 7 (2000): 339–59. <http://www.tau.ac.il/%7Etsurxx/Stock_Responses.html>.

Turner, Mark. "Aspects of the Invariance Hypothesis." *Cognitive Linguistics* 1.2 (1990): 247–55.

---. *Cognitive Dimensions of Social Science: The Way We Think About Politics, Economics, Law, and Society*. Oxford: Oxford UP, 2001.

---. "Cognitive Science and Literary Theory." Special issue, *Stanford Humanities Review* 4.1 (1994). <http://www.stanford.edu/group/SHR/4-1/text/toc.html>.

---. "The Cognitive Study of Art, Language, and Literature." *Poetics Today* 23.1 (2002): 9–20. <http://dx.doi.org/10.1215/03335372-23-1-9>.

---. *Death Is the Mother of Beauty: Mind, Metaphor, Criticism*. Chicago: U of Chicago P, 1987.

---. *The Literary Mind: The Origins of Thought and Language*. New York: Oxford UP, 1996.

---. *Reading Minds: The Study of English in the Age of Cognitive Science*. Princeton: Princeton UP, 1994.

---, ed. *The Artful Mind: Cognitive Science and the Riddle of Human Creativity*. New York: Oxford UP, 2006.

---, ed. *Blending and Conceptual Integration*. Web page. 2012. <http://www.markturner.org/blending.html>.

Turner, Mark, and Gilles Fauconnier. "A Mechanism of Creativity." *Poetics Today* 20.3 (1999): 397–418.

van Oort, Richard. "Cognitive Science and the Problem of Representation." *Poetics Today* 24.2 (2003): 237–95. <http://dx.doi.org/10.1215/03335372-24-2-237>.

Veeser, H. Aram. "The New Historicism." *The New Historicism Reader*. Ed. H. Aram Veeser. New York: Routledge, 1994. 1–32.

---, ed. *The New Historicism*. New York: Routledge, 1989.

---, ed. *The New Historicism Reader*. New York: Routledge, 1994.

Verspoor, Marjolijn, Kee Dong Lee, and Eve Sweetser, eds. *Lexical and Syntactic Constructions and the Construction of Meaning*. Amsterdam: John Benjamins, 1997.

West, Cornel. "The New Cultural Politics of Difference." *The Cultural Studies Reader*. Ed. Simon During. London: Routledge, 1995. 203–17.

Weston, Jessie L. *From Ritual to Romance*. 1920. Garden City: Doubleday, 1957.

Wheelwright, Philip. *Metaphor and Reality*. Bloomington: Indiana UP, 1962.

White, Hayden. "Frye's Place in Contemporary Cultural Studies." *The Legacy of Northrop Frye*. Ed. Alvin Lee and Robert Denham. Toronto: U of Toronto P, 1994. 28–39.

---. "Ideology and Counterideology in the *Anatomy*." *Visionary Poetics: Essays on Northrop Frye's Criticism*. Ed. Robert D. Denham and Thomas Willard. New York: Peter Lang, 1991. 101–11.

---. *Metahistory: The Historical Imagination in Nineteenth-Century Europe*. Baltimore: Johns Hopkins UP, 1973.

Willard, Thomas. "Alchemy and the Bible." *Centre and Labyrinth: Essays in Honour of Northrop Frye*. Ed. Eleanor Cook, Chaviva Hošek, Jay Macpherson, et al. Toronto: U of Toronto P, 1983. 115–27.

---. "Archetypes of the Imagination." *The Legacy of Northrop Frye*. Ed. Alvin Lee and Robert Denham. Toronto: U of Toronto P, 1994. 15–27.

Williams, Raymond. *Culture and Materialism: Selected Essays*. 1980. London: Verso, 2005.

---. *Keywords: A Vocabulary of Culture and Society*. Glasgow: Fontana, 1976.

Wolfe, Tom. "Sorry, But Your Soul Just Died." *Hooking Up*. New York: Farrar, Straus, and Giroux, 2000. 89–109.

Zerbisias, Antonia. "Men's Rights Activists Drive Harper's Policies." *Toronto Star* 3 Feb. 2010. <http://www.thestar.com/living/article/759534--men-s-rights-activists-drive-harper-s-policies>.

Zunshine, Lisa. "Introduction: What Is Cognitive Cultural Studies?" *Introduction to Cognitive Cultural Studies*. Ed. Lisa Zunshine. Baltimore: Johns Hopkins UP, 2010. 1–33.

---, ed. *Introduction to Cognitive Cultural Studies*. Baltimore: Johns Hopkins UP, 2010.

Index

www.ingramcontent.com/pod-product-compliance
Lightning Source LLC
LaVergne TN
LVHW090156080826
844660LV00013B/825/J

* 9 7 8 1 4 4 2 6 4 3 9 1 8 *